Disparaged Success

A volume in the series

Cornell Studies in Political Economy

EDITED BY PETER J. KATZENSTEIN

A full list of titles in the series appears at the end of the book.

Disparaged Success

LABOR POLITICS IN POSTWAR JAPAN

IKUO KUME

CORNELL UNIVERSITY PRESS

Ithaca and London

First published 1998 by Cornell University Press.

Printed in the United States of America

Cornell University Press strives to utilize environmentally responsible suppliers and materials to the fullest extent possible in the publishing of its books. Such materials include vegetable-based, low-VOC inks and acid-free papers that are also either recycled, totally chlorine-free or partly composed of nonwood fibers.

Cloth printing   10   9   8   7   6   5   4   3   2   1

Library of Congress Cataloging-in-Publication Data

Kume, Ikuo, 1957–
    Disparaged success: labor politics in postwar Japan / Ikuo Kume.
        p.   cm.
    Includes index.
    ISBN 0-8014-3364-9 (cloth: alk. paper)
    1. Labor policy—Japan—History—20th century.   2. Trade-unions—Japan—Political activity—History—20th century.   3. Industrial relations—Japan—History—20th century.   I. Title.
    HD8726.5.K775   1997
    322′.2′095209045—dc21   97-30568

To Tomoko

Contents

Figures and Tables

FIGURES

TABLES

Acknowledgments

I am grateful to Peter J. Katzenstein, Theodore J. Lowi, and T. J. Pempel. They patiently encouraged me to complete this work and gave me much advice. Professor Katzenstein helped me to straighten my argument; without his persistent encouragement over these ten years, this work would never have been completed. Professor Pempel, though his understanding of Japanese labor politics differs from mine, consistently helped me to elaborate my argument by giving critical but very positive criticism. It was Professor Lowi who first introduced me to the fertile field of political economy, and his sober view of interest group politics led me to a demystification of Japanese labor politics.

Sidney Tarrow deserves special mention. I learned a lot from his lectures on social movements, which gave me ways to think about Japanese labor politics. John C. Campbell, Miriam Golden, Martin Kenney, Jonas Pontusson, Kathleen Thelen, and anonymous reviewers gave me valuable comments and criticism on various parts of the manuscript. I also benefited greatly from discussions with Nils Elvander, Michael Goldfield, and Åke Sandberg.

On the other side of the Pacific, where I conducted research and have spent most of my career, I am also indebted to many people. First, I am most grateful to Michio Muramatsu. Professor Muramatsu taught me how interesting Japanese politics is long before the recent political turmoil started in Japan and has continuously encouraged me. Two of my best friends, Masaru Mabuchi and Toshiya Kitayama, gave me thoughtful advice that helped me to elaborate my argument. Substantial parts of the manuscript have been published in Japanese. Takeshi Inagami, Mitsutoshi Ito, Tetsuro Kato, Takashi Kawakita, Ichiro Miyake, Keisuke

Nakamura, Hideo Otake, Toshimitsu Shinkawa, Toru Shinoda, Kuniaki Tanabe, Shoko Tanaka, and Yutaka Tsujinaka read parts of the manuscript in Japanese and gave helpful comments. Discussions with Takenori Inoki, Makoto Iokibe, Junko Kato, Taro Miyamoto, Konosuke Odaka, Hideo Okamoto, Masayuki Tadokoro, Masahiko Tatebayashi, and colleagues on the Faculty of Law at Kobe University inspired various ideas formulated in the manuscript.

I owe a great debt to the many institutions and people who have supported my work. A Fulbright Scholarship enabled me to complete my work at Cornell. The Kikawada Foundation provided financial support for extensive interviews with union leaders. The Matsushita International Foundation supported comparative research. Financial support from the Ministry of Education and logistical support from Bert Edström of the Center for Pacific Asia Studies at Stockholm University made possible two months of research in Sweden, which added a comparative dimension to this book. The Nitobe Fellowship made it possible for me to stay at Cornell for two years. I also thank union leaders, officials at the Ministry of Labor, Nikkeiren, and the Japan Productivity Center who answered my various questions. Keiko Higuchi, Kiyoko Iwasaki, Nahoko Morita, and Tomoko Sakai were my highly qualified research assistants. Martha Walsh and Stephen Weldon made this manuscript readable by their patient copyediting. Carol Betsch and Roger Haydon at Cornell University Press gave me helpful advice through editing and production.

I thank my parents, Toshio and Masako Kume, for their bet on my future career from the beginning of my graduate study. My sons, Isaka and Haruki, supported my study in their own cheerful ways. Finally, I am deeply indebted to my wife, Tomoko, for her belief in me and her always optimistic way of thinking.

I. K.

Kobe, Japan

CHAPTER ONE

Introduction: The Puzzle
of Japanese Labor Politics

Since the 1980s, unions have faced difficulties in most of the advanced industrial democracies. In the United States, union power has eroded drastically, especially under the Reagan administration, and British unions under Thatcher fared no better. Nor in Germany was Kohl's conservative government an ally to labor. Even in Sweden, Social Democrats lost the 1991 election, and a conservative coalition government was formed, so that now many scholars are discussing the end of the long-cherished Swedish model.[1]

At the same time, a common change is occurring in all of these countries: the decentralization of labor-management relations. This change is often regarded as either a cause or a symptom of union decline. Management offensives in the United States, the emergence of company unions in Britain, the increasing importance of work councils rather than collective bargaining in Germany, and the demise of centralized wage bargaining and tripartite negotiation in Sweden, all appear to offer evidence of union decline.[2] Scholars and analysts citing such evidence usually take it

[1] Thomas A. Kochan, Harry C. Katz, and Robert B. McKersie, *The Transformation of American Industrial Relations* (New York: Basic Books, 1986), pp. 3–4; Joel Krieger, *Reagan, Thatcher, and the Politics of Decline* (New York: Oxford University Press, 1986); Victor A. Pestoff, "Towards a New Swedish Model: From Neo-Corporatist to Neo-Liberal Priorities for the Welfare State," paper presented at the seminar "Transformation Process in Eastern Europe—Challenges for Socio-Economic Theory," in Cracow, Poland, March 10, 1992; see also *Western European Politics, Special Issue*, ed. Jan-Erik Lane, *Understanding the Swedish Model* 14-3 (July 1991).

[2] Harry C. Katz, "The Decentralization of Collective Bargaining: A Literature Review and Comparative Analysis," *Industrial and Labor Relations Review* 47-1 (October 1993); Colin Crouch, "Generalized Political Exchange in Industrial Relations in Europe during the Twentieth Century," in Bernd Martin, ed., *Governance and Generalized Exchange: Self-*

for granted that decentralized labor is destined to lose power in a capital-ist political economy.

In Japan, however, a decentralized labor structure based on enterprise unionism presents an interesting anomaly to this conventional under-standing of labor politics. In 1993, after thirty-eight years of continuous rule by the conservative Liberal Democratic Party, a non-LDP coalition government was established. Although the new government was by no means a social democratic one—conservative parties remained influential in the administration—the national labor confederation, Rengō (Japa-nese Trade Union Confederation) fully supported the change. Even when the Japan Socialist Party deserted the coalition in April 1994 and formed a new government with the LDP in July labor unions continued to play a critical role in the political transformation. It is true that this transforma-tion was brought about by a split within the LDP, not by increasing power on the left. Nevertheless, it is still worth asking why the world's most decentralized union structure is becoming an important actor in national politics. I attempt to answer this question by analyzing the historical development of Japanese labor politics since World War II.

The most conspicuous development in Japanese labor politics is labor's intensified participation within the political economy by its expansion from company-wide to national policymaking. Through the confron-tational labor offensive immediately after the war and subsequent management counterattacks, labor and management finally reached a reconciliation: labor achieved status as a legitimate member of the com-pany beyond its presence as a production factor. It chose to collaborate with management to increase productivity in exchange for its fair share of the profits. Based on this accommodation, labor began participating in production and management decision making through various institu-tional mechanisms. This dense network of interactions between manage-ment and labor contributed to the flexible production system in Japanese manufacturing industries.[3]

In the late 1960s, when management and labor in manufacturing industries realized the necessity of competing fully with foreign compa-

---

Organizing Policy Networks in Action (Boulder: Westview, 1990); Michael Goldfield, *The Decline of Organized Labor in the United States* (Chicago: University of Chicago Press, 1987); Bob Jessop, Kevin Bonnett, Simon Bromley, and Tom Ling, *Thatcherism: A Tale of Two Nations* (Cambridge: Polity Press, 1988), p. 151; Claus Offe, *Disorganized Capitalism: Contemporary Transformations of Work and Politics*, ed. John Keane (Cambridge: Polity Press, 1985), pp. 162–63; Pestoff, "Towards a New Swedish Model."

[3] E.g., James P. Womack, Daniel Jones, and Daniel Roos, *The Machine That Changed the World* (New York: Rawson Associates, 1990).

nies as a result of the opening of Japanese financial and product markets, they established industry-level labor-management councils in various industries to discuss necessary industrial adjustments. Furthermore, labor unions gradually participated in government-industry negotiations on industrial policy formulation.[4]

In the 1970s, labor unions, especially in the private sector, deepened their participation in national policymaking. In 1970, an informal semimonthly tripartite meeting, Sanrōkon (Discussion on Industry and Labor), was established. Union participation in government deliberation councils (*shingikai*) broadened. These networks among labor, management, and the government at the industry and national levels allowed flexibility in adjusting to new economic situations, especially after the first oil crisis. Labor unions restrained their wage demands in exchange for a government promise to stop inflation. This informal incomes policy worked well owing to extensive information exchange among labor, business, and the government.[5] Since then, union presence in national policymaking has further increased and did not decline in the 1980s with the conservative resurgence.

In sum, Japanese decentralized labor unions have steadily institutionalized their participation within the political economy from the company level to the national level. This development made industrial and economic adjustments in Japan easier and less costly for Japanese workers.

Most scholars, however, have characterized Japanese labor as docile and powerless and have neglected its achievements. Political scientists often claim that labor has been powerless in the policymaking process under the continuous conservative Liberal Democratic rule from 1955 to 1993, and they frequently attribute this fact to the decentralized and underdeveloped labor movement. For instance, T. J. Pempel and Keiichi Tsunekawa, using a neocorporatist framework, described Japan as "corporatism without labor," a common view among Japanese political scientists.[6] Takeshi Ishida argued that Japanese political groups were in

---

[4] Ronald Dore shows this development in his study of the Japanese textile industry. *Flexible Rigidities: Industrial Policy and Structural Adjustment in the Japanese Economy, 1970–1980* (London: Athlone Press, 1986). See also Susumu Hisamura, *Sangyōseisaku to rōdōkumiai* (Industrial policy and labor unions) (Tokyo: Nihon Rōdō Kyōkai, 1988).

[5] Haruo Shimada, "Wage Determination and Information Sharing: An Alternative Approach to Incomes Policy?" *Journal of Industrial Relations* 25-2 (June 1983). He calls this network "functional corporatism." Ikuo Kume, "Changing Relations among the Government, Labor, and Business in Japan after the Oil Crisis," *International Organization* 42-4 (Autumn 1988).

[6] T. J. Pempel and Keiichi Tsunekawa, "Corporatism without Labor?" in Philippe C.

two camps, the mainstream and the outsiders, and the latter, which included labor, was almost totally excluded from the policymaking process.[7] Very often this weakness of labor is attributed to decentralized enterprise unionism.

Many labor sociologists as well as economists also regard enterprise unionism as a cause of labor's weakness in negotiation with employers on wages and other working conditions.[8] They usually argue that because Japanese unions are not industrial unions but enterprise unions, they are easily manipulated by management into accepting poorer working conditions than what centralized industrial unions could have achieved. According to this argument, management can divide and rule workers and can mobilize workers in an intensive production process with lower wages.

These scholars generally see Japan's dual economic structure—a highly unionized modern industrial sector coexisting with a poorly unionized small and medium-sized corporate sector—as an inevitable result of decentralized enterprise unionism. The end result is allegedly a weak labor movement in wage bargaining, at the workplace, and in national politics. These scholars point out how Japan's leftist labor movement was defeated in the 1950s and docile enterprise unionism appeared in the 1960s, and then they use those events as evidence for the weak labor thesis. Often described as a critical turning point, for example, is the defeat of the union movement of the communist-led Sanbetsu (Japanese Congress of Industrial Unions), in which private-sector enterprise unionism is seen as demolishing the radical leftist labor movement.[9] Second, these scholars note the erosion of leftist unionism in public-sector dominated Sōhyō (General Council of Trade Unions of Japan).[10] This occurred in the 1960s when the International Metalworkers' Federation–Japan Council (IMF-JC) united big business unions in the metal and machine industries under

---

Schmitter and Gerhard Lehmbruch, eds., *Trends towards Corporatist Intermediation* (London: Sage, 1979).

[7] Takeshi Ishida, *Gendai soshikiron* (Modern organization) (Tokyo: Iwanami Shoten, 1961).

[8] E.g., Walter Galenson, "The Japanese Labor Market," in Hugh Patrick and Henry Rosovsky, eds., *Asia's New Giant: How the Japanese Economy Works* (Washington: Brookings Institution, 1976), and Toshimitsu Shinkawa, "Dualism to sengo Nihon no seijikeizai" (Dualism and postwar Japanese political economy), *Leviathan*, no. 5 (Autumn 1989).

[9] Sanbetsu was organized in August, 1946, under the strong influence of the Japan Communist Party. It was one of the two major union movements in Japan immediately after World War II.

[10] Sōhyō was organized in 1950 as a democratic union federation in opposition to the communist-led union movement, but it later changed from democratic to leftist. It was the largest national labor federation in Japan until 1987.

4

the banner of business unionism. The establishment of hegemony of the private-sector unions in the 1980s, represented by the formation of Rengō in 1989, has been seen as the completion of this process of the domestication of the labor movement in Japan.[11]

These orthodox views, however, have recently faced substantial criticism from two groups of revisionist scholars. The first group emphasizes the positive role of Japanese unions within the enterprise. An increasing number of economists and sociologists are now demonstrating that Japanese enterprises are more employee-oriented than American firms. Ronald Dore characterizes the Japanese enterprise in terms of a "community model," in which the firm is defined as a social unit made up of all of its full-time workers. By contrast, he characterizes the Anglo-Saxon enterprise in terms of a "company law model," in which the firm is defined as the property of the shareholders, whose rights are paramount. Masahiko Aoki has shown that Japanese firms tend to take employees' interests into consideration in managerial decision making. Kazuo Koike found that employees in Japanese firms actively participate in personnel decision making, although he does not regard this as a uniquely Japanese phenomenon. Michio Nitta demonstrated how the Japanese steel workers' union influenced managerial decisions in restructuring the production system.[12] This counter-evidence to the orthodox view requires us to develop a new understanding of Japanese labor politics. These revisionists, however, are more inclined to analyze how the corporate organization or the management system functions than how it originated. This perspective makes their argument somewhat static and apolitical. What is missing is an analysis of labor's role in setting up the employee-oriented management system. I take this role seriously in understanding how an employee-oriented company system emerged in Japan.[13]

[11] The Japanese Private-Sector Trade Union Federation (Rengō) was founded in 1987. The private-sector Rengō absorbed Sōhyō in 1989, and represented 65 percent of organized workers in Japan, thereby unifying private- and public-sector workers in one large national organization.

[12] Ronald Dore, *Taking Japan Seriously: A Confucian Perspective on Leading Economic Issues* (London: Athlone Press, 1987), p. 54; Masahiko Aoki, *Information, Incentives, and Bargaining in the Japanese Economy* (Cambridge: Cambridge University Press, 1988); Kazuo Koike, *Shokuba no rōdō kumiai to sanka* (The union on the shopfloor and its participation) (Tokyo: Tōyōkeizai Shinpōsha, 1975); and Michio Nitta, *Nihon no rōdōsha sanka* (Workers' participation in Japan) (Tokyo: Tokyodaigaku Shuppankai, 1990). For similar analyses showing Japanese labor's influence in the firm, see Ronald Dore, *British Factory—Japanese Factory: The Origins of National Diversity in Industrial Relations* (Berkeley: University of California Press, 1973); Noriyuki Itami, *Jinponshugi kigyō* (Human capital enterprise) (Tokyo: Chikuma Shobo, 1987); James C. Abegglen and George Stalk, Jr., *Kaisha: The Japanese Corporation* (New York: Basic Books, 1985).

[13] Dore focuses on the effects of late development and Confucian culture to explain the

The second group of revisionists sheds new light on the role of labor at the national level. If Japanese labor played an important and independent role, rather than a passive one in establishing and running the employee-oriented enterprise, how would labor pursue its interests at the national level? The nationalization and coordination of wage bargaining in the form of the Shuntō (Spring Offensive) annual wage negotiation was crucial. In 1954, Japanese private-sector unions introduced this strategy to increase their leverage. Through coordinated wage bargaining in spring, a union coordinating body chose the most successful industry and had unions in that sector lead the wage bargaining and set the basic pattern. A number of labor economists argue that this strategy enabled workers to enjoy relatively egalitarian and better wages.[14] Recently some political scientists have joined this revisionist camp by demonstrating the increasing role of labor in national politics. Especially after the first oil crisis, the unions in the private sector achieved substantial success in their bid for benefits such as employment security.[15]

These revisionists explicitly or implicitly pose a question to the orthodox scholars: Why has Japanese labor succeeded in gaining important benefits, such as secure employment and participation in the production system, despite its "weakness" characterized by a decentralized enterprise union structure? Indeed, orthodox scholars have not considered Japanese labor's performance in a systematic manner because of their obsession with the "weak labor" interpretation. We must therefore start our analysis with an examination of that performance.

LABOR PERFORMANCE IN POSTWAR JAPAN

The weak labor thesis implies that Japanese workers have been unable to enjoy benefits that stronger union movements have achieved. For those

employee orientation of the Japanese enterprise, whereas Koike emphasizes company-specific skill formation. A more political approach can be found in Andrew Gordon, *The Evolution of Labor Relations in Japan: Heavy Industry, 1853–1955* (Cambridge: Harvard East Asian Monographs, 1988); Martin Kenney and Richard Florida, "Beyond Mass Production: Production and Labor Process in Japan," *Politics and Society* 16-1 (March 1988). A brief historical review of Japanese firms from this perspective is in Aoki, *Information, Incentives, and Bargaining*, chapter 5.

[14] E.g., Shuntō Kenkyukai, *Shuntō kawarunoka* (Will Shuntō change?) (Tokyo: Eideru Kenkyusho, 1989).

[15] Kume, "Changing Relations"; Yutaka Tsujinaka, "Rōdōkai no saihen to 86 nen taisei no imi" (Transformation of the labor movement and the meaning of the 1986 system), *Leviathan*, no. 1 (Autumn 1987); Mitsutoshi Ito, "Daikigyō rōshirengō no keisei" (Formation of

who support this view, it is almost self-evident that Japan's decentralized and fragmented enterprise unionism has not produced favorable results for workers. Therefore, proponents of the weak labor thesis refer to the poor working conditions of Japanese workers, such as comparatively long work hours by international standards and slow nominal wage increases after the oil crisis, seldom taking a comprehensive view of labor's achievements in postwar Japan. In fact, however, according to several indexes (although the performance mix varies over time as well as across countries), Japanese labor has come to enjoy a level of benefits comparable to those in other advanced industrial countries.

Though not truly a performance index, let us start by examining the characteristics of the union movement, since the advocates of the weak labor thesis rely most heavily on these characteristics. First, the organization rate in Japan has been low in comparison with those in small social democratic European countries such as Sweden. In 1980 the Japanese rate was 31 percent, while that of Sweden was 90 percent. However, among large industrialized democracies, the Japanese rate has not been distinctively low. Those rates in 1980 were 57 percent for Britain, 55–60 percent for Italy, 42 percent for West Germany, 28 percent for France, and 25 percent for the United States.[16]

The organization rate has recently been declining in Japan, though this is not unique to Japan. The Japanese union organization rate soared from zero at the end of World War II to about 50 percent in 1949, and then gradually declined to around 30 percent. It rose to 34.4 percent in 1975, but again steadily declined to 24.4 percent in 1992. It is true that this decline, if it continues, would pose a serious challenge to the Japanese labor movement in the future. However, we should keep in mind the fact that despite this decline, Japanese unions organize a substantial number of workers and that total number has not declined as much as the percentage. In 1992, the total number of union members was 12,541,000, which constituted 10.1 percent of the nation's population.[17]

Second, many observers tend to emphasize the cooperative and peaceful nature of Japanese industrial relations. For example, the rate of labor conflicts in Japan, especially after the first oil crisis, has been low. Days lost

---

the big business–labor coalition), *Leviathan*, no. 2 (Spring 1988); Toru Shinoda, *Seikimatsu no rōdōundo* (The labor movement at the end of the century) (Tokyo: Iwanami Shoten, 1989).

[16] Michael Goldfield, *The Decline of Organized Labor in the United States*, p. 16. The original source is unpublished data from the U.S. Department of Labor, BLS, Division of Foreign Labor Statistics.

[17] Ministry of Labor, *Rōdō hakusho* (White paper on labor, annual) (1993).

in strikes per 1,000 workers per year declined from 219.9 in 1975 to 3.8 in 1988. But a review of the postwar history of Japanese industrial relations shows it to have been highly contentious in the earlier period. The occupation reforms spawned an upheaval in the Japanese labor movement during the late 1940s and the early 1950s. Before the seventies, labor unions were prone to strikes, in contrast to the common view of a country with harmonious industrial relations. While in the 1980s the average number of days lost in strikes in Japan became the lowest among the OECD countries, from 1955 to 1964 the average was more than that in Great Britain, West Germany, or Sweden.[18]

If we further analyze the shape of strikes, we find that in the late 1940s and 1950s the length of strikes—that is, average days lost in one strike—was longer, while their size—the average number of participants per strike—was larger than in the later period (figs. 1 and 2).[19] In those days the Japanese unions were more militant and actively appealed to their members to strike. Then, while the length and size of strikes decreased drastically in the 1960s and early 70s, the number of strikes increased to its peak in 1974 (fig. 3). In that period, there were more strikes of shorter length and smaller size. Finally, after the first oil crisis, the number of strikes as well as their length and size decreased.

These data seem to show that the postwar Japanese labor movement has become less militant. Scholars of the orthodox school regard this as evidence of labor's loss of power. However, another reason for less militant behavior is that labor was able to achieve what it wanted without appealing to such tactics.[20]

What were those achievements? The students of the weak labor thesis argue that Japanese enterprise unionism is responsible for poorer working conditions than those in other countries with an "authentic" union movement. To the contrary however, much evidence suggests that Japanese workers have come to enjoy working conditions comparable to those of other OECD countries.

First, Japanese workers in the postwar era gained rapid wage increases

---

[18] Kazuo Koike, *Shigoto no keizaigaku* (Economics of jobs) (Tokyo: Tōyōkeizai Shinpōsha, 1991), p. 195.

[19] Edward Shorter and Charles Tilly, "The Shape of Strikes in France, 1830–1960," *Comparative Studies in Society and History* 133-1 (January 1971).

[20] Walter Korpi argues that Swedish labor was so strong that it did not need to appeal to strikes. This point is significant for understanding change in the 1960s in Japan, too. Decrease in the intensity of strikes does not necessarily mean weakness of unions, but may result from the establishment of stable labor-management relations. Korpi, *Working Class in Welfare Capitalism: Work, Unions and Politics in Sweden* (London: Routledge & Kegan Paul, 1978), pp. 45–47.

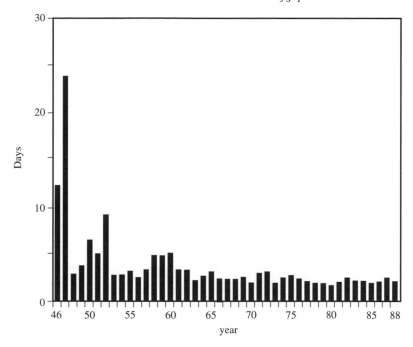

Figure 1. Length of strike: Average number of days lost per strike. From *Shōwa kokusei sōran* (Tokyo: Tōyōkeizaishinpōsha, 1992).

and are now enjoying wages as high as those in other OECD countries. According to Bank of Japan statistics, in 1960 American workers received 982.6 percent of Japanese workers' average hourly wage, and German workers received 273.9 percent. In 1976 the disparity had dropped, and American workers received 146.6 percent, British workers received 79.2 percent, and German workers 115.4 percent of Japanese wages. In 1987 American workers received 81.8 percent, British workers 62.1 percent, and German workers 80.6 percent.[21] According to Ministry of Labor statistics, in 1991 Americans received 99 percent and Germans 140 percent of their Japanese counterparts' wages. These comparisons have some problems because of volatile exchange rates. Thus, the Japanese wage increase is partly a result of the strong yen. But even if we take into

[21] Bank of Japan, *Gaikoku keizai tōkei nenpō* (Annual statistics of foreign economies). Japanese data include workplaces with more than 30 employees. U.S. data are for all blue-collar workers. British data include male adult blue-collar workers. German data are for all blue-collar workers in workplaces with more than 10 employees. Cf. ILO, *Yearbook of Labor Statistics.* Cited in Yoshimitsu Kagiyama and Shigeru Ota, *Nihon niokeru rōdōjōken no tokushitsu to shihyo 1990 nenban* (Nature and index of working conditions in Japan, 1990 edition) (Tokyo: Hakutō Shobō, 1990), p. 86.

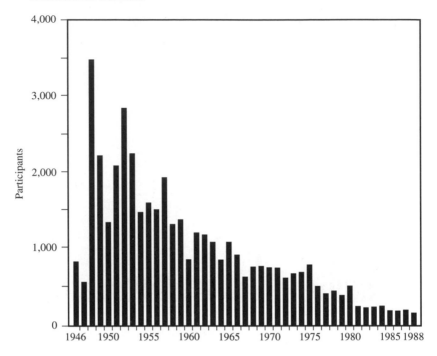

Figure 2. Size of strike: Average number of participants per strike. From *Shōwa kokusei sōran.*

account the increase in the yen's value to the dollar, that is, 360 yen = 1 dollar in 1960 and 134.7 yen = 1 dollar in 1991, Japanese wage increases are still comparable.

In terms of the average annual increase in the nominal hourly wage, which is not directly influenced by exchange rate variations, Japanese labor also enjoyed a favorable performance. Those average annual increases in manufacturing industries from 1960 to 1990 were 9.7 percent for Japan, 6.9 percent for West Germany, and 5.4 percent for the United States. These data show that Japanese workers were not forced to accept cheaper wages in the high economic growth period, and the data discredit the weak labor thesis.[22]

---

[22] Neoclassical economists would argue that this wage increase is the result of a tight labor market because they believe that wage is a function of supply and demand of labor. However, as neoinstitutionalist economists argue, in the real world wage settlements are mediated by such things as collective bargaining and union movements. I believe that supply and demand in the labor market play an important role in wage determination, but this does not mean one definite equilibrium exists a priori. There may be multiple equilibrium points, given a market with transaction costs. In this sense, Japanese wage increases should not be regarded as an automatic outcome of market forces. In fact, many labor economists, using

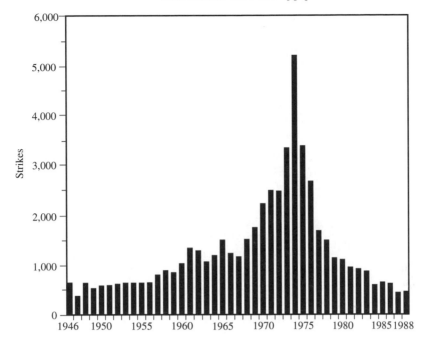

Figure 3. Number of strikes. From *Shōwa kokusei sōran.*

The nature of wage settlement, however, changed after the first oil crisis, at least in Japan. It is well known that Japanese unions began restraining their wage demands after the oil crisis. Students of the weak labor thesis regard this as further evidence for their position. It is true that the nominal Japanese wage stopped its rapid increases after the first oil crisis, from 17.4 percent per year for the period from 1968 to 1973 to 4.2 percent for the period from 1979 to 1990. But this average increase in the latter period is no less than those in West Germany and the United States

---

econometric analyses, have found substantial "union effects" on the wage level in Japan independent of market situations. E.g., Akira Ono, *Sengo Nihon no chingin kettei* (Wage determination in postwar Japan) (Tokoy: Tōyōkeizai Shinpōsha, 1973); Yoko Sano, *Chingin kettei no keiryōbunseki* (Econometric analysis of wage determination) (Tokyo: Tōyōkeizai Shinpōsha, 1970); Keisuke Nakamura, Hiroki Sato, and Takuhei Kamiya, *Rōdōkumiai wa hontoni yakunitatte irunnoka* (Does the union work?) (Tokyo: Sōgō Rōdō Kenkyusho, 1988), chap. 1. It is sufficient for my argument to conclude that Japanese enterprise unionism did not prevent Japanese workers from achieving wage increases comparable with those of the American and European labor movements. Or we may say that favorable outcomes of the tight labor market in the high growth period were not hampered by a "structurally weak" labor movement. But I show in later chapters that Japanese labor used favorable market conditions to achieve high wage increases.

(4.3 percent and 4.5 percent, respectively). The trends in the real hourly wage, though, are interesting. Real hourly wage increases in Japan in this period were higher than those in the United States and comparable to those in West Germany. The average rate per year for Japan from 1979 to 1990 was 1.6 percent, while those for West Germany and the United States were 1.4 percent and −1.0 percent, respectively.[23] Furthermore, French and Italian workers achieved higher nominal wage increases than Japanese workers in the same period (7.9 percent and 11.4 percent, respectively), but their real wage increases were less than the Japanese (0.9 percent and 0.7 percent). Japanese unions changed their goal from nominal wage increases to real wage increases after the first oil crisis, and this tactic was effective. In fact, this success was not an automatic result of their wage restraint, but rather a result of their efforts in the national political process to commit the government to an anti-inflationary policy. In this sense, labor's role was instrumental in achieving success. Given the increase in real wages in this period, it is difficult to argue that Japanese labor was defeated by management after the first oil crisis.

However, although Japanese wages have become among the world's highest, especially given the drastic yen revaluation to around 104 yen to the dollar in the spring of 1994, the real purchasing power of Japanese workers were still lower than that of American and German workers. According to a Ministry of Labor estimate, American and (West) German workers' hourly wages in terms of purchasing power parity were 140 percent and 146 percent, respectively, of their Japanese counterparts in 1991.[24] This is one major reason why Japanese management and labor in the 1980s became interested in changing government policy so as to reduce consumer prices, as I describe in chapter 7. It is a reflection of these changing interests that the Ministry of Labor has published these data since 1980 in its widely distributed publication, Summary of Labor Statistics.

Wages are not the only way to measure labor's performance. A second important measure is employment security. Japanese employment security has been the highest in the OECD countries. From 1964 to 1973, of the G7 countries, Japan, West Germany, and France boasted low unemployment rates below 3 percent. However, in the period 1980–1990, Japan was the only country to maintain its unemployment rate below 3 percent. The unemployment rate is closely related to the overall eco-

---

[23] OECD, *Economic Outlook: Historical Statistics, 1960–1990* (Paris: OECD, 1992), p. 94.
[24] Ministry of Labor, Rōdōdaijin Kanbō Seisakuchōsabu, ed., *Rōdō tōkei yōran* (Summary of labor statistics) (1994), p. 259.

nomic performance of the nation. However, a closer look at the data tells us that the unemployment rate is also influenced by management practice; Japanese employers were more committed to keeping their workers employed than were their American and German counterparts. Although industrial adjustment after the first oil crisis forced many nations to reduce production output, the ways to reduce it varied across nations. In Japan, while production output was reduced by 19.8 percent, employment reduction was only 7 percent. In the United States, the numbers were 13.1 percent and 10.7 percent, respectively, and in West Germany, 10.9 percent and 11.5 percent. This means that American and German employers more easily dismiss workers to adjust their business to changing market situations.[25] Japanese management's tendency to retain its employees has been institutionalized through postwar labor politics. The Japanese union movement has put the highest priority on employment security.

A third measure of labor performance is working hours. Japanese workers cannot boast of short working hours, but that must be understood in perspective. In 1990 the average annual working hours per worker in Japan were 2,124, the longest of the G7 countries. By comparison, they were 1,948 in the United States, 1,953 in Britain, and 1,598 in Germany.[26] Nevertheless, working hours have become shorter over time in Japan. Total annual working hours decreased steadily from 1960 (2,432) to 1975 (2,064) and stayed at around 2,100 hours until 1988. After that, they fell to 1,972 hours in 1992.[27] The longer working hours in Japan are partly a result of the fact that management and labor prefer employment security and tend to use working hours as a buffer mechanism to adjust to economic changes. When faced with business downturns, management usually cuts overtime hours rather than lays off workers.

Fourth, labor performance can be measured by participation in decision making. Within the company, labor has deepened its participation in managerial decision making. Various institutional networks provided labor with strong foundations for such participation. Furthermore, Japanese unions deepened their participation in public policymaking and won numerous victories, especially after the first oil crisis. The Japanese gov-

[25] Nihon Keizai Shimbunsha, *Zeminaru Nihon keizai nyūmon* (Seminar: Japanese economy) (Tokyo: Nihon Keizai Shimbunsha, 1985), p. 472; Kuramitsu Muramatsu, "Nihon no koyōchousei" (Employment adjustment in Japan), in Takenori Inoki and Yoshio Higuchi, eds., *Nihon no koyō shisutemu to rōdōshijo* (The Japanese employment system and labor market) (Tokyo: Nihon Keizai Shinbunsha, 1995).

[26] Ministry of Labor, *Rōdō hakusho* (1991). These are total working hours, which are normal working hours plus overtime.

[27] Ministry of Labor, *Maitsuki kinrōtōkei chōsa* (Monthly labor statistics survey).

ernment introduced various public policies to facilitate employment. The conservative government committed itself to full employment and established consistent and extensive employment policies, such as the Employment Insurance Law and the Special Law for Structurally Depressed Industries. Even the Nakasone administration of the 1980s, which was supposedly following neoliberalism and the Reagan and Thatcher philosophy of small government, was concerned seriously about employment, at least in the private sector.

Of course, Japanese labor has not always achieved what it wanted, but neither has it always failed. The data reviewed above imply that Japanese labor's performance has been at least comparable to those of other advanced industrial democracies. This, then, is our problematic: given the alleged structural weakness of Japanese labor, why did it achieve such favorable results? The answer, I argue here is that Japanese labor played an active and crucial role in institutionalizing the postwar Japanese political economy in a way that allowed it to secure substantial improvements for its members.

It is important to understand that the performance of labor has changed over time. The orthodox approach tends to see labor politics in a dichotomous way, that is, in terms of victory or defeat, and thus misses the complexity of Japanese labor politics. In contrast, I focus on the dynamic political process that produces various outcomes in a capitalist political economy. I analyze labor's performance in the context of political negotiations between labor, management, and the government. Neither management nor government could unilaterally control workers, but neither could Japanese labor unilaterally achieve its goals. We must pay attention to the dynamic political process in which labor negotiates with management and/or the government on a relatively equal footing. This approach requires great care in judging labor's performance. One measure of performance at a particular time may not be an accurate or fair measure at another time. Furthermore, some unions may realize benefits to themselves at the expense of others. Or their achievements may produce positive spill-over effects that benefit other groups. These spill-over effects are determined by the nature of political negotiation and the way that the outcome is institutionalized. Thus the scope of each outcome must be empirically analyzed. We should not try to judge the results of labor politics in terms of the "real collective interest of the working class as a whole" and thereby regard partial benefits for labor as evidence of the cooptation of labor. I go beyond the strong/weak dichotomy of the class-politics approach and propose a more dynamic understanding of labor politics, focusing on labor's changing goals and its performance mix over time. This approach requires us to analyze Japanese labor politics historically.

The indexes of labor's performance in Japan fall into three stages: period I, 1945–60; period II, 1961–75; and period III, 1976–present. In the first period, the labor movement was more militant and the relations among labor, management, and the government were rather turbulent and chaotic. Long and large strikes were common. In the second period, labor-management relations became well institutionalized. The number of strikes increased, but they became shorter in duration. This change occurred as a result of the development of the Shuntō wage negotiation pattern. Every spring, many unions called for strikes, but these were part of an institutionalized wage bargaining pattern. In the third period, strikes became rare because wage negotiations became more institutionalized and the information exchange between management and labor increased. The two sides thus came to share a basic understanding of the economic situations each one faced.

The relationship between wage and productivity increases has also changed over time in postwar Japan and shows a similar periodization (figs. 4 and 5). In period I, nominal wage increases greatly exceeded productivity (value added per worker) increases in the earlier years, then productivity increases exceeded wage increases in the 1950s, enabling management to easily reinvest its profits. In period II, wage and productivity increases became balanced, and then wage increases once again surpassed productivity increases in the early 1970s. Although the excess was not as large as that in the late 1940s, it is substantial. But again, in period III productivity exceeded wage increases.

This periodization leads us to two questions: How and why did labor politics change from period I to period II, and then change again in period III? The data show that labor politics stabilized in period II after the turbulent times in period I. Japanese workers came to share a similar wage increase pattern with workers in Western countries in period II. Table 1 shows that, in this period in all the selected OECD countries including Japan, both high real wage increases and high productivity increases coexisted. These data suggest that through this transformation, Japanese labor politics came to resemble the "politics of productivity" in postwar Western Europe, where labor and management accepted a principle of high wage increases based on high productivity increases.[28]

[28] Charles Maier, *In Search of Stability: Explorations in Historical Political Economy* (Cambridge: Cambridge University Press, 1987); Stephen Bornstein, "States and Unions: From Postwar Settlement to Contemporary Stalemate," in Bornstein, David Held, and Joel Krieger, eds., *The States in Capitalist Europe: A Casebook* (London: George Allen & Unwin, 1984).

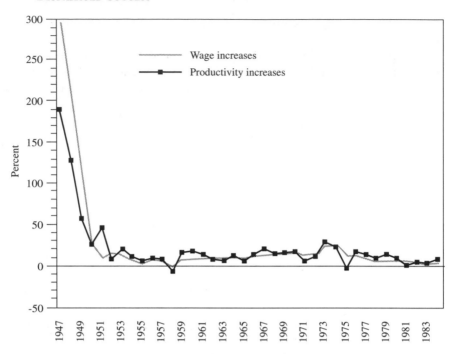

Figure 4. Wage and productivity increases in manufacturing industries. *Wage increase* is the annual average increase in monthly cash earnings of regular workers in manufacturing industries. *Productivity increase* is the annual average increase in value added per person in manufacturing industries. Both figures are not adjusted to the consumer price increase and are nominal. From Statistics Bureau, Management and Coordination Agency, *Historical Statistics of Japan* (Tokyo: Japan Statistical Association, 1987).

In period III, Japanese labor politics diverged from its European counterpart. The "politics of productivity" was challenged in this period in all of these countries. The wage-productivity configuration became unstable and ceased to show a coexistence. The Japanese situation however, seems to stand out. In period III, Japan could maintain relatively high real wage increases based on high productivity increases. While various "incomes policy" experiments failed in European countries and the United States, the Japanese informal "incomes policy" seems to have been successful without any formal government role. Scholars of the orthodox view tend to regard this as a defeat for the union movement. However, as shown above, labor's performance in period III was substantial. Although the nominal wage stopped its rapid increase, real wage increases were better than in other OECD countries. Furthermore, employment security was

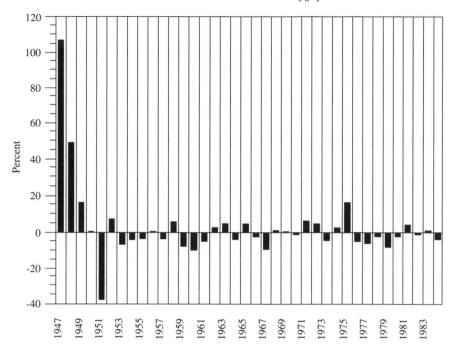

Figure 5. Difference between wage and productivity increases in manufacturing industries in postwar Japan. Difference is calculated by subtracting productivity increase from wage increase in Figure 4. From *Historical Statistics of Japan.*

higher and labor's participation in company decision making as well as national policymaking was strengthened.

In chapter 2 I situate the Japanese experience in a theoretical framework, reviewing the existing conceptualization of the power of labor and summarize the main argument of the book.

Chapter 3 describes how Japanese labor achieved and maintained its legitimate status within the company, during the labor offensive in the late 1940s and the management counter-offensive in the early 1950s. The chapter shows that while labor failed to nationalize the achievements it made at the company level, management also failed to win dominance in labor-management relations within the company. As labor and management collided at the national level in the early 1950s, an end result was the formation of a productivity coalition between management and labor within the private company. The national-level forces were not powerful enough to determine the nature of this coalition. Management sought to

Table 1. Difference between wage and productivity increases, compared by country, 1960–89

Period	Increase	Japan	U.S.	Germany	France	U.K.	Italy	Sweden
1960–68	Wage	5.2%	1.6%	4.3%	4.0%	na	3.9%	na
	Productivity	9.0	3.2	4.7	6.8	3.4%	7.2	5.2%
	Difference	−3.8	−1.6	−0.4	−2.8	na	−3.3	na
1968–73	Wage	9.7	1.2	2.6	3.2	2.0	2.8	1.8
	Productivity	10.4	3.5	4.5	5.8	3.9	5.6	5.4
	Difference	−0.7	−2.3	−1.9	−2.6	−1.9	−2.9	−3.6
1973–79	Wage	1.7	0.0	2.4	3.7	0.9	5.2	1.2
	Productivity	4.5	0.3	3.1	3.7	na	5.4	1.2
	Difference	−2.8	−0.3	−0.7	0.0	na	−0.2	0.0
1979–89	Wage	1.5	−0.9	1.3	0.9	2.6	0.7	0.5
	Productivity	4.5	2.3	1.0	2.7	na	4.1	3.0
	Difference	−3.0	−3.2	0.3	−1.8	na	−3.4	−2.5

SOURCE: OECD, *Historical Statistics*.

NOTE: *Wage increase* is the average annual real wage increase in manufacturing. *Productivity increase* is the average annual increase of real value added per person in manufacturing. The difference is calculated by subtracting productivity increase from wage increase.

minimize labor unrest within their companies and strove for cooperation from workers, while private enterprise unions sought wage increases in line with productivity increases and participation in decision making. This set the initial conditions for the postwar Japanese labor movement, which I call the micro-level labor accommodation.

Chapter 4 takes up two tasks. First, it analyzes how enterprise unions succeeded in nationalizing their wage negotiations in Shuntō, which brought about high wage increases broadly across sectors. This was a result of inter- and intra-class politics. Second, the chapter describes how Shuntō wage practices contributed to Japanese economic growth and at the same time drove unions to advance micro- and macro-level agendas, specifically participation in management decision making and in the formation of industrial policy. The public-sector-dominated, leftist Sōhyō refused to follow this path and gradually lost its leadership in the labor movement to the private sector unions.

Chapters 5, 6, and 7 focus on the unions' activities in national policymaking. Chapter 5 describes the politicization of the labor movement in the 1970s. Initially, Sōhyō succeeded in achieving various welfare policy victories based on its social democratic strategy. Sōhyō's main focus was on distributive issues. The first oil crisis, however, drove private-sector unions to politicize their activities with regard to the issues of employment and industrial restructuring. The private-sector unions developed these activities based on micro-level labor accommodation, and this eroded the Sōhyō movement.

Chapter 6 analyzes how enterprise unions succeeded in achieving various policies to protect their members' employment security by comparing the cases of the coal-mining industry in the early 1960s and the manufacturing industries in the 1970s. The chapter shows that a coalition between unions and management in the given sectors and the governing LDP's effort to expand its support base provided labor with an important opportunity to achieve its policy victories.

Chapter 7 describes how the private-sector unions survived the era of conservative resurgence in the 1980s, and increased their political significance in national policymaking.

In Chapter 8 I conclude this book, puting the Japanese labor movement in comparative perspective and showing its implications for the study of labor more generally.

CHAPTER TWO

Reenvisioning the Role of Labor in Japan

Among students of labor politics, the Japanese experience has not attracted significant interest. The implications of the Japanese experience for the study of labor politics seem to have been all too evident: the most decentralized labor movement in the advanced industrial democracies failed to enjoy prolabor policies let alone establish a labor party government. The end result has been continuous conservative rule. This interpretation fits well with the conventional view of labor politics. But the conventional understanding has a bias that disparages what the Japanese labor movement achieved. An emerging notion of labor politics, which focuses on the micro level, provides us with a new lens with which to analyze the Japanese experience. Furthermore, I believe, the Japanese case has critical implications for this new notion of labor politics.

THE CONVENTIONAL VIEW OF LABOR POLITICS

Most scholars studying labor usually presume that labor's power is a function of its resources—the number of workers organized and the degree to which they are unified. The emergence of a neocorporatist approach in the late 1970s and the early 1980s further consolidated this conception of labor's political power.[1] Students of corporatism usually assume that the existence of a highly centralized and broadly organized union is a prerequisite for the corporatist political arrangement.[2] Such a

[1] Schmitter and Lehmbruch, eds., *Trends toward Corporatist Intermediation.*

[2] For instance, Philippe C. Schmitter, "Interest Intermediation and Regime Governability in Contemporary Western Europe and North America," in Suzanne Berger, ed., *Organizing*

union movement will be so strong, it is thought, that the government and/or capital will have to accommodate the unions' demands during tripartite central bargaining. Corporatist scholars thus tend to treat the centralization of labor organizations as a surrogate variable for strength, rather than analyzing the process itself, namely, what labor actually achieved and how. Korpi's "power difference model of conflict," for instance, tends to focus on the "power resources" of labor rather than on the way labor is actually mobilized.[3]

It is not surprising that this conventional theorizing of labor power leads people to the conclusion that Japanese labor is comparatively weak. Andrew Taylor, for example, proposes that "a centralised union movement composed of few industrial unions with a collective ethos enjoying a high density of membership will be more influential than a decentralized movement with many unions and a low density of membership. . . . Union political ineffectiveness would thus seem to be maximised in Japan: multiple levels of organization (enterprise, region, industry, and national) with authority concentrated at the lowest level."[4] He continues, however, by arguing that "the system of company consultation and the annual wage bargaining (Shuntō) have given some unions, especially those in the very large, export oriented manufacturing companies, a voice in government. . . . Economic difficulties in the 1970s and 1980s boosted the political influence of the unions, encouraging 'labor front unification.' " Following conventional wisdom, he believes that a unified labor movement is a necessary condition for success.

Pempel and Tsunekawa, drawing directly from the neocorporatist framework, argue that while the Japanese political economy resembles corporatism in that various economic interests have been incorporated in intensive negotiation with the government, "the major exception to the broad trend of encorporatization in the national economic interest was labor which although it became extremely powerful in the postwar period was consistently allied with political parties on the 'outs.' "[5] They carefully

---

Interests in Western Europe (Cambridge: Cambridge University Press, 1981); Walter Korpi and Michael Shalev, "Strikes, Industrial Relations, and Class Conflict in Capitalist Societies," *British Journal of Sociology* 30-2 (June 1979); David Cameron, "Social Democracy, Corporatism, Labor Quiescence, and the Representation of Economic Interest in Advanced Capitalist Society," in John H. Goldthorpe, ed., *Order and Conflict in Contemporary Capitalism* (London: Oxford University Press, 1984).

[3] Korpi, *Working Class in Welfare Capitalism*, pp. 45–47. John Stephens argues in a similar vein in *The Transition from Capitalism to Socialism* (London: Macmillan, 1979).

[4] Andrew J. Taylor, *Trade Unions and Politics: A Comparative Introduction* (London: Macmillan, 1989), pp. 19–21.

[5] Pempel and Tsunekawa, "Corporatism without Labor?" pp. 261–64.

sort out various reasons why such strength on the part of labor in the immediate postwar period was not turned into a formalized role for labor in the making of state policy or in the political economy: an early collapse of the socialist government; labor's division into two peak associations, one of which was completely hostile to any coalition with business; the Allied occupation policy change; the prolabor parties' inability to attract significant numbers of non-union voters; and so forth. Throughout, they emphasize the fact that persistent enterprise unionism undergirds labor's weakness.

This conventional theorizing presumes the centralized and unified labor organization to be a precondition for power. This claim consists of two distinct propositions. First, vertical diversification (that is, decentralization) necessarily results in a co-optation of labor within the company. Second, the horizontal diversification of labor organizations (that is, fragmentation) endangers labor's power because the capitalists and/or the state can easily dominate a divided labor movement. However, recent analyses of labor politics strongly cast doubt on these two assertions.

LABOR'S MICRO-LEVEL POWER

The 1980s witnessed important changes in labor-management relations in the industrialized democracies. Political and economic pressures to decentralize the collective bargaining system were pervasive in all these countries, and many scholars tend to associate these pressures with a weakening of labor power.[6]

However, several recent studies show that decentralized union structures are not so hazardous to the power of labor, but rather may constitute a basis for renewed power. Based on his well-organized comparative analysis of work reorganization in the American and German automobile industries, Lowell Turner demonstrates that a strong shop-floor workers'

---

[6] Katz, "Decentralization of Collective Bargaining." For instance, Scott Lash and John Urry, *The End of Organized Capitalism* (Madison: University of Wisconsin Press, 1987); Offe, *Disorganized Capitalism*, chap. 6. Offe, focusing on the decentralization tendency in the firm-specific work council in Germany, argues as follows: "The work council, both because of its relative weakness and the fact that it quite naturally deals primarily with particular problems and interests within the firm, is a body whose noticeable strengthening *vis-à-vis* the wage-contract level must lead to 'centrifugal' tendencies in trade union policy, and this means an intensification of the problem of unification" (p. 162). "What is crucial for trade unions is that they are only capable of action as *organizations* to the extent that their membership base is prepared to act in solidarity in the service of interests that are recognized as common interests" (p. 164).

institution (for example, a work council) in Germany helped the union to make reorganization more favorable to workers.[7] German labor succeeded in gaining access to management decision making, as a result of this plant-level institution.

Kathleen Thelen, from her study of plant bargaining in three industries adversely affected by macroeconomic developments in the 1970s and 1980s, shows that industrial adjustment and economic adaptation to these crises in West Germany have by and large been accomplished with and not against labor. She argues that the key to the German negotiated adjustment lies not in closed sessions of tripartite bargaining in Bonn but rather in the interaction of central unionism and the institutions for labor-management negotiation at various sub-national levels. Decentralized negotiations and labor's subsequent participation at the plant and company level contributed to this success. A recent article of hers further strengthens this argument by comparing the Swedish and German situations.[8] She finds that unions in Sweden—which are clearly stronger than those in Germany by standard measures such as higher membership levels, closer links to the Social Democratic Party, and centralization of union organization—were faced with an all-out attack on national-level bargaining by employers in the 1980s. By contrast, German unions maintained their centralized industrial bargaining. Because of the dual system in Germany, the pressures for shop-floor flexibility were resolved through a process of "negotiated decentralization." These studies require us to reconsider the conventional measures of labor's strength by showing that unions can maintain their power even at the micro level.[9]

Students of the orthodox view, however, argue that labor's participation in managerial decision making is just a co-optation of labor. This assertion has been forcefully made in the study of Japanese labor. Kunth Dohse, Ulrich Jürgens, and Thomas Malsch describe the Japanese company system as "Toyotism," a system in which management prerogatives are largely unlimited. Michael Burawoy calls it "hegemonic despotism" and claims that it allows management's super-exploitation of workers. However, as

---

[7] Lowell Turner, *Democracy at Work: Changing World Markets and the Future of Labor Unions* (Ithaca: Cornell University Press, 1991).

[8] Kathleen A. Thelen, *Union of Parts: Labor Politics in Postwar Germany* (Ithaca: Cornell University Press, 1991) and Thelen, "West European Labor in Transition: Sweden and Germany Compared," *World Politics* 46-1 (October 1993).

[9] The Italian case also demonstrates that decentralized unions show resilience against management offensives. Richard M. Locke, "The Resurgence of the Local Unions: Industrial Restructuring and Industrial Relations in Italy," *Politics and Society* 18-3 (September 1990). Cf. Kathleen A. Thelen, "Beyond Corporatism: Toward a New Framework for the Study of Labor in Advanced Capitalism," *Comparative Politics* 27-1 (October 1994).

Martin Kenney and Richard Florida argue, this super-exploitation thesis "misses the critical organizational innovations which have propelled Japanese industry to the forefront of global capitalism and have led to dramatic increases in living standards for Japanese workers."[10] Given those conditions, the potential of labor's power within the company itself should not be discounted.

What are labor's "power resources" at the micro level? Indeed, what do we mean by power in the workplace?[11] Neo-Marxists emphasize that capitalist industrialization evoked a relentless process of homogenization and simplification of work, which they regard as a deskilling of workers. In the quintessential book describing this process, Harry Braverman argues that workers whose craft skills allow them to control the labor process are able to resist management's demands. To overcome this resistance scientific management, or Taylorism, was developed to "dissolve the labor process as a process conducted by the worker and reconstitute it as a process conducted by management."[12] The purpose was to remove conceptual functions from workers' tasks and to make workers more like machines that would smoothly execute management's directions.

This neo-Marxist thesis has recently come under attack due to a lack of empirical support and for its theoretical problems.[13] One critical flaw is the craft/Taylorism dichotomy. In other words, management's problem in dealing with workers is not easily solved by the introduction of Taylorism or degradation of skill. This flaw is related to another flaw, that is, the implicit presumption that workers are passive and unable to resist the pressure from management.[14] However, various studies demonstrate that management has had to invent manifold managerial systems to control the labor process. For instance, Richard Edwards writes, "Continuing

[10] Kunth Dohse, Ulrich Jürgens, and Thomas Malsch, "From 'Fordism' to 'Toyotism'? The Social Organization of the Labor Process in the Japanese Automobile Industry," *Politics and Society* 14-2 (1985). Michael Burawoy, *The Politics of Production: Factory Regimes under Capitalism and Socialism* (London: Verso, 1985), p. 143. Martin Kenney and Richard Florida, *Beyond Mass Production: The Japanese System and Its Transfer to the U.S.* (Oxford: Oxford University Press, 1992), p. 37.

[11] For an excellent literature review on this issue, see Steven Peter Vallas, *Power in the Workplace: The Politics of Production at AT&T* (Albany: State University of New York Press, 1993), chap. 2. My argument is indebted to this review.

[12] Harry Braverman, *Labor and Monopoly Capital: The Degradation of Work in the Twentieth Century* (New York: Monthly Review, 1974). Quote on p. 170.

[13] See Paul Adler, "Automation, Skill and the Future of Capitalism," *Berkeley Journal of Sociology* 33 (1988); Paul Adler and Bryan Borys, "Automation and Skill: Three Generations of Research on the NC Case," *Politics and Society*, 17-3 (September 1989); and Vallas, *Power in the Workplace*, pp. 22–24.

[14] E. g., David Stark, "Class Struggle and the Transformation of the Labor Process," *Theory and Society* 9-1 (January 1980).

conflict in the workplace and employers' attempts to contain it have thus brought the modern American working class under the sway of three quite different systems for organizing and controlling their work: simple control, technical control (with union participation), and bureaucratic control."[15] When workforces were small and the boss was both close and powerful, simple control, in which power over workers was exercised arbitrarily, was prevalent. Technical control, in Edwards' terms, is quite similar to what is commonly understood as scientific management or Taylorism, which has flourished in modern large firms. However, Edwards does not believe that technical control defines the management system in modern industries. There, he finds a third system, bureaucratic control, which "rests on the principle of embedding control in the social structure or the social relations of the workplace."[16] In this system, rule of law replaces "rule by supervisor command," and supervisors and workers alike become subject to the dictates of company policy. This system goes hand in hand with the development of an internal labor market in which workers develop company-specific skills and ascend the career ladder within the firm. This system is effective as long as workers regard the company policy to be fair. In a similar formulation, Michael Burawoy finds that the management system has changed from one of despotism and coercion, to one of hegemony and consent.[17]

Although these scholars pay needed attention to the complexity of management system developments, their thesis still has problems. For example, they assume that management can always finally control the process of labor. They regard any management concession to workers as a cleverer and more elaborate way to control the labor process. Despite the fact that they try to understand political dynamics on the shop floor, their analysis tends to produce a deterministic view of managerial hegemony.

Several scholars are more confident that technological development would make the work structure less hierarchical by enskilling industrial workers.[18] The new technology requires more educated and technically skilled workers who can perform conceptual functions on the shopfloor. If this is the case, the bureaucratic control or hegemonic regime based on

---

[15] Richard Edwards, *Contested Terrain: The Transformation of the Workplace in the Twentieth Century* (New York: Basic Books, 1979), p. 21. See also, David M. Gordon, Richard Edwards, and Michael Reich, *Segmented Work, Divided Workers: The Historical Transformation of Labor in the United States* (Cambridge: Cambridge University Press, 1982).

[16] Edwards, *Contested Terrain*, p. 21.

[17] Burawoy, *Politics of Production*.

[18] E.g., Michael J. Piore and Charles F. Sabel, *The Second Industrial Divide* (New York: Basic Books, 1984); Larry Harschborn, *Beyond Mechanization* (Cambridge: MIT Press, 1984).

workers' consent may not be management's unilateral success, but rather its concession to labor. Worker influence increases with the increasing importance of their skills in the production process.

The literature on internal labor markets supports this assertion. The internal labor market (ILM) is an organizational unit, such as a plant or a company, in which the pricing and allocation of labor is governed by a set of administrative rules and procedures. Many observers have found a growth of ILMs within firms and subsequent developments such as the growth of company-specific skills among workers and on-the-job training practice.[19] Although there is no consensus among scholars about the theoretical concept and the origins of ILMs, nor any empirical measure of them, they agree that firm-specific skills are an important component of ILMs and that having such skills makes employees a valued asset not easily replaced from the outside.[20] Employees with these skills will tend to want to remain with their employer because such skills lack value to other employers. But the development of ILMs enables workers to stand on a relatively equal footing with their employer.

It is in Japan that ILMs have been most highly developed and workers' involvement in the production process has received the most attention. Kazuo Koike demonstrates that Japanese blue-collar workers in large companies develop wide-ranging skills in a career over a long period within a company. Many other labor scholars have also found that Japanese workers acquire many skills because of the practice of job rotation or intra-workplace job movement.[21] Workers devise better methods of production on the shop floor. This skill formation contributes not just to high worker morale but also to their technological knowledge. This skill has two implications. First, according to Koike, as this skill is company-specific, workers prefer to stay in the same company because of the high cost of "exiting." As a result, if workers are not satisfied with working conditions, they tend to voice their complaints within the company rather than choosing to leave.[22] This results in intensive intra-company politics.

---

[19] E.g., Peter B. Doeringer and Michael J. Piore, *Internal Labor Markets and Manpower Analysis* (Lexington, Mass.: DC Heath, 1971).

[20] Robert P. Althauser, "Internal Labor Markets," *Annual Review of Sociology* 15 (1989).

[21] For instance, Koike, *Shokuba no rōdō kumiai*; Kikuji Yoneyama, *Gijutsu kakushin to shokuba kanri* (Technological change and shop floor management) (Tokyo: Bokutakusha, 1978); Takashi Kawakita, *Sangyō hendō to rōmu kanri* (Industrial change and personnel management) (Tokyo: Nihon Rōdō Kenkyukikō, 1989).

[22] Albert O. Hirschman, *Exit, Voice, and Loyalty* (Cambridge: Harvard University Press, 1972). Kazuo Koike, "Josetsu: Howaitokaraka kumiai moderu" (Introduction: The model of the white-collarized union), in Nihon Rōdō Kyōkai, ed., *80 nendai no rōshikankei*.

Second, skill can be a power resource for workers because management depends on their skill for productivity increases.

If this enskilling thesis is true, it calls our attention to a wider context. Some scholars focus mainly on endogenous developments on the shop floor resulting from new technology. However, this development has exogenous causes, particularly, the nature of market competition and the timing of industrialization. In Japan, management's dependence on workers' skill was enhanced by the historically backward state of Japanese industry and the harsh competition that Japanese manufacturing companies faced domestically as well as internationally. Japanese management was in a vulnerable position with regard to labor, because it had to utilize its production facilities in the most effective way.

The impact of an international force on the work organization is now widely shared by students of labor. Wolfgang Streeck, concurring on the enskilling thesis, argues that management, faced with the new world competition which requires flexible production, is dependent upon the development of workers' skill. Turner also emphasizes the change in world market competition as a driving force for changes in the workplace. If this is the case, Streeck maintains, the "economic structure of capitalism continues to offer important political opportunities for trade unions."[23]

Management in Japan had to be careful not to alienate workers in order to catch up with the fast-starters and survive the market competition.[24] In a word, Japanese management was dependent on workers for their cooperation, and this dependence gave labor much power.

Many organizational sociologists assume the critical role of dependence in creating power. For instance, Richard Emerson writes: "Thus it would appear that the power to control or influence the other resides in control over things he values, which may range all the way from oil resources to ego support. In short, power resides implicitly in the other's dependence."[25] Broadly based on this perspective, organization sociologists

[23] Wolfgang Streeck, "Skills and the Limits of Neo-Liberalism: The Enterprise of the Future as a Place of Learning," discussion paper #FS I 88-16, Wissenschaftszentrum Berlin für Sozialforschung (October 1988), p. 9; Turner, *Democracy at Work*, p. 9.

[24] Many Japanese companies financed capital by borrowing money from banks. For their sense of vulnerability, see Kent E. Calder, *Crisis and Compensation: Public Policy and Political Stability in Japan* (Princeton: Princeton University Press, 1988).

[25] Richard M. Emerson, "Power-Dependence Relations," *American Sociological Review* 27-1 (February 1962), p. 32. See also Peter M. Blau, *Exchange and Power in Social Life* (New York: John Wiley, 1964); James D. Thompson, *Organizations in Action* (New York: McGraw Hill, 1967).

argue that the power of the actors within an organization is a function of the actor's ability to cope with uncertainty, which has its theoretical origin in the works of Richard Cyert, James March, and James Thompson.[26]

Michel Crozier, in his analysis of French tobacco processing plants, found that maintenance workers had more power than their formal status would suggest. He argues that they could maintain power by coping with the only major, unpredictable uncertainty—machine breakdowns—in otherwise highly routinized plants.[27] The ability to cope with uncertainty made other actors in the plant dependent on maintenance workers. D. J. Hickson and his colleagues made this argument in an operationalized hypothesis in order to explain the difference of power among organizational subunits:

> Thus, intraorganizational dependency can be associated with two contributing variables: (1) the degree to which a subunit copes with uncertainty for other subunits, and (2) the extent to which a subunit's coping activities are substitutable. But if coping with uncertainty, and substitutability, are to be in some way related to power, there is a necessary assumption of some degree of task interconnection among subunits. By definition, organization requires a minimum link. Therefore, a third variable, centrality, refers to the varying degree above such a minimum with which the activities of a subunit are linked with those other subunits.[28]

These scholars do not deal with unions in their theoretical frameworks because they are analyzing the power of the formal subunit of organization.[29] However, if management becomes dependent on a group of workers, this theoretical perspective can be extended to analyze workers' power. It will enable us to understand how workers can utilize their skill to influence management decisions.

---

[26] Richard M. Cyert and James G. March, *A Behavioral Theory of the Firm* (Englewood Cliffs, N.J.: Prentice-Hall, 1963); Thompson, *Organizations in Action.*

[27] Michel Crozier, *The Bureaucratic Phenomenon* (Chicago: University of Chicago Press, 1964).

[28] D. J. Hickson, C. R. Hinings, C. A. Lee, R. E. Schneck, and J. M. Pennings, "A Strategic Contingencies' Theory of Intraorganizational Power," *Administrative Science Quarterly* 16-2 (June 1971). They first tested this hypothesis in 1974. C. R. Hinnings, D. J. Hickson, J. M. Pennings, and R. E. Schneck, "Structural Conditions of Intraorganizational Power," *Administrative Science Quarterly* 19-1 (March 1974). The *Social Science Citation Index* lists citations in journal articles of these works from 1975 to 1985. See Carol Stak Saunders, "The Strategic Contingencies Theory of Power: Multiple Perspectives," *Journal of Management Studies* 27-1 (January 1990).

[29] Their lack of interest in the unions' role is itself interesting. This might reflect the conventional view of labor as a production factor, as opposed to a legitimate participant in the firm.

The problem of this approach, however, resides not in its applicability to labor-management relations, but in its own theoretical framework. This view of power is rather static and deterministic. It assumes that power is a function of dependence, which is determined by the ability to cope with uncertainty. Dependence, however, may not be transformed into actual power in the form of influence over the parts of the decision process.[30] Furthermore, uncertainty is not just produced through technological process but is created politically.[31] What the organizational subunits value and feel responsible for is also socially constructed. Here intra-organizational politics is very important.

This criticism requires us to further consider the relation between skill and power. We should not see the enskilling of workers and the subsequent increase in workers' influence within the firm as an automatic process, determined by technological development.[32] Rather it is a political process. David Noble argues that the process of enskilling becomes political when management resists the technical and economic pressures to increase the workers' skill level. This is because of management's ideological and political commitment to the older management system, which ensures its traditional superior status over workers. Noble claims that the market force at this stage is on the side of labor because greater competition forces management to make its business more competitive by introducing a new management system.[33] However, breaking with the traditional management system is a political act because of management's likely resistance. The political opportunity created by management's dependence on workers' skill does not directly guarantee one definite political outcome, in this case an increase in the influence of labor. Instead, political negotiation intermediates between opportunity and outcome.

Steven Vallas in his analysis of the labor process at AT&T, finds a decoupling of skill and power. He demonstrates that the introduction of new information technology brought about a new situation for workers:

[30] Jeffrey Pfeffer, *Power in Organizations* (Marshfield, Mass.: Pitman, 1981), p. 115.

[31] Andrew M. Pettigrew focuses on the tactical manipulation of information to acquire power. *The Politics of Organizational Decision-Making* (London: Tavistock, 1973).

[32] On this point, these scholars differ from the earlier industrial sociologists who had a pluralist perspective and saw that industrialization inevitably brought about pluralistic industrialism with less overt protest. They focused more on political dynamics. One prominent text of this pluralist school is Clark Kerr, John T. Dunlop, Frederick H. Harbison, and Charles A. Myers, *Industrialism and Industrial Man* (Cambridge: Harvard University Press, 1960).

[33] David Noble, *Forces of Production: A Social History of Industrial Automation* (New York: Knopf, 1984).

"Even when their jobs remain highly complex, their skills no longer confer the same power or control over the work process as was previously the case. . . . While management has indeed extended its control over production, it has done so not by uprooting workers' skills but by placing information systems at the directive nodes of the productive circuitry and progressively removing workers to more peripheral locations in the labor process."[34] His conclusion, however, leads us to a broader interpretation. He argues that one structural support underpinning management's control of the labor process after the introduction of new technology is the institutional pattern of collective bargaining that has emerged in the wake of the Wagner Act. The argument goes as follows:

> As information technologies have reduced workers' capacity to informally negotiate with their supervisors, workers have grown increasingly dependent on the formal levers of union power. . . . Workers therefore find themselves caught in a web of legal obligations that shifts the initiative away from the shop floor and seems only to institutionalize managerial control over production. The combined effect has been to reduce the resources with which workers can challenge the company, leaving workers little choice in their everyday working lives but to submit to management control.[35]

In other words, labor failed to actualize its potential for power because of institutional constraints rather than as an inevitable byproduct of new technology.[36]

In Japan, enterprise unions were in better institutional settings to transform their skill into power, based on ILM and technological innovation. This type of skill is the basis of the semi-autonomous work peer groups in Japanese companies.[37] Many labor scholars have pointed out the existence of semi-autonomous work peer groups on the shop floor in Japanese companies, very often being the union leaders themselves. Labor-management consultation within the plant also provides a important institutional setting for labor to develop their power.

However, the power of the union is not determined solely by the nature

---

[34] Vallas, *Power in the Workplace*, pp. 186–87.

[35] Ibid., p. 189.

[36] Cf. Robert J. Thomas, "Participation and Control: A Shopfloor Perspective on Employee Participation," in Richard J. Magjuka and Samuel B. Bacharach, eds., *Research in the Sociology of Organizations: Structuring Participation in Organizations*, vol. 7 (London: JAI Press, 1989).

[37] Keisuke Nakamura and Michio Nitta, "Developments in Industrial Relations and Human Resource Practices in Japan," paper prepared for the first phase of the International Network on Industrial Relations and Human Resource Policy and Practice, March 1993. This is the best review of recent studies on Japanese industrial relations available in English.

of the intra-company institutional setting nor by skill formation. Union power can be political in nature. Japanese management in the 1950s needed to be conciliatory to the moderate unions in order to keep radical leftist groups out of union leadership. This was another reason for management dependence on the union, and it facilitated the formation of a dense network of interaction between the moderate union and management, which in turn gave labor a stronger institutional base. The labor offensive in the late 1940s also left an important legacy for unions by consolidating their status as legitimate actors within the enterprise. Labor became a member of the enterprise, not just a production factor. Given these conditions, management needed to mobilize workers in the production process in order to survive.[38] These opportunities enabled private-sector unions to form a "productivity coalition" with management within the firm. This was the bottom line of Japanese postwar labor politics.

Scholars should pay more careful attention to how unions develop their negotiations with management, taking into account political opportunities as well as constraints. Labor, even if isolated as a result of enterprise unionism, has the potential to develop power within the enterprise. Of course, this does not mean these political opportunities within the enterprise automatically provide labor with favorable outcomes. The degree and nature of success is contingent on intra-company political dynamics. I argue that Japanese enterprise unions succeeded in promoting their interests based on their intra-organizational power and through political dynamics.

LABOR'S MACRO-LEVEL POWER

The second theoretical question is whether a unified labor organization is a precondition for labor's power at the national level. This point is

[38] Daniel Ross, James Womack, and Daniel Jones, from a slightly different perspective, focus on the introduction of a new production strategy, i.e., lean production, as opposed to mass production, and claim that lean production can scarcely be more oppressive than mass production. They stress the role of trust and confidence as the foundation of this system. "If management fails to lead and the work force feels that no reciprocal obligations are in force, it is quite predictable that lean production will revert to mass production." Employee involvement is quintessential for effective production. In this context, workers may enjoy intra-organizational power, which has been studied by many organizational theorists. James P. Womack, Daniel Jones, and Daniel Roos, *The Machine That Changed the World* (New York: Rawson Associates, 1990), p. 103. Cf. Charles C. Heckscher, *The New Unionism: Employee Involvement in the Changing Corporation* (1988; rpt. Ithaca: Cornell University Press, 1996); Kenney and Florida, *Beyond Mass Production.*

important in understanding Japanese labor politics. First, Japanese enter-prise unions lack organizational unity—which industrial unions enjoy at the national level—often because of company loyalty. Second, the Japa-nese labor movement has undergone a deep ideological cleavage between the right and the left. This horizontal division is regarded as a source of weakness, by conventional theorists.

An implicit assumption behind the conventional understanding of the power of labor is that the capitalists and/or the government are a unified and powerful force controlling the political economy. In that view, labor has to mobilize enough resources to overwhelm these forces in order to realize its own interests. This "resource-centered" view has faced some recent criticism from the related field of social movement studies. Sidney Tarrow writes that studies of the constraints on collective action of the poor are well-developed, but much less developed are studies of the political situations in which the state becomes vulnerable to collective action. Here the concept of "political opportunity structure is developed." First, Peter Eisinger uses this concept to explain black urban protest. He argues that the openness of city government to black protest determined movement forms. Frances Fox Piven and Richard Cloward regard the instability of political alignment as an important component of political opportunity. J. C. Jenkins and Charles Perrow focus on the availability of allies and support groups. Herbert Kitschelt shows that policymaking structures may determine opportunities. The political opportunity struc-ture is certainly less a variable than a cluster of variables, but a message for the study of labor seems to be clear. If the social movement, which usually possesses fewer resources than labor unions, sometimes enjoys successes, why is the amount of resources a determining condition for the labor movement's success? We should focus instead on the political op-portunities for labor unions in order to explain their influence and successes.[39]

In this study, I borrow the concept of political opportunity structure as

---

[39] Sidney Tarrow, "National Politics and Collective Action: Recent Theory and Research in Western Europe and the United States," *Annual Review of Sociology* 14 (1988), pp. 429–30; J. Craig Jenkins and Kurt Schock, "Global Structures and Political Processes in the Study of Domestic Political Conflict," *Annual Review of Sociology* 18 (1992); Peter K. Eisinger, "The Conditions of Protest Behavior in American Cities," *American Political Science Review* 67-1 (March 1973); Frances Fox Piven and Richard A. Cloward, *Poor People's Movements: Why They Succeed, How They Fail* (New York: Vintage, 1977); J. Craig Jenkins and Charles Perrow, "Insurgency of the Powerless Farm Workers Movements (1946–1972)," *American Sociological Review* 42-2 (April 1977); Herbert Kitschelt, "Political Opportunity Structures and Political Protest: Anti-nuclear Movements in Four Democracies," *British Journal of Political Science* 16-1 (January 1986). The labor movement is not usually treated as a social movement in this literature, with some exceptions.

a frame of reference. Tarrow formulated five types of opportunities: institutional opportunities, the stability of coalitions and alignments, elite divisions and/or tolerance for protest, the presence of support groups and allies, and the policymaking capacities of states.[40] In this analysis, I further simplify the concept and introduce two aspects of the political opportunity structure for labor: (1) political coalition formation and (2) labor policy networks.[41]

Political coalition formation is a variable reflecting the extent to which labor can be incorporated into the governing coalition. I focus on the alliance politics of labor unions. The policy network for labor is a variable that shows how favorable the institutional setting is for labor's participation in the policymaking process. The policy network is an institutionalized interrelationship between state and society within a domestic structure.[42] Political coalition formation represents the political situation for labor unions created by interaction among political actors, while the policy network represents institutional situations for labor unions.

Recent studies show that cross-class politics is a more important determinant of labor politics than labor's resource mobilization. Much of the literature on social democracy has depicted its consolidation as a process in which capital has been politically tamed by a strong labor movement. The Swedish model was regarded as a typical case.[43] However, several recent studies criticize this interpretation. Adam Przeworski emphasizes the point that capital and labor rationally chose social democracy based on their distinct calculations of advantages of such institutional settings. Peter Katzenstein focuses on the cross-class coalition formation as one important base of democratic corporatism in the small European states.[44] Peter Swenson also emphasizes this cross-class politics, by disaggregating capital and labor, and shows a dynamic process behind the consolidation of social democracy in Sweden as well as in Germany. He demonstrates that the consolidation of centralized bargaining, a definitive characteristic of Swedish social democratic corporatism, was more "the product of a

---

[40] Tarrow, "National Politics and Collective Action," pp. 429–30.

[41] See Peter J. Katzenstein, "Introduction: Domestic and International Forces and Strategies of Foreign Economic Policy," in Katzenstein, ed., *Between Power and Plenty: Foreign Economic Policies of Advanced Industrial States* (Madison: University of Wisconsin Press, 1978).

[42] Ibid., p. 19.

[43] E.g., Korpi, *Working Class in Welfare Capitalism* and Stephens, *Transition from Capitalism to Socialism*.

[44] Adam Przeworski, *Capitalism and Social Democracy* (Cambridge: Cambridge University Press, 1985); Peter J. Katzenstein, *Small States in World Markets: Industrial Policy in Europe* (Ithaca: Cornell University Press, 1985); and idem, *Corporatism and Change: Austria, Switzerland, and the Politics of Industry* (Ithaca: Cornell University Press, 1984).

cross-class, interfactional coalition of interests than an armistice between classes at war, for there were to be losers in each camp."[45] Cross-class coalitions between employers and workers in export-oriented industries were a driving force for centralized bargaining. There were inter- and intra-class politics rather than a unilateral and overwhelming power of labor behind a corporatist political economy.

These analyses demonstrate the insufficiency of arguments that labor and capital as unitary and homogeneous entities. Such criticisms are not new, of course. Pluralist political scientists, like Robert Dahl, criticized the elitist approach over thirty years ago, while in the field of labor studies the theory of pluralistic industrialism also did this.[46] However, the assumption that the two classes were homogeneous, either in reality or in potentiality, has obsessed students of labor for a long time. Even among pluralists, two prominent scholars, Dahl and Charles Lindblom, changed their views and now regard business as a dominant political force based on its privileged position within the capitalist economy.[47] Recently, various students have cast renewed doubt on this assumption. As David Vogel eloquently argues, the class consciousness of the bourgeoisie varies over time, and business is not a unified political entity. "There is nothing about the nature, scope or magnitude of the power wielded by business that cannnot be accounted for within the framework of a sophisticated model of interest-group politics."[48] The capitalist class unity is criticized even among neo-Marxists. Fred Block, for instance, argued that a diversity of interests exists among particular capitalists, interests which could not be generalized across the class.[49]

[45] Peter Swenson, *Fair Shares: Unions, Pay, and Politics in Sweden and West Germany* (Ithaca: Cornell University Press, 1989). Swenson formulates this point more clearly in "Bringing Capital Back In, or Social Democracy Reconsidered: Employer Power, Cross-Class Alliances, and Centralization of Industrial Relations in Denmark and Sweden," *World Politics* 43-4 (July 1991). See also James Fulcher, *Labour Movements, Employers, and the State: Conflict and Co-operation in Britain and Sweden* (Oxford: Clarendon Press, 1991); Jonas Pontusson, "Behind and Beyond Social Democracy in Sweden," *New Left Review* 143 (January–February 1984).

[46] Cf. Robert A. Dahl, *Who Governs? Democracy and Power in an American City* (New Haven: Yale University Press, 1961); Kerr, Dunlop, Harbison, and Myers, *Industrialism and Industrial Man*.

[47] Charles Lindblom, *Politics and Markets: The World's Political Economic Systems* (New York: Basic Books, 1977); Robert A. Dahl, *A Preface to Economic Democracy* (Berkeley: University of California Press, 1985).

[48] David Vogel, "Political Science and the Study of Corporate Power," *British Journal of Political Science* 17-4 (October 1987). See also Vogel, "Why Businessmen Distrust Their State: The Political Consciousness of American Corporate Executives," *British Journal of Political Science* 8-1 (January 1978) and Vogel, "The Power of Business in America: A Re-appraisal," *British Journal of Political Science* 13-1 (January 1983).

[49] Fred Block, *Revising State Theory: Essays in Politics and Postindustrialism* (Philadelphia: Temple University Press, 1987), chap. 3.

Post-materialist labor historians discuss diversity beyond that based on economic interests. For them, the political identity of workers is formed through political conflicts. William Sewell, for instance, writes: "Labor historians' materialist predilections, I would argue, have made them willing to accept proletarianization as a sort of universally valid material explanation. As a consequence, they have paid less attention to the profoundly uneven and contradictory character of changes in production relations, not to mention the role of discourse and politics in labor history."[50] This "materialist commonsense" is by no means limited to Marxists, he continues, but is shared by a wide range of liberals, populist radicals, and free-market conservatives. What he is attacking is economic reductionism, and he advocates an autonomy of the political realm. From this perspective, there is no reason to believe that labor is a unitary entity. Political identity is more plastic. Although the degree of autonomy of the political realm must be studied empirically, this perspective theoretically supports the cross-class political analysis.[51]

The post-materialist perspective is echoed in the statist approach. The statists argue that bureaucrats and political parties are not agents of societal forces, but have their respective interests.[52] This perspective asserts that these state actors are also autonomous participants in cross-class politics. Bureaucrats and politicians have their own interests in forming an alliance with societal actors, and vice versa, in their efforts to create a governing coalition. This coalition formation provides labor or a segment of labor with political opportunities to participate in the policy process and to pursue their interests. The Roosevelt coalition and the populist coalition in Latin America are two examples of this.[53] The governing

[50] William H. Sewell, Jr., "Toward a Post-materialist Rhetoric for Labor History," in Lenard R. Berlanstein, ed., *Rethinking Labor History* (Urbana: University of Illinois Press, 1993). Examples of such analysis are William Reddy, *The Rise of Market Culture: The Textile Trade and French Society, 1750–1900* (Cambridge: Cambridge University Press, 1984) and Victoria C. Hattam, *Labor Visions and State Power: The Origin of Business Unionism in the United States* (Princeton: Princeton University Press, 1993). Such an effort went back to the work of E. P. Thompson, *The Making of the English Working Class* (New York: Vintage Book, 1963).

[51] For an empirical study, cf. Ronald Aminzade, "Class Analysis, Politics, and French Labor History," in Berlanstein, ed., *Rethinking Labor History.*

[52] Theda Skocpol, "Bringing the State Back In: Strategies of Analysis in Current Research," in Peter Evans, Dietrich Rueschemeyer, and Skocpol, eds., *Bringing the State Back In* (New York: Cambridge University Press, 1985).

[53] E.g., Benjamin Ginsberg and Martin Shefter, "The Presidency and the Organization of Interests," in Michael Nelson, ed., *The Presidency and the Political System*, 2d ed. (Washington: CQ Press, 1987) for the United States; Guillermo O'Donnell, *Modernization and Bureaucratic Authoritarianism* (Berkeley: Institute of International Studies, 1973), and Ruth Berins Collier and David Collier, *Shaping the Political Arena: Critical Junctures, the Labor Movement, and Regime Dynamics in Latin America* (Princeton: Princeton University Press, 1991) for Latin American

coalition in Switzerland, dominated by international business, also incorporated labor in order to mobilize consent for coping with economic change.[54] Given the nature of this process of the formation of governing coalitions, we have no reason to believe that a fragmented labor movement is predestined to be a political loser in national politics. Rather, the outcome depends on the particular configuration and interaction of political forces.

The orthodox interpretation of Japanese labor politics presumes that labor can benefit little because it failed to mobilize enough resources to threaten management or government. This perspective takes it for granted that Japanese management and government are unilaterally dominant and united against labor on all issues and is unable to depict the actual dynamics of Japanese labor politics. Management was not a unified camp and often depended on labor's cooperation. The degree of dependence varied due to several factors, such as market competition and the nature of work organization. Management in individual private manufacturing companies, faced with severe market competition and dependent upon workers' cooperation, were more accommodationist than the national level management association, Nikkeiren. Even at the national level, we can find a division between the confrontationist Nikkeiren and the accommodationist management group, Doyukai. By the same token, the unions' perceived self-interests differed across sectors. The unions in the manufacturing sector were more accommodationist and more eager to cooperate with management in pursuing productivity increases than those in the public and service sectors. Accommodationist cross-sectoral alliance was a basis of the Shuntō wage bargaining and politics of productivity in the 1960s.

The conservative LDP government was not unified against labor either. The LDP governing coalition originally consisted of agricultural interests, small merchants and industrialists, and big business, but the LDP gradually became eager to build electoral support among urban workers. More and more LDP politicians tried to represent workers' interests. Even the conservative LDP government introduced a series of pro-labor policies. After the first oil crisis, it sought labor's cooperation in running the national economy because private sector union cooperation was crucial for the LDP government in controling inflation. The Ministry of Labor has been another important actor in labor politics and has

---

experiences. See also Dietrich Rueschemeyer, Evelyne Huber Stephens, and John D. Stephens, *Capitalist Development and Democracy* (Chicago: University Chicago Press, 1992).

[54] Katzenstein, *Corporatism and Change.*

maintained a pro-labor policy preference. Consequently, we can find accommodationists and confrontationists in all camps—labor, management, and government—in various stages of Japanese labor politics. These are the bases of an inter- and intra-class politics, which enabled private manufacturing sector unions to enjoy their victories. Given these cross-class configurations of poilitical actors at the national level, again we can observe a political dynamic, in which accommodationist management and state actors become conciliatory toward accommodationist unions in order to contain confrontationist unions. The developments of postwar Japanese labor politics witnessed a gradual consolidation of an accommodationist alliance across business, labor, and the political actors.

The second variable is the policy network. The ways in which political interaction among state and societal actors is institutionalized influences the power of labor. This institutional feature is relatively independent of political coalition formation, and provides labor with political opportunities. Margaret Weir and Theda Skocpol, in their comparative analysis of Sweden, Britain, and the U.S., found that the introduction of Keynesian welfare policy was contingent upon past institutional developments.[55] In a more direct finding, Bo Rothstein demonstrates that a voluntary but publicly supported unemployment insurance scheme administered by unions or union-dominated funds (the Ghent system) was an important institutional source of labor power in Sweden. He argues that "organized class power stems not only from socioeconomic factors but also from the power that social classes at times are able to invest in political institutions."[56]

More interesting theoretically is Katzenstein's analysis of Swiss liberal corporatism and Austrian social democratic corporatism. He finds that these variants of corporatism lead to a similar consequence, a succcssful mobilization of consensus to deal with economic change. He shows that "weak" Swiss unions, internally divided and less centralized, came to be legitimate members, of the social coalition, although subordinate to business, and were entitled to be consulted on various policy choices. Labor's success owes to the nature of the policy network in Switzerland, which has institutionalized intensive bargaining among the state and societal actors.

---

[55] Margaret Weir and Theda Skocpol, "State Structures and the Possibility for 'Keynesian' Responses to the Great Depression in Sweden, Britain, and the United States," in Evans, Rueschemeyer, and Skocpol, eds., *Bringing the State Back In.*

[56] Bo Rothstein, "Labor-market Institutions and Working-class Strength," in Sven Steinmo, Kathleen Thelen, and Frank Longstreth, eds., *Structuring Politics: Historical Institutionalism in Comparative Analysis* (Cambridge: Cambridge University Press, 1992), p. 52.

"The central feature of this complex process of political bargaining is the fact that all interested groups are directly represented at every site of the policy debate and at every stage of the process." A similar corporatist setting functioned in the opposite direction in Austria. Consequently, "in Austrian capitalism the power of the strong, business, and the state is circumscribed; in Swiss capitalism the power of the weak, the unions, and the state is inflated."[57] The policy network, that is, an institutionalized interrelationship between state and society within a domestic structure, may provide labor with favorable political opportunities and may increase labor's influence in the political economy.

The existence of intensive and extensive networks within the Japanese political economy provided labor with favorable political opportunities. The following brief review of the Japanese political economy debate shows its network nature and the implication of this characteristic for labor. Japan's postwar rapid economic growth has been a popular research topic, and many scholars have tried to find the causes of its success. Two popular understandings of Japanese success have emerged, the state-centered thesis and the market-centered thesis.[58] The former, which attributes Japan's success to state policy, has been proposed by many political economists. Its most typical argument is one that can be labeled the "Japan, Inc." approach.[59] This states that the powerful government in Japan's hierarchically ordered society successfully controlled the economy in order to catch up with the Western economies. The best and brightest bureaucrats exercised dominant power, formulating the optimal program for economic success and implementing it effectively. Chalmers Johnson's pioneering work, although more nuanced, can be read in this way.

On the other hand, many neoclassical economists argue that effective market competition in Japan after World War II contributed to its success.[60] They believe that government intervention provided a favorable environment for market-driven activity. The most efficient entrepreneurs

[57] Katzenstein, *Corporatism and Change,* pp. 124, 136.

[58] This typology is often made. See David Friedman, *The Misunderstood Miracle: Industrial Development and Political Change in Japan* (Ithaca: Cornell University Press, 1988) and Gregory W. Noble, "The Japanese Industrial Policy Debate," in Stephan Haggard and Chung-in Moon, eds., *Pacific Dynamism: The International Politics of Industrial Change* (Boulder: Westview Press, 1989).

[59] For instance, Eugene J. Kaplan, *Japan: The Government-Business Relationship* (Washington: U.S. Department of Commerce, 1972).

[60] For instance, Patrick and Rosovsky, eds., *Asia's New Giant;* Hugh Patrick, "The Future of the Japanese Economy: Output and Labor Productivity," *Journal of Japanese Studies* 3-2 (Summer 1977); and Ryutaro Komiya, Masahiro Okuno, and Kotaro Suzumura, eds., *Nihon no sangyōseisaku* (Industrial policy of Japan) (Tokyo: Tokyo Daigaku Shuppankai, 1984).

won out over other, less efficient competitors in a freely operating market system independent of, or inspite of, government intervention. Consequently, they conclude, the Japanese economy as a whole became successful because of this market competition. For these students, Japan is not special in any sense, but rather similar to other market economies.[61]

However, these two theses have recently come under strong criticism. The state-centered thesis has been discredited by many studies showing that the Japanese government was not so omnipotent and the "famous" industrial policy often failed to achieve its original goal.[62] The market-centered thesis has also been shown to be incomplete, in that it does not explain why Japan could have had such an effective market. As David Friedman writes, "If Japanese producers did a better job of responding to market demands, we need to know why they were more capable than manufacturers elsewhere. If the market operated more efficiently in Japan and hence disciplined producers more effectively, we again need to know why this was so."[63]

Interestingly enough, both pure economists and political economists recently have focused their arguments in a similar direction. A neoinstitutionalist perspective has become popular among economists, while many studies in political economy show growing emphasis on state-society networks. An increasing number of economists are focusing on institutions defined as "humanly devised constraints on human actions that determine the structure of incentives."[64] Departing from the presumption of the textbook market, they try to incorporate transaction costs into their analysis. Institutions are important in this type of analysis, because they determine transaction costs.[65] Once we admit that institutions matter in the economy, we are led to an analysis of the state and the society in which the market is embedded. Firm organizations, interfirm networks, and firm-bank relations, to name a few, are important elements of this analysis. Furthermore, a neoinstitutionalist approach has pushed economists to analyze the relations between the government and business.

Neoinstitutionalism is gaining popularity among students of the Japa-

---

[61] Chalmers Johnson, *MITI and the Japanese Miracle: The Growth of Japanese Industrial Policy, 1925–1975* (Stanford: Stanford University Press, 1982).

[62] E.g., Komiya, et al., *Nihon no sangyōseisaku.*

[63] Friedman, *Misunderstood Miracle*, p. 5.

[64] Douglass C. North, *Institutions, Institutional Change, and Economic Performance* (Cambridge: Cambridge University Press, 1990), p. 3.

[65] E.g., Oliver E. Williamson, *Markets and Hierarchies: Analysis and Antitrust Implications* (New York: Free Press, 1975) and Thrainn Eggertsson, *Economic Behavior and Institutions* (Cambridge: Cambridge University Press, 1992).

nese economy.[66] Masahiko Aoki, a leading economist in the field, uses this approach as a basis for his analysis of various aspects of the Japanese firm: company organization, corporate financing, and industrial organization (including subcontracting and corporate grouping).[67] He also includes an analysis of Japanese state-society relations in his main analysis. These scholars focus not just on various networks within and among firms, but also on the broader social and political networks in which the market is embedded. Neoinstitutionalist analysis here comes very close to that of political economists, although the pure economists are still less interested in state-society relations than political economists.

Political economists in recent studies have also emphasized networks. Many have analyzed the state-society networks, as is most typical of the corporatist approach, but in studies of Japanese political economy, they tend to focus mainly on the state apart from the society. This is because the Japanese state is regarded as strong. Many political economists thus assume that the promulgation of industrial policy is proof of its effectiveness. However, recent studies examine how state intervention actually influences society and vice versa, by focusing on the relations between state and society. Richard Samuels argues that Japanese industrial policy was effective when there existed "reciprocal consent" between the government and the targeted industry. Daniel Okimoto shows that the networks between the Ministry of International Trade and Industry (MITI) and market actors were important in formulating and implementing industrial policy. Michio Muramatsu and Ellis Krauss characterize state-society relations in Japan as "patterned pluralism," in which such relations are canalized into various networks. Gary Allinson emphasizes that political negotiation is a pervasive and important feature of Japanese politics, summarizing various studies in a book coedited with Yasunori Sone.[68] All

---

[66] E.g., Ken'ichi Imai, "Japan's Corporate Networks," in Shumpei Kumon and Henry Rosovsky, eds., *The Political Economy of Japan*, vol. 3: *Cultural and Social Dynamics* (Stanford: Stanford University Press, 1992); Yasusuke Murakami, "The Japanese Model of Political Economy," in Kozo Yamamura and Yasukichi Yasuba, eds., *The Political Economy of Japan*, vol. 1: *The Domestic Transformation* (Stanford: Stanford University Press, 1987); Kozo Yamamura, "The Role of Government in Japan's 'Catch-up' Industrialization: A Neo-institutionalist Perspective," in Hyung-Ki Kim, Michio Muramatsu, T. J. Pempel, and Kozo Yamamura, eds., *The Japanese Civil Service and Economic Development* (Oxford: Clarendon Press, 1995).

[67] Masahiko Aoki, *Information, Incentives, and Bargaining in the Japanese Economy*.

[68] Richard J. Samuels, *The Business of the Japanese State: Energy Markets in Comparative and Historical Perspective* (Ithaca: Cornell University Press, 1987); Daniel I. Okimoto, *Between MITI and the Market* (Stanford: Stanford University Press, 1989); Michio Muramatsu and Ellis S. Krauss, "The Conservative Policy Line and the Development of Patterned Pluralism," in Yamamura and Yasuba, eds., *The Political Economy of Japan*, vol. 1; Gary D. Allinson,

these scholars focus on the interaction between state and society rather than on unilateral state control over society. At the same time, they regard Japanese state-society relations as not sporadic but institutionalized in dense networks. In this sense, these scholars share their academic interests with the neoinstitutionalist economists.

These studies of Japanese political economy all show that the existence of intensive and extensive social, economic, and political networks is characteristic of the Japanese political economy. One interesting outcome is that such networks often helped Japanese industries to meet economic challenges with relative ease. In the 1950s, when the prospects of the Japanese steel industry were still uncertain, government intervention in that industry created intensive information exchange among steel makers and the government on prospects for the future steel industry and facilitated a bold management investment decision by reducing uncertainties. In the 1970s, structurally depressed industries (for example, ship building and textiles) were helped by various industrial policy measures, such as authorizing recession cartels and arranging investment coordination, in adjusting their production to new economic situations. In order to implement these policy measures, it was essential for the given companies to coordinate among themselves, as the government did not have the legal power to ensure implementation. In that process, the network within the industry played a critical role.[69]

What actually happened in Japanese labor politics was that labor was gradually incorporated into these extensive networks. Many scholars have argued that such incorporation owed a great deal to labor's defeat. Industrial rationalization and adjustment, in this view, occurred because of weak labor unions. This understanding is very problematic, however. If labor was forced to accept industrial adjustment, why would it voluntarily cooperate with management or government in implementing those policies. Management needed more than workers' subordination; an active and voluntary commitment from them was critical to running a flexible production system. The government also had to maintain a cooperative relationship with unions in order to steer the economy in new directions after the oil crisis. Thus it had to commit itself to increasing workers' real

---

"Introduction: Analyzing Political Change: Topics, Findings, and Implications," in Allinson and Yasunori Sone, eds., *Political Dynamics in Contemporary Japan* (Ithaca: Cornell University Press, 1993).

[69] Ken'ichi Imai, "Komento" (Comment), in Komiya, et al., *Nihon no sangyōseisaku*; Merton J. Peck, Richard C. Levin, and Akira Goto, "Picking Losers: Public Policy toward Declining Industries in Japan," *Journal of Japanese Studies* 13-1 (Winter 1987); Dore, *Flexible Rigidities*; and Samuels, *Business of the Japanese State.*

wages with an anti-inflation policy and tax cuts in order to compensate for the slowed increases in nominal wages.

An intensive network can function effectively to reduce transaction costs if consensus is achieved voluntarily among the network's actors.[70] Not domination, then, but consensus reduces costs. The recent neoinstitutionalist and network analyses of the Japanese political economy implicitly show that Japanese labor has been a strong actor in the Japanese political economy, not just a passive, powerless tool of government and business. This understanding is potentially contradictory to the orthodox view of weak Japanese labor.

The domestic political opportunity structure, however, is not created through an endogenous political process, but is affected by international forces.[71] Many political economists, have focused on the interaction between domestic and international forces to explain political outcomes. Some of these studies give us an important clue to understanding the impact of international forces, mediated by domestic forces, on labor's status. On the basis of statistical comparison among highly industrialized democracies, David Cameron demonstrates that a country's openness or economic dependence tends to result in large public sectors because the government plays a large role in compensating the possible damages caused by this openness. Katzenstein, elaborating on Cameron's argument, shows that the international vulnerability or economic openness of the small European states results in democratic corporatism. Unlike Cameron, he demonstrates that, when faced with economic vulnerability, the domestic differences among these states lead to different types of corporatism, for example, liberal corporatism in Switzerland and social corporatism in Austria.[72] What is noteworthy here is the fact that a shared sense of vulnerability in Switzerland, caused by its international dependence, drove the dominant coalition member—business—to incorporate labor. International forces influenced political opportunities for labor.

[70] Yasusuke Murakami and Thomas P. Rohlen, "Social-Exchange Aspects of the Japanese Political Economy: Culture, Efficiency, and Change," in Kumon and Rosovsky, eds., *The Political Economy of Japan*, vol. 3.

[71] Jenkins and Schock claim that the study of domestic political conflict should incorporate two distinct theories: a "political process theory," which includes the concept of political opportunity structure, and a theory of global structures, like world system and dependency theories. These scholars mainly focus on conflicts in the third world, however, when they treat global structures. See "Global Structures and Political Processes."

[72] Katzenstein, *Between Power and Plenty*; Peter Gourevitch, *Politics in Hard Times: Comparative Responses to International Economic Crises* (Ithaca: Cornell University Press, 1986); David Cameron, "The Expansion of the Public Economy: A Comparative Analysis," *American Political Science Review* 72-4 (December 1978); Katzenstein, *Small States in World Markets*; Katzenstein, *Corporatism and Change*.

This was also true for the Japanese case. Management, labor (especially in the private manufacturing sector), and government have all been obsessed by a sense of vulnerability to international competition. This sense of vulnerability was one of the important causes of accommodationism within the export-oriented private manufacturing sector and the economic bureaucracies. Political opportunities created by political coalition formation and the policy network provided Japanese labor with the potential for power and the possibility to realize its interests.

JAPANESE LABOR POLITICS: LINKING MICRO TO MACRO

This review demonstrates that enterprise unions are not isolated within their enterprises. I argue that it is necessary to analyze labor's role both within the enterprise and at the national level in order to make sense of Japanese labor politics. The potential of labor's power within the company itself should not be discounted. Even those who emphasize the important role of unions within the plant and company, however, seem not to fully evaluate the possibility of micro-level labor power. For instance, Turner, while admitting the importance of plant-level participation for labor politics, argues that without macro-level corporatist bargaining or laws to regulate management behavior for unions, union participation ends up as a co-optation of labor:

> Most important, statutory or corporatist regulation narrows managerial discretion concerning both work reorganization and union integration, which allows for a more stable and extensive union role. . . . By contrast, where no such statutory or bargaining arrangements exist and the labor movement is fragmented (as in Japan), the union has little independent basis from which to develop its own information and analysis. . . . [C]ollaboration that occurs does so on management's terms (Japan, numerous plant-level cases in the United States, Britain, and Italy). Weak labor is integrated into managerial decision making in a decidedly subordinate way.[73]

Many labor students, who admit the importance of labor's participation in the workshop, concur with this assertion.[74]

---

[73] Turner, *Democracy at Work*, p. 13. Thelen also emphasizes the legalistic nature of the German dual system, which guarantees labor's plant-level rights. This legalism allegedly helped to shore up negotiated adjustments. However, she seems to be careful to conclude that this is a necessary condition for labor's successful participation in plant-level production decisions. Thelen, *Union of Parts*.
[74] For instance, Christian Berggren, *Alternatives to Lean Production: Work Organization in the*

Is macro-level labor power a precondition for successful labor participation in the workplace? Our theoretical review suggests that the answer might be no. Political opportunities at the micro and macro levels may enable labor to develop its power from below without prior consolidation of labor's power at the national level. But this question should be answered empirically. Because decentralized and fragmented unions in Japan were able to earn substantial achievements—such as a voice in production decisions, secure employment, and pro-labor policies—the Japanese case requires further reconsideration of the conventional understanding of labor politics. I am not trying to minimize the significance of labor's achievements at the national level, but I do want to take micro-level labor politics seriously.

If we look only within the enterprise, however, we tend to overlook an important achievement at the national level. Japanese unions succeeded in developing a national movement out of decentralized enterprise unionism. An example of this, for instance, is how enterprise unions cooperated with each other under the leadership of the industrial federation of enterprise unions; in that situation enterprise unions developed wide political demands and organized their movement across enterprise boundaries. The Shuntō wage bargaining is another example that shows how effectively enterprise unions cooperated. It is clear that enterprise unionism was not dominated by management if we look at what happened at the national level.

Conversely, labor politics within the enterprise illuminates labor's achievement at the national level. Tsujinaka argues that due to their successful participation in the national-level political networks, Japanese unions became able to play an important role in national policymaking.[75] A typical criticism made by orthodox scholars against this view is that labor unions succeeded in participating in policymaking only because they gave up workers' real interests and moderated their demands. A study of Japanese labor politics focusing on national-level developments alone cannot address this criticism sufficiently, because it does not grasp the nature of Japanese labor politics. The inadequacy of the co-opted labor view becomes clear only when we review the development of labor politics from the workshop level. One of the main goals of unions in the post-

---

Swedish Auto Industry (Ithaca: ILR Press, 1992). Paul C. Weiler advocates a legalistic approach to understanding the development of workers' involvement in the production process. *Governing the Workplace: The Future of Labor and Employment Law* (Cambridge: Harvard University Press, 1990).

[75] Yutaka Tsujinaka, "Rengō and Its Osmotic Networks," in Allinson and Sone, eds., *Political Dynamics in Contemporary Japan.*

oil-crisis period was to maintain employment, and the unions successfully lobbied for government policies that helped companies restructure production in order to maintain employment. In due course, unions cooperated with management to moderate wage demands and to rationalize the production system. For students of the orthodox view, this is just one example of the unions' concession to management and government. However, if we recall how militantly the unions fought to maintain employment within their companies in the 1950s, we see this labor strategy in the post-oil-crisis period not as a concession to management and government but as a development of the Japanese unions' deeply rooted strategy. Starting from participation in enterprise-level decision making to protect jobs and improve working conditions, Japanese labor has gradually increased its participation within the political economy to the industrial level and then the national level.

Without examining developments at the micro level, we tend to overlook the characteristic features of Japanese labor politics. Japanese labor developed its strategy from the micro level to the national level. In due course, labor helped to create the opportunities and constraints in Japanese labor politics. In this book, I show that the unions succeeded in reducing the cost of economic adjustment in the 1970s and survived the neoconservative tide of the 1980s. I argue that these successes are attributable to the combination of their activities within the enterprise and at the national level. It is important to analyze labor politics by focusing on the interaction between firm-level and national-level events. By doing this, I take the private sector labor movement more seriously than do orthodox scholars, who treat the private-sector unions as losers in Japanese labor politics and their hegemony over the leftist public-sector unions as the end of the authentic labor movement in Japan. In my view, this hegemony is part of the development of the Japanese labor movement, starting from micro-level accommodation in the private sector. Organized labor in the private sector is thus the key to understanding Japanese labor politics. This approach reverses the orthodox view of Japanese labor and offers a new and more comprehensive understanding of Japanese labor politics.

LABOR IN POLITICAL ECONOMY: A GENERAL FRAMEWORK.

It is convenient to have a two-dimensional theoretical framework to understand the arena of labor politics in the capitalist political economy, so I have divided union activity into two categories: distributive activity, which seeks a share of the profit, and productive activity, which attempts

	Micro or enterprise level	Macro or national level
Distributive activity	Sphere I Intra-firm wage negotiations	Sphere II National wage negotiations
Productive activity	Sphere III Participation in managerial decision making	Sphere IV Participation in national policymaking

Figure 6. The arena of labor politics: Spheres of political activity in labor relations.

to influence the production process. I have also categorized the arena of unions activity as either enterprise or national. Although it can be further categorized into industrial and national levels, for my argument, it is sufficient and convenient to distinguish between the enterprise (micro) level and the national (macro) level. Thus we end up with four categories, or spheres, of union activity (fig. 6).

The orthodox view of Japanese labor politics argues that Japanese unions were locked within the enterprise and failed to organize effective action at the national level. The unions allegedly also failed to establish autonomous and sufficient control within the enterprise. This view assumes that labor's power is greatly limited without a united labor organization and strategy. In other words, orthodox scholars argue that union activity in Japan in sphere II was so limited that practically, it was confined to sphere I activities and that labor consequently suffers from low wages and poor working conditions.

This understanding is problematic in two ways. First, it ignores the importance of the national-level Shuntō wage negotiations and overlooks the fact that Japanese workers, not only unionized workers in the core economy but also those in the small and medium-sized companies, have enjoyed a dramatic wage increase since the 1950s. Japanese labor activity in sphere II should not be discounted.

Second, as many revisionists now argue, Japanese firm organization has an employee-orientation and thus workers' voices can be heard in management decision making. Activity in sphere III is be one of the most impressive aspects of Japanese labor-management relations. The orthodox view, however, tends to regard this aspect as just a co-optation of labor into the production system.

Immediately after World War II, thanks to reforms by the Allied occupation, the power balance between labor and management became very favorable to labor. Unions were organized rapidly and the organization rate soared from almost zero to more than 50 percent, being strongly supported by the Supreme Commander of the Allied Powers (SCAP). At the same time, the highly concentrated financial combines (zaibatsu) were broken down and many prewar high-ranking corporate managers were purged from companies. This resulted in a massive labor offensive for the first time in Japan. Unions organized militant activities in all four spheres. Within companies, they demanded higher wage increases and sometimes attempted to control production, giving rise to what is called the "production control struggle." It was very common for management to agree to give unions veto power in most managerial decision making. At the national level, labor tried to organize industry-wide, centralized wage bargaining and also pursued socialist control over the economy, either through general strikes or a corporatist strategy.

This labor offensive eventually faced a management counterattack after 1949, led by the Japan Federation of Employers' Associations (Nikkeiren). The beginning of the cold war and a change in SCAP political objectives from democratization to economic recovery enabled this counterattack to be effective. The management strategy, especially that of Nikkeiren, was to confine union activity to sphere I, arguing that management should recapture the managerial prerogatives lost in the postwar labor offensive. In addition, Nikkeiren originally did not want labor to have an active role in sphere III because it feared such participation would again result in a loss of managerial prerogatives.

In this book I show why and how labor succeeded in gaining influence in sphere III after its initial defeat and how labor successfully developed its national-level activities in spheres I and IV. In analyzing these aspects of Japanese labor politics, I will focus on labor's power in relation to management and government. Most scholars analyze labor power in terms of its own resource mobilization, such as the organization rate and degree of centralization. I instead focus on the political opportunity structure of the Japanese labor movement as a more important factor.[76] This perspective brings attention to intra- and inter-class political dynamics, which produced an accommodationist cross-class alliance in Japanese labor politics.

The configuration of accommodationists and confrontationists in the political economy is contingent on labor politics. Drawing on Theodore Lowi's seminal work which distinguished distributive, regulatory, and

[76] Jenkins and Schock, "Global Structures and Political Processes"; Tarrow, "National Politics and Collective Action."

redistributive policies, David Vogel wrote: "It would seem reasonable to assume that the political consciousness of the business community would vary along parallel lines. Thus, the more the political agenda is dominated by redistributive issues, the more likely are businessmen to think in terms of their class interests. Similarly, the more distributive issues predominate, the more likely businessmen are to evaluate political decisions exclusively in terms of the welfare of their own company."[77] We can hypothesize that some political issues facilitate the confrontationist tendency within labor, business, and government, and others facilitate an accommodationist one. In the model I propose here, I link this perspective to my typology of labor politics. The accommodationist approach will prevail more on productive issues than on distributive issues because the former tends to produce "positive-sum" results and the latter "zero-sum" results. It will also prevail more at the micro level than at the macro level, because a positive-sum accord between labor and management is more likely at the micro level, where a "free rider problem" is less serious since there are fewer participants.[78] In addition, national-level interaction is more likely to raise class consciousness. As Japanese private sector labor developed its activity from the micro to the macro level as well as from the distributive to the productive arena, the micro-level productivity coalition further developed into a national-level accommodationist alliance. The developmental path of postwar Japanese labor politics from the micro level to the macro level and its early emphasis on productive issues therefore facilitated the consolidation of an accommodationist cross-class alliance rather than a confrontationist condition.

This perspective, I believe, leads to a more dynamic analysis, one which is necessary to understand the paradox of Japanese labor politics: why did Japanese labor succeed in gaining important benefits, such as secure employment and participation in the production system, despite its apparent "weakness," characterized by a decentralized enterprise unionism?

[77] Vogel, "The Power of Business in America," p. 36. See also Theodore J. Lowi, "American Business, Public Policy, Case-Studies and Political Theory," *World Politics* 16-4 (July 1964).

[78] Mancur Olson, *The Logic of Collective Action* (Cambridge: Harvard University Press, 1965).

CHAPTER THREE

Institutionalizing Labor
Accommodation within the Company

This chapter reviews the development of labor-management relations from 1945 to the 1950s, which became the basis of the labor accommodation between 1960 and 1974. Political conflicts among labor, management, and government in this period gave rise to a characteristic labor accommodation within the company which became institutionalized.[1] Labor played an important role in this transformation.

THE LABOR OFFENSIVE (1945–51)

In this early postwar period, wage increases were much higher than productivity increases, and the correlation between the two was not strong. These were the days of the labor offensive, which resulted from the occupation reform and which liberated unions and demoralized capitalists for a time. Labor achieved a high wage increase in this period, following a new wage demand principle, the "Densan wage pattern" which arose in the electric power industry (Densan) as a result of the unions' wage negotiation tactics. The Densan unions in 1946 set up a new wage demand formula based mainly on the cost of living and succeeded in forcing management to accept it as their wage pattern.[2] They demanded "a fixed minimum wage based on the cost of living, adjusted to reflect regional

---

[1] This view has been cogently proposed by Martin Kenney and Richard Florida. I owe a great deal to their brilliant work, *Beyond Mass Production*.

[2] The Densan union's demand is quoted in Kazuo Okochi, ed., *Shiryō sengo 20 nen-shi*, vol. 4: *Rōdō* (Postwar documents, the first 20 years, vol. 4: Labor) (Tokyo: Nihon Hyōronsha, 1966), p. 27.

variation, additional pay to reward ability, seniority, and attendance, the elimination of imbalances based on rank or educational background, and a commitment to adjust wages in the future to reflect price changes."[3] This wage demand was quickly picked up by unions across most industries in Japan. It was the leftist Sanbetsu union federation that advocated this wage demand nationally, but the unions affiliated with the moderate Sōdōmei (Japan Labor Federation) and independent unions also adopted this wage model. Although these unions did not get all that they demanded, they mostly succeeded in forcing management to accept the wage principle, in which the wage was "closely linked, in its major component, to objective characteristics of age and seniority that were likely to rise with need."[4] This type of wage has been characterized as a "livelihood wage" which guarantees the worker enough money to live on.[5] In this sense, the livelihood wage demand was an effort to decommodify labor and was based on strong egalitarian norms that developed among workers after the war. Although coordination of union wage demands at the industrial or national level was not effective (with notable exceptions in some industries, such as electric power), the livelihood wage demands themselves solidified wage demands across industries.

This was a victory for the liberated labor movement in Japan. But it was made possible partly because of postwar hyperinflation. Faced with inflation, people tended to seek a minimum stipend to live on rather than better living conditions, and this situation gave support to wage demands based on the livelihood wage. The postwar economy was so chaotic that workers could not anticipate certain economic growth in the near future. It was out of the question for them to support a productivity-linked wage increase, which would be the basis for a "politics of productivity." Even the Nikkeiren could not commit itself to the principle of a productivity-linked wage increase at that time. Faced with the labor offensive, management was put on the defensive. In 1948, for instance, Nikkeiren adopted the principle "Basic Attitudes toward Wage Demands," arguing that, although the efficiency wage was preferable and inevitable for a reconstructed Japanese economy, there was no way to reject some base wage calculated on the cost of living and not related to productivity/efficiency increases. The result was that wage increases were much higher than productivity increases.

[3] Gordon, *Evolution of Labor Relations in Japan*, p. 352.
[4] Ibid., p. 356. Rōdō Sōgi Chōsakai, ed., *Sengo rōdō sōgi jittai chōsa*, vol. 10: *Rōdō kyōyaku o meguru rōshifunsō* (Study on the postwar labor conflicts, volume 10: Conflicts on labor contracts) (Tokyo: Chuōkōronsha 1958), pp. 111–23.
[5] Gordon, *Evolution of Labor Relations in Japan*, p. 349.

The unions' idea of decommodification of labor was based on the democratic notion of the enterprise as a community consisting of equal members. Their argument that workers should be compensated, not in terms of output or ability, but in terms of needs led naturally to the idea that all workers were equal members of the enterprise. This egalitarianism drove the unions to pursue enterprise democratization. Most unions at the outset demanded the abolition of the status distinction between white-collar staff (shokuin) and blue-collar workers (kōin). In the prewar period, workers received daily wages, while staff received monthly salaries and annual bonuses, and there were many differences in the fringe benefits between them, such as paid holidays. Unions were very eager to abolish this discrimination within the company. As a result, the union took on the characteristics of an enterprise union consisting of both white-collar staff and blue-collar workers. Management mostly accepted these union demands, and the enterprise system in Japan was substantially democratized. Consequently, wage differentials as well as status differences among employees in the enterprise decreased dramatically.[6]

Labor's notion of the enterprise as a community, coupled with the economic destruction and higher unemployment rate after the war, drove unions to demand secure employment within the enterprise. "The labor movement tried to lay the permanent job as one cornerstone in its remaking of the Japanese structure of labor relations."[7] Many unions demanded a policy prohibiting lay offs, and some forced management to commit itself to that policy. In their initial manifestos, the Sōdōmei and Sanbetsu federations proclaimed their goal to be forcing capitalists to run production so as to provide workers with places to work.[8] In the iron and steel industry, for instance, unions at the NKK (Nippon Kōkan) Kawasaki steel mill and Tsurumi shipyard succeeded in concluding labor contracts with management that required management to get consent from the union before firing workers.[9] It is true that labor unions by definition try to protect employment. But Japanese unions in those days went further, fiercely demanding no dismissals at all. It was rational for unions to demand no dismissals, because the Japanese economy was in such terrible shape and its recovery was so uncertain that the dismissal of workers

[6] Kuniyoshi Urabe and Kihei Omura, *Nihonteki rōshi kankei no tankyu* (Tokyo: Chuōkeizaisha, 1983), p. 85.

[7] Gordon, *Evolution of Labor Relations in Japan*, p. 365.

[8] Sōdōmei, "Kessei taikai sengen" (Manifesto of the first conference), August 3, 1946. Sanbetsukaigi, "Kōryō" (Platform of the first conference), August 21, 1946. Both quoted in *Shiryō sengo 20 nen-shi*, pp. 13–16.

[9] *Tekko rōren undō-shi: 30 nen no ayumi* (Tokyo: Nihon Tekkō Sangyō Rōdō Kumiai Rengōkai, 1981), p. 15.

meant that they would be faced with starvation. As a result of this communitarian ideology, the factory or enterprise became the basic unit of union organization.[10] It was thus natural for unions to try very hard to keep workers within the community.

If workers regarded the factory or enterprise as their community and were determined to stay there, it was natural for workers to try to exercise some voice regarding the managerial and production decisions within the enterprise. Immediately after World War II, workers tried not just to gain a voice in the enterprise, but to take over production from the hands of management. This was the so-called production control tactic. This type of labor dispute was found in the newspaper firm *Yomiuri shimbun* in 1945, and in Tōshiba (the electric equipment firm), NKK (iron and steel), Mitsubishi Coal Mining, Tōhokuhaiden (electric power), and others in 1946. In that year, 400 out of 1,258 labor disputes were categorized as production control struggles.[11] In those days, faced with uncertainty in business environments and enormous inflation, managers were hoarding materials, and thus strikes were not an effective tactic. Rather, unions resorted to production control to guarantee employment and wages.[12]

Although some reformist managers within the progressive Dōyūkai (Japan Council for Economic Development) were somewhat sympathetic, this production control was denounced by the Yoshida cabinet and management as an infringement on the right of private property.[13] Furthermore, in July 1946, the General Headquarters of the Allied Occupation (GHQ) strongly condemned production control as the confiscation of property without compensation, and consequently it became more difficult for unions to resort to this strategy.[14]

[10] There are many efforts to explain enterprise unionism in Japan. A brief review can be found in Taishiro Shirai, "A Theory of Enterprise Unionism," in Taishiro Shirai, ed., *Contemporary Industrial Relations in Japan* (Madison: University of Wisconsin Press, 1983), pp. 121–24. More historical analysis is available in Takeshi Inagami and Takashi Kawakita, eds., *Nihon no shakaigaku*, vol. 9: *Sangyō-rōdō* (Sociology in Japan, vol. 9: Industry and labor) (Tokyo: Tokyo Daigaku Shuppankai, 1987).

[11] Hirosuke Kawanishi, *Kigyōbetsu kumiai no riron: Mō hitotsuno Nihonteki rōshikankei* (A theory of enterprise unionism: Another Japanese labor-management relationship) (Tokyo: Nihon Hyōronsha, 1989), p. 122.

[12] Sanbetsu Kanjikai, "Seisankanri danatsu ni taisuru seimeisho" (Communique on the government repression of production control), March 20, 1948. Quoted in *Shiryō sengo 20 nen-shi*, p. 10.

[13] Hideo Otake, "The Zaikai under the Occupation: The Formation and Transformation of Managerial Councils," in Robert E. Ward and Yoshikazu Sakamoto, eds., *Democratizing Japan: The Allied Occupation* (Honolulu: University of Hawaii Press, 1987).

[14] Originally GHQ was not opposed to this tactic but supported it. For instance, in the production control struggle in the NKK Tsurumi mill in 1946, union leaders visited GHQ

It is, however, noteworthy that the government did not try to nullify all union activity that participated in production decision making. Instead it endeavored to channel workers' participation into management councils (*keieikyōgikai*), the labor-management consultation mechanism within the enterprise and the plant. In June 1946, on the same day that it declared production control to be illegal, the government also publicized the Comments of the Chief Secretary of the Cabinet concerning the Management Council. His comments advocated the establishment of such councils within all enterprises:

> Union and management should cooperate in a democratic way in order to increase production by setting up a management council consisting of the same number of members from each side. . . . Management should explain its enterprise plan and financial situations as well as general principles of personnel management to union representatives in the council and should take the union's reasonable views into consideration in managerial decision making.[15]

Management also supported the establishment of management councils. Obviously, it hoped that the councils would function to preempt industrial conflicts.[16]

Table 2 shows that many unions had such councils in the immediate postwar years. (Their decrease in 1950 and their later resurgence will be a topic analyzed later.) The increase in 1947–48 does not necessarily mean that government and management co-opted labor by forcing it to adopt the enterprise system. Rather, as we have seen, the unions also found the management council advantageous to further strengthen, or at least maintain, their say within the enterprise system.

Sōdōmei, from the beginning, took participation in enterprise decision making seriously as a result of its social democratic industrial democracy orientation. It vigorously pursued the establishment of management councils.[17] The leftist Sanbetsu, led by the communists, was reluctant to be

and received support for unions from the officials there. Nihon Kōkan Tsurumi Seitesusho Rōdōkumiai, ed., *Tsurutetsu rōdō undōshi* (History of Tsurutetsu union), 1956, pp. 59–61, quoted in Eiji Takemae, Akimasa Miyake, and Koji Endo, eds., *Shiryō Nihon senryō 2: Rōdō kaikaku to rōdō undō* (Documents: Occupation of Japan, vol. 2: Labor reform and the labor movement) (Tokyo: Ōtsuki Shoten, 1992), pp. 48–49.

[15] Ministry of Labor, *Shiryō rōdō undōshi* (1945–46) (Documents labor history)(Tokyo: Rōmugyōsei Kenkyusho, annual), p. 804. Translated by the author.

[16] Hideo Otake, "The Zaikai under the Occupation," p. 372.

[17] Urabe and Omura, *Nihonteki rōshikankei*, pp. 72–73. Sōdōmei Kakudai Chuōjunbi Iinkai, "Tōmen no undōhōshinsho" (Urgent tactics), January 17, 1993, quoted in *Shiryō sengo 20 nen-shi*, p. 13.

Table 2. Development of management councils

	Number of councils	Percentage of unions with councils (%)
1947	11,837	42.4
1948	15,005	44.3
1949	13,344	38.5
1950	6,383	23.6
1951	8,401	30.4
1952	9,625	34.0
1953	10,770	35.7
1954	10,825	34.4

SOURCE: Urabe and Omura, *Nihonteki rōshi kankei no tankyū*, p. 79. This data originally appeared in Toshitada Tateyama, "Sengo no sangyo minshushugi" (Industrial democracy in the postwar period), in Minshu Shakaishugi Kenkyūkaigi and Sangyō Minshushugi Kenkyūiinkai, eds., *Sangyō mishushugi: Gendai no rōshikankei* (Industrial democracy: Democracy in modern times) (Tokyo: Daiya-mondosha, 1963), p. 220.

involved in the reformist industrial democracy movement, but they used management councils as well—as a means for class struggle, especially after the crack-down on production control tactics. The Sanbetsu unions, however, were eager to democratize the company production system. Their strategic focus was on the factory or enterprise because they followed the principle of union organization advocated by the World Federation of Trade Unions, that is, "one single union per plant."[18]

Although there were significant ideological differences in the conception of the management council between the Sanbetsu and Sōdōmei federations, both went beyond management's conception of it. As the demobilization of the military proceeded and unemployment was expected to soar in 1946, unions became seriously concerned about protecting employment. Many unions began to press labor contracts that mandated that management seek consent from the union through the management council before dismissing workers or changing their job assignments. This was true for the Sanbetsu-affiliated unions as well as the Sōdōmei-affiliated ones.[19] Furthermore, in most managerial decisions, management had to consult with the union through the management council.

---

[18] Hisashi Kawada, "Workers and Their Organization," in Kazuo Okochi, Bernard Karsh, and Solomon B. Levine, eds., *Workers and Employers in Japan: The Japanese Employment Relations System* (Tokyo: Tokyo University Press; and Princeton: Princeton University Press, 1973).

[19] Rōdō Sōgi Chōsakai, ed., *Sengo rōdō sōgi jittaichōsa*, vol. 10, pp. 189, 240–41.

It is true that Sanbetsu was cautious about the possibility of being co-opted by management through this management council, but its member unions often committed themselves more and more to running the production system within the enterprise. The more actively the unions pursued such tactics, the deeper they became involved in the production system. For instance, one Sanbetsu-affiliated union, Japan Machine Equipment Union Federation (Zen Nihon Kiki Rōsō) advocated that individual enterprise unions should figure out ways to promote production increases based on their members' work experiences.[20] The logic expressed there is very close to the Quality Control Circle Movement of today, although it was a union perspective. Moreover, a substantial number of labor contracts had clauses stating that the union should be responsible even for maintaining work discipline at the shop floor level. Unions regarded themselves as an essential and legitimate member of the enterprise—in Sanbetsu's view, superior to management, and in Sōdōmei's view, an equal partner with management—and they deepened their participation in the enterprise production system.

Failures in Linking the Micro Accommodation to National Politics

We can find two trends toward a national-level movement based on these micro-level developments in this period, although both failed. The first was the leftist effort led by Sanbetsu, while the second was the social democratic/corporatist movement led by Sōdōmei. Sanbetsu was organized in August 1946, under the influence of the communists. Its basic strategy was to build a national-level labor movement from plant-level struggles. It sought first to take control of the production system at the plant level, which was the organization's power base, and then to take control of national politics through national general strikes. Sanbetsu argued that it was inevitable that labor should resort to strikes, overthrow the conservative government, and set up a new democratic government, in order to reconstruct the Japanese economy. In the successful October Offensive of 1946 over livelihood wages and secure employment, a Sanbetsu leader, Matsuta Hosotani, announced that a labor struggle was no longer an economic struggle but a political one to overthrow the reactionary Yoshida government and that Sanbetsu should be a driving force toward a national general strike and aim at establishing a demo-

---

[20] Zen Nihon Kiki Rōsō, "Shirei dai 7 go: Tōsō hōshin wareware wa ikani tatakauka" (Directive no. 7, struggle principles: How we will fight), quoted in *Shiryō sengo 20 nen-shi*, pp. 9–10.

cratic popular government.[21] This strategy strongly reflected the Communist party's strategy of establishing a people's democratic government by overthrowing the Yoshida government.

This strategy was at first faced with criticism not only from the Yoshida government but also from the Socialist Party and Sōdōmei. They were opposed to extra-parliamentary and violent struggle. However, faced with the government's uncompromising response to the wage demands of public-sector workers, the public-sector unions formed the Allied Struggle Committee of All Public-Sector Unions in November 1946, and all member unions declared their willingness to resort to confrontational tactics against the Yoshida government. This escalation by the public-sector union movement pressed Sōdōmei and the socialists to come close to Sanbetsu's strategy. In his New Year Statement, Prime Minister Yoshida denounced this union strategy, stating that it was being promoted by a "lawless gang." This antagonism from the government further helped unions consolidate their solidarity. In January 1947, public sector unions declared that they would organize a general strike starting on February 1.[22] This tactic was supported by the newly formed Zentō (National Alliance Council of Unions), which was a loosely coupled, overarching organization of thirty major unions including Sanbetsu and Sōdōmei. Thus, Sanbetsu's strategy for nationalizing the union movement seemed victorious. But just before its commencement GHQ banned the strike using the supreme authority of the occupational force. In the following April election for the House of Representatives, although the Socialist Party won 143 out of 466 seats and succeeded in organizing the Katayama cabinet with the Democratic and the National Cooperation parties, the Communists and Sanbetsu-affiliated candidates lost badly, falling from 35 seats to 4. This demonstrated that the general strike led by Sanbetsu had not gained sufficient popular support and had indeed alienated the public. After these losses, Sanbetsu began to lose its strength gradually, as it was faced with internal dissidents who criticized the communist-led union movement as well as with outside critics who attacked its radical-political orientation.[23] Even worse for Sanbetsu, GHQ became antagonistic to the

---

[21] Kazuo Okochi and Hiroshi Matsuo, *Nihon rōdō kumiai monogatari sengo-hen Jou* (A tale of Japanese labor unions: Postwar, vol. 1) (Tokyo: Chikuma Shobō, 1969), p. 171. His recollection on this point can be found in Akira Takanashi, ed., *Shōgen sengo rōdō kumiai undōshi* (Testimony: Postwar history of the labor movement) (Tokyo: Tōyō Keizai Shinpōsha, 1985), p. 14.

[22] For the process of the February 1 general strike, see Ministry of Labor, *Shiryō rōdō undōshi* (1947), pp. 7–153.

[23] Ministry of Labor, *Shiryō rōdō undōshi* (1948), pp. 543–73. Cf. Takanashi, ed., *Shōgen sengo rōdō kumiai undōshi*, pp. 19–22.

communists and their supporters' unions. Sanbetsu's strategy to national-ize the labor movement thus failed, and the membership of Sanbetsu itself decreased until the union dissolved in 1958.

From the beginning, Sōdōmei pursued a corporatist strategy to nation-alize its movement. It advocated labor's participation in the process of economic reconstruction at both the national and company levels. In December 1946, Sōdōmei succeeded in establishing the Preparation Committee for the Economic Recovery Conference with the progressive management organization, the Japan Committee for Economic Develop-ment (Dōyūkai), as well as Sanbetsu and Nichirō (Japan Labor Union Congress).[24] Its aim was to set up a corporatist institution in which labor and management would work out a way to democratize and reconstruct the Japanese economy. The urgent need for reconstruction, emergence of reformist managers, and strengthened labor unions all provided Sōdōmei with a good opportunity to realize its corporatist strategy. On February 6, 1947, the Economic Recovery Conference was officially estab-lished. All major labor and management groups participated; Sōdōmei, Sanbetsu, and Nichirō were the participants from the labor side, and Dōyūkai, Nissankyo (Japan Industry Federation), Kankeikyo (Kantō Man-agers Association), and Kansaikeikyo (Kansai Managers Association) were from the management side. Similar recovery conferences were established at each industry level, including the National Coal Industry Recovery Conference and the National Steel Industry Recovery Conference.

This success for Sōdōmei, however, was not long-lived. Although Sanbetsu participated in the recovery conference, it was reluctant to be involved in this corporatist arrangement, because it was afraid that the labor movement would be co-opted and would lose its revolutionary potential. Thus, after agreeing to participate, Sanbetsu did not cooperate with the other participants but tried to use this conference as a means to propagate its leftist agenda. According to Hideo Otake, "whenever the executive committee met or rallies were held, the representatives of the Sanbetsu made speeches featuring ideological propaganda and the theme of struggle.... [C]onsequently, few meaningful decisions were made."[25] The socialist Katayama cabinet began supporting this conference financially, but the stalemate in the executive committee caused by the leftist Sanbetsu did not change, driving management interest away from the conference as a vehicle for labor-management collaboration. Manage-ment finally dissolved the Economic Recovery Conference on April 28,

[24] Nichirō was a small, middle-of-the-road labor federation formed in October 1946. It had only 300,000 members in the beginning.
[25] Otake, "The Zaikai under the Occupation," p. 376.

1948, responding to Sōdōmei's call for its reorganization.[26] Here Sōdōmei's strategy to nationalize the labor movement failed due to Sanbetsu's opposition. Consequently, two separate paths to nationalizing the labor movement were closed.

THE PERIOD OF ACCUMULATION (1950–1959)

At the same time that these national strategies of the labor unions failed, the extremely favorable environment for labor unions began to vanish. The U.S. occupational policy goals changed from democratization to reconstructing Japan as a fortress against communism. The United States forced the Japanese government to adopt the drastic deflationary policy of the Dodge Line in 1949. Joseph Dodge, a Detroit banker, was sent by the U.S. government to Japan to end postwar hyperinflation by slashing government expenditures and forcing Japan's government to move toward budget surpluses. The policies brought about a severe economic recession. In addition, the communist activists, who started extra-parliamentary revolutionary activities, were purged in 1950. This was a serious blow to Sanbetsu, which was already losing strength due to internal criticism by its members of the communists' arbitrary leadership. All these factors put the unions on the defensive. Management, on the other hand, gradually regained its self-confidence. Furthermore, within management groups, economic liberals took the lead over progressives and began advocating the normalization of labor-management relations that had been constructed under the labor offensive.

Nikkeiren was the principal managerial organization that fought back against this labor offensive. It was organized in 1948 as a national organization of management, and its slogan was "management should be self-confident and tough." The management offensive started by first attacking labor's tight grip on the managerial and personnel decision making within the company. It then tried to transform the wage system from one based on the cost-of-living index (the livelihood wage) into one that was economically rational. This offensive was necessary for management, because the Dodge Line had eliminated the conditions that enabled management to respond to labor's demands. Management could no longer give in easily to labor's demands because government subsidies for such industries as iron and steel, which had been providing manage-

[26] Ibid., p. 377.

ment with extra profits, were drastically slashed.[27] Market discipline was imposed on management and labor.

Managerial Authority vs. Labor Participation

The first thing that management had to do was retake control over managerial and personnel decision making, which had been eroded by unions in the postwar labor offensive. In the existing labor-management relationship, management could not rationalize the production system. Management had to try to normalize this labor-management relationship first, before it could streamline business by dismissing redundant workers and survive in this new economic climate.

Nikkeiren issued its Appeal for Securing Managerial Prerogatives in May 1948, made it clear that management should recoup its managerial authority, and demanded that the government support this effort. In December 1948, the Ministry of Labor (MOL) with support from GHQ ordered its local offices and the local governments to regulate unions.[28] MOL claimed that many unions were dominated by a small number of leaders in a totalitarian and non-democratic way, and the ministry announced its plan to revise the Labor Union Law. Although the formal goal of this revision was to encourage union openness and independence, it weakened labor's power within the company. For instance, full-time union officials could no longer take salaries from the company, and lower-ranking managers were required to become non-unionized. The bills to revise the Labor Union Law and the Labor Relations Adjustment Law passed the Diet in May 1949, despite labor's strong opposition. These bills put some limitations on union tactics in the public utility industries.

Following its success at the national level, management fortified its efforts to regain managerial authority at the company level. The goal was to revise labor contracts that had prescribed that management should get consent from labor on a wide range of managerial issues, such as firing and hiring.

[27] Ikuo Kume, "A Tale of Twin Industries: Labor Accommodation in the Private Sector," in Gary D. Allinson and Yasunori Sone, eds., *Political Dynamics in Contemporary Japan* (Ithaca: Cornell University Press, 1993), pp. 168–74.
[28] Nikkeiren, "Keieiken kakuho nikansuru ikensho" (Opinion on how to regain managerial authority), May 10, 1948, quoted in *Shiryō sengo 20 nen-shi*, pp. 102–3; Ministry of Labor, "Rōdōshō tūchō: Minshuteki rōdō kumiai oyobi minshuteki rōdōkankei no jochō nitsuite" (A notice by the Ministry of Labor: How to promote democratic labor unions and labor-management relations), December 22, 1948, quoted in *Shiryō sengo 20 nen-shi*, p. 134.

After Nikkeiren's announcement of the Appeal for Securing Manage-rial Prerogatives, management in the private sector sought to secure managerial authority through a revised labor contract. In this move, management at the Nissan Chemical Industry Company, for instance, proposed a new labor contract plan in 1949.[29] In this new plan, the union was required to admit that all power to make decisions on personnel management should belong solely to management. In addition, manage-ment proposed to abolish the management council. A new mechanism for ex post facto conflict-solving and complaint-hearing was set up instead. This proposal naturally met strong union opposition.

It was difficult for management to revise the existing labor contracts, however, because in many cases it was required that the labor contract be renewed automatically if both parties did not agree to revisions. The revision of the Labor Union Law in 1949 removed this bottleneck for the management offensive by prescribing that the automatic renewal clause in labor contracts would not bind the parties concerned after the contract term had expired. This law strengthened management's efforts to conclude new labor contracts, by unilaterally terminating the old contracts.

Nevertheless, management did not get a free hand. Unions were fiercely opposed to the newly proposed contracts, and refused to con-clude them. Consequently, the percentage of workplaces covered by labor contracts decreased from 62.8 percent in 1948 to 45.1 percent in 1950. A decrease in the number of the management councils also resulted (table 2). Management, however, had a stake in stabilizing labor-management relations, and they began making compromises with union demands. For instance, in the Toyo Rayon Company, after two years of conflict, manage-ment and union accepted a mediation plan by the Labor Council in 1952.[30] The new contract prescribed that management should give notice to the union in case of job rotation and transfer; it should consult with the union in case of massive job transfers; and it should get consent from the union in case of transfers of union officials. The end result was a compro-mise between management and labor. This was a common pattern in many labor disputes over new labor contracts.

Furthermore, although Nikkeiren took a hard-line position against labor's participation within the company management system, other national-level actors, such as the Japan Productivity Center and the Minis-try of Labor, took a more conciliatory stance on this issue. They advocated

[29] Rōdōsōgi Chōsakai, ed., *Sengo rodo sogi jittaichosa*, vol. 10, pp. 209–70.
[30] Ibid., p. 286.

the incorporation of labor within the company system in order to achieve industrial harmony and higher economic growth. This national-level process will be dealt with in the next chapter.

Management regained the power to control the management system in the company, but labor maintained its right to be consulted in the case of personnel as well as managerial decision making. Management councils increased in numbers after the drop in 1950 (table 2). Recently, many studies have found that Japanese enterprise unions established various rules, formal and informal, to control the ways that management could change work organizations in the process of rationalization.[31] According to Hiroki Sato and Takashi Umezawa's study based on an extensive survey of 682 private enterprise unions in 1981, most unions have some mechanism by which management consults with them or gives them prior notification on a wide range of issues (table 3).[32] 21.4 percent of the surveyed unions have the right to be consulted and 39.0 percent to be notified in advance when the company introduces a new management plan. Furthermore, 67.8 percent of the unions in the former category succeeded in revising the management plan, and in the latter category, 42.3 percent. These findings show that this labor-management consultation mechanism is not a token institution for the union but an actual channel of influence.[33] Labor continued to be a legitimate participant within the company rather than devolve into a mere production factor.

Economic Rationality vs. Egalitarian Wages

Following its assault on labor's influence in decision making, management attacked labor's high wage demands which had been based upon the notion the livelihood or need-based wage. The livelihood wage was solidaristic because it did not count a worker's ability or the company's profitability. Based on this wage system, it was easier for unions to organize industry-wide wage negotiations. Management began challenging this wage system and trying to isolate wage demands within individual companies. Again, Nikkeiren started the offensive. In its 1950 paper "Management's Attitudes toward Wage," Nikkeiren contended that "man-

---

[31] E.g., Koike, *Shokuba no rōdō kumiai to sanka*; Nitta, *Nihon no rōdōsha sanka*.

[32] Hiroki Sato and Takashi Umezawa, "Rōdōkumiai no 'hatsugen' to kumiairuikei" (The union's 'voice' and the union typology), in Nihon Rōdō Kyōkai, ed., *80 nendai no rōshikankei* (Labor-management relations in the 1980s) (Tokyo: Nihon Rōdō Kyōkai, 1983).

[33] Many scholars conducted research and found an intensive communication between union and management. For instance, Koike, *Shokuba no rōdō kumiai to sanka*; Takeshi Inagami, *Rōshikankei no shakaigaku* (Sociology of industrial relations) (Tokyo: Tokyo Daigaku Shuppankai, 1981); Nitta, *Nihon no rōdōsha sanka*.

Table 3. Union participation in management decisions

Issue	Type of participation required by union contracts					
	Agreement (%)	Consultation (%)	Prior notice (%)	Report (%)	None (%)	N.A. (%)
Management plan	2.80	21.40	39.00	16.10	20.20	0.40
Introduction of new equipment	3.20	21.50	42.30	12.20	20.80	—
Personnel plan for new equipment	10.70	29.30	31.20	10.90	17.80	—
Personnel relocation	14.70	23.80	29.60	12.30	17.70	1.90
Designation of workers to be relocated	9.50	17.60	33.30	14.40	24.40	0.70
Overtime	34.60	29.90	11.30	8.70	9.70	5.90
Necessary personnel allocation	8.10	22.90	23.30	12.50	32.10	1.20

SOURCE: Sato and Umezawa, "Rōdōkumiai no 'hatsugen' to kumiairuikei," p. 420.
NOTE: Data from 682 private enterprise union contracts in 1981.

agement should reject wage demands based upon the cost-of-living and should seek to institutionalize the rational wage system based on workers' ability and output, because wage is a reward for labor."[34] This aggressive statement contrasts with the more reserved statement of Nikkeiren in 1948.

In 1952, the newly organized Sōhyō responded by advocating a "market basket" wage principle, in which wage demands were formulated by calculating the minimum cost to sustain "healthy and cultured" living, which was a constitutional right.[35] Sōhyō conducted a survey asking how much members would need in order to sustain a modest life style, and it set wage demands on this basis. This was merely a development of the livelihood wage, but this new calculation let Sōhyō demand more than twice as much as the average 1951 wage. Sōhyō tried to rally unions for a solidaristic wage struggle against Nikkeiren's offensive. However, even among the unions, this new wage struggle tactic was criticized as unrealistic because it ignored the existing economic situation of Japanese industries.[36] Practically speaking, after bitter confrontation between labor and management, Sōhyō failed to generate serious support for this new wage tactic, especially in light of management's strong opposition during the Densan-Tanro (electric power and coal-mining) strikes in 1952. Wage increases in this period were far below what the unions demanded through the market basket formula.[37] In addition, management supported by Nikkeiren cracked down on wage struggle tactics at the industry level, the aim of which was to overcome the weakness of enterprise union. The Densan dispute of 1952 and the Nissan Motors dispute of 1953 were the watershed cases. Following these, the industry-wide union movement was dissolved into an enterprise union movement.

However, Nikkeiren did not totally transform the wage settlement at the company level. Nikkeiren advocated the introduction of a regular wage increase (abolishing what was called a "base up") and a job-based wage system. A "base up" was a raise in the total wage bill of the company, which would result in wage increases for the entering wage as well as all other wages. A regular raise (*teiki shōkyū*) would increase the pay of each indi-

---

[34] Nikkeiren, "Tōmen no chinginmondai ni taisuru keieisha no taido" (Employers' attitude toward wage issues), quoted in Nihon Keieisha Dantai Renmei, *10 nen no ayumi* (10 years of Nikkeiren) (Tokyo: Nikkeiren, 1958), p. 141.

[35] Sōhyō, "Chingin kōryō soan" (A draft of wage principles), February 22, 1957, quoted in *Shiryō sengo 20 nen-shi*, p. 185.

[36] Okochi and Matsuo, *Nihon rōdōkumiai monogatari*, vol. 2, p. 88.

[37] For instance, the Toshiba union demanded a 15 percent raise but could not avoid accepting a 4.7 percent raise in 1954. Gordon, *The Evolution of Labor Relations in Japan*, p. 378. Cf. Ministry of Labor, *Shiryō rōdō undōshi* (1954).

vidual worker by an agreed percentage, which usually would not increase the company's wage bill if retirees and newly hired people were in proper balance.[38] Management preferred a regular raise, while labor preferred a base up, because the latter was more solidaristic in nature. Faced with union resistance, individual managements made compromises with unions to establish a new wage settlement pattern. As Andrew Gordon shows, the base up was not completely superseded by the regular raise within company wage negotiations even in the 1950s.[39] At the company level, some element of egalitarianism continued.

We can find this continuity in the process by which management tried to introduce a job-based wage system in place of the livelihood wage. From the beginning, Nikkeiren advocated the "rational" wage system based upon job rather than the cost-of-living index or workers' needs. For Nikkeiren, a job-based wage system was seen to be necessary to integrate workers into the company production system. As such, it was regarded as a basis for economic growth. However, at the company level, it was very difficult to introduce such a job-based wage system. In the 1950s, Sōhyō consistently opposed any job-based wage.[40] A job-based wage seemed to individualize or commodify workers and caused negative reactions from unions, which feared it would undermine key union principles.

In the shipbuilding and steel industries, for instance, management planned to rationalize the wage system to facilitate productivity increases. But management had to be very careful in introducing the job-based wage in anticipation of labor's negative reaction. One union leader in the shipbuilding industry said, "The introduction of a job-based wage would undermine the existing seniority wage system and would make rank-and-file workers uneasy about their living conditions.... Workers employed for more than twenty years tend to need a large amount of money for their families.... We could not but keep the seniority wage system while incorporating a job-based wage principle within that system." A labor management staff member of Yahata Steel said, "I originally thought a job-based wage was very good.... However, it caused a lot of problems once we tried to introduce that wage principle. It took a long

---

[38] Gordon, *Evolution of Labor Relations in Japan*, p. 376. He further explains, "Considered in graphic terms, the base-up 'lifted' the wage curve, increasing the area underneath it (wage cost), whereas the regular raise only moved individuals along the curve, leaving the wage curve untouched and the cost to the firm unchanged."

[39] Ibid., pp. 374–81.

[40] Sōhyō, "Chingin sutoppu o dahasuru tōmen no tōsō hōshin" (Struggle tactic to overcome the zero wage increase), June 10, 1954, quoted in *Shiryō sengo 20 nen-shi*, p. 261.

time to domesticate it in the Japanese wage system." In Yahata too, the existing seniority wage system was not completely replaced by the job-based wage.[41]

Management, thus, had to change a job-based wage plan to a job "capability" based wage. As job capability is learned in the company over time, it is somewhat similar to the seniority wage, although it takes merit into account. Explicit and implicit reactions from labor toward the job-based wage system eventually kept the seniority wage principle—which is theoretically closer to the livelihood wage—alive at the company level. According to Akira Ono's statistical analysis, the Japanese wage system maintained its characteristics of a livelihood wage well into the 1980s.[42] In other words, labor's egalitarianism or moral economy did prevent the seniority wage system from being fully transformed into an efficiency-oriented, economically rational one. Within the company, labor maintained its egalitarian wage system.

This brief review shows that while labor did not nationalize its movement in the late 1940s and also suffered from a management offensive led by Nikkeiren in the 1950s, it did maintain its achievements of the earlier labor offensive period. Unions maintained their say in the company's management system and kept the wage system based on a solidaristic wage principle. Japanese unions within the company maintained their position as legitimate actors even after the management offensive of the 1950s. This I have called micro-level labor accommodation.

THE POWER OF THE UNION WITHIN THE ENTERPRISE

The enterprise union can utilize the member workers' skill as a possible power resource. The practice of job rotation and job movement gives Japanese blue-collar workers in large companies wide-ranging skills in a career over a long period within a single company.[43] This skill formation increases worker morale. Kazuo Koike argues, "This kind of wide ranging skill contains such knowledge and promotes the ability of workers to determine the causes of problems on the shop floor and thus to contrib-

[41] Quoted passages from Ekonomisuto, ed., *Shōgen kōdo seichōki no Nihon Ge* (Testimony: Japan in the high growth era), volume 2 (Tokyo: Mainichi Shimbunsha, 1984), pp. 265 and 223. See also Shin Nihon Seitetsu, *Honoo to tomoni: Yahata seitetsu kabushiki kaisha shi* (A history of Yahata Steel Company) (Tokyo: Shin Nihon Seitetsu, 1981), pp. 651–52.

[42] Akira Ono, *Nihonteki koyōkankō to rōdō shijō* (Japanese employment practices and the labor market) (Tokyo: Tōyōkeizai Shinpōsha, 1989), chap. 2.

[43] For instance, Yoneyama, *Gijutsu kakushin to shokuba kanri*; Kawakita, *Sangyō hendō to rōmu kanri.*

ute to productivity."[44] This enskilling has two implications: First it is company-specific, thus creating loyal workers who tend to stay in the company.[45] Second, it gives workers power, and makes management dependent on them.

This enskilling is also the basis of the semi-autonomous work peer groups in Japanese companies.[46] Many labor scholars have pointed out the existence of these groups. Kazuo Koike, based on extensive research, argues that there are some spheres of work in which neither union nor management holds as much control as peer groups, which really control how work is organized.[47] Peer groups do not completely control work, but they enjoy a substantial amount of self-control. Keisuke Nakamura, based on an intensive historical analysis of the implementation of the managerial method in the NKK steel company demonstrates that cooperation of the semi-autonomous groups was indispensable in establishing the quality control (QC) circle practice.[48] Originally, management tried to establish QC circles unilaterally but failed. Management needed voluntary cooperation from the autonomous work peer groups to successfully establish it. In this context, the blue-collar workers with some managerial responsibilities play an indispensable role. They are usually central figures in peer groups, and at the same time, union representatives on the shop floor. They tend to represent their peer groups' interests against management, using their peer groups' semi-autonomous control over work as their power resource.[49] Nakamura also found that middle-rank managers on the production line allied themselves with the union to resist the implementation of the new managerial method of industrial engineering advocated by the staff office.

As Michio Nitta found, intra-company politics forced the management of Shin Nihon Steel to make consecutive concessions to union leaders to maintain cooperative relations with the union, even though its union was known as one of the most cooperative in Japan. Its power was based on the

---

[44] Kazuo Koike, "Human Resource Development and Labor Management Relations," in Yamamura and Yasuba, eds., *Political Economy of Japan*, vol. 1, p. 327.

[45] Koike, "Josetsu: howaitokarāka kumiai moderu."

[46] Nakamura and Nitta, "Developments in Industrial Relations and Human Resource Practices in Japan."

[47] Koike, *Shokuba no rōdō kumiai to sanka*, pp. 217–28.

[48] Keisuke Nakamura, "Nihonkōkan niokeru QC sākuru no seiseikatei" (The formation process of the QC circle in NKK), working paper no. 23, Center for Business and Industrial Research, Hosei University, 1992.

[49] Akira Takanashi, in his study of the steel industry, found that blue-collar workers with some managerial responsibilities represented their peer groups against management. *Nihon tekkōgyō no rōshikankei* (Labor-management relations in the Japanese iron and steel industry) (Tokyo: Tokyo Daigaku Shuppankai, 1967), p. 291.

power resources described above. In addition, the need to rationalize steel making in order to catch up with foreign competitors increased management's dependence on the union. The fact that the Shin Nihon Steel union strengthened the labor-management consultation mechanism when management introduced a new rationalization plan is further evidence of this interpretation.[50]

The power of the union, however, is not determined solely by the nature of work organization. Union power can be more political in nature. Management needs to be conciliatory to the moderate union in order to keep radical leftist groups within the company out of union leadership. Even in the case of Shin Nihon Steel's Yahata Mill, which has been a bastion of moderate labor activity in the steel industry, leftist candidates for positions of union officials often won more than 30 percent in the 1960s.[51] Management supported moderate union leaders also because the existence of the radical left within the union enhanced its power.[52] This point leads to a more political and dynamic understanding of union power within the enterprise.

POLITICAL DYNAMICS WITHIN THE ENTERPRISE

The case of labor-management conflict in the automobile industry illustrates the political dynamics conducive to union power. The All-Japan Auto Workers' Union (*Zenjidōsha*, AJAWU) was organized in 1948 and was known for its radical leftist character. The unions within the Toyota and Nissan Motor Companies were affiliated with this industry union, and both companies experienced harsh labor-management conflicts in the 1950s. Two critical events for Toyota's labor-management relations were the strikes of 1950 and 1953. In 1950 the Dodge Line and its subsequent economic downturn put Toyota on the edge of bankruptcy. In July 1950 the company's debt was three times its capital, and the creditor banks demanded that management dismiss redundant workers and split the company into manufacturing and sales companies. Management had to accept this offer, although it had earlier promised not to fire workers. This naturally enraged the union and resulted in a bitter conflict. When the

---

[50] Nitta, *Nihon no rōdōsha sanka*, p. 161.

[51] Heihachiro Kawabe, "Tekkō sangyō" (The iron and steel industry), in Tomio Makino, ed., *Nihonteki rōshikankei no henbō* (Changing Japanese labor-capital relations) (Tokyo: Ōtsuki Shoten, 1991), p. 22.

[52] Nobuhiro Hiwatari, "The Political Economy of Enterprise Unionism and Industrial Collaboration in Japan: Explaining Union Strategies to Cope with Economic Stagnation and Aging Work Force," paper presented at the Workshop on the Shifting Boundaries of Labor Politics, March 12–14, 1993, Center for European Studies, Harvard University.

company called for 1,600 volunteers for retirement in April 1950, the union went on strike against this plan. However, faced with the strong resolve of management and the crisis of the company, the union eventually agreed to this plan in June. This was the beginning of the end of leftist hegemony in the Toyota union. In the course of this 1950 conflict, the skilled workers who had graduated from the training school within the Toyota Company played an important role in criticizing the leftist union leaders, and after the strike they organized themselves within the union as opponents to the leftists. The shop floor supervisors and lower-rank managers, who were union members too, also joined the opposition forces within the union. These opposition groups were implicitly supported by company management.[53]

In 1953, after the Korean War boom helped the company to revive, the Toyota union, following AJAWU's strategy, went on strike and demanded an industry-wide guaranteed minimum seniority wage. However, despite the fifty-five-day-long conflict, management rejected the union's demand and instead cut the wages of the workers on strike. This management offensive was typical in those days.[54] In the process of the 1953 strike, the company-educated skilled workers again played an important role in opposing the leftist union leadership, and the union backed off after the company promised a bonus raise in August.[55] In 1954 this opposition group eventually won the union election supported by the rank-and-file workers who worried about the future of the company and took leadership of the new Toyota Union by dissolving the Toyota Local of the AJAWU. This new union established the new principle that workers' well being, on the one hand, and the development of the auto industry and the company, on the other, should be mutually reinforcing. The Labor-Management Co-Declaration of 1962 clearly advocated labor-management cooperation for productivity increases based on mutual trust. Since then the Toyota union has been known as the most cooperative union in Japan. The opposition to this cooperative union leadership has been weak, and even in 1971 when the opposition gathered its largest vote share in a union election, it received only 20.1 percent.[56] This coop-

[53] Hideo Totsuka and Tsutomu Hyodo, *Rōshikankei no tenkan to sentaku: Nihon no jidōshasangyo* (Transformation and choice of labor-management relations: The Japanese automobile industry) (Tokyo: Nihon Hyōronsha, 1991), p. 142.

[54] Yoshinari Maruyama and Mitsuo Fujii, *Toyota/Nissan* (Tokyo: Ōtsuki Shoten, 1991), p. 18.

[55] *Sōzō kagirinaku: Toyota jidōsha 50 nen-shi* (Unlimited creativity: fifty years of the Toyota Automobile Company) (Nagoya: Toyota Jidōsha Kabushiki Kaisha, 1987), p. 309.

[56] Masaki Saruta, "Jidōsha sangyō" (The automobile industry), in Makino, *Nihonteki rōshikankei no henbō*, p. 45.

erative union has been one of the foundations for the famous flexible production system that has flourished at Toyota.[57]

The AJAWU Nissan Local in 1953 simultaneously organized a strike, demanding the same industry-wide guaranteed minimum seniority wage, the same rules regarding the hiring of temporary workers as regular employees, the improvement of retirement benefits, and so forth. The Nissan union was regarded as the strongest union within the AJAWU, and union representatives at the shop floor, who were usually lower-rank managers, controlled the production process, so management was highly dependent on the union. This strong Nissan union, however, also faced a hard-line response from management similar to that in Toyota. All union demands were turned down, and management counter-proposed the non-unionization of lower-ranking managers and the "no work, no pay" principle. The latter principle meant that the company would not pay that portion of the worker's wage covering the time that he was engaged in union activity during working hours. When the union escalated their tactics from a wave of one-hour strikes to a strike with an unlimited term, management in return locked out workers. The conflict became violent, and union members broke the lockout. Management responded by dismissing the top union leaders. The union still tried to escalate its pressure on management, but opposition to such tactics gradually appeared within the union. The opposition group, consisting of shop-floor supervisors, established a second union. This second union rapidly expanded its membership, was supported by management, and finally established hegemony within the company.[58]

These two cases show a typical, successful management offensive in the 1950s. The aftermath of these two events was very different, however. A recent intensive study of the labor-management relations within the Nissan Motor Company and the Toyota Motor Company demonstrates that the Nissan union had a much more autonomous status and exerted stronger influence over managerial decisions than did the Toyota union.[59] For instance, according to one study, "if the company intends to promote Mr. X to foreman it first has to submit a suggestion to that effect to the union chairman. . . . Then the union examines the person, and having

---

[57] Roos, Womack, and Jones, *Machine That Changed the World*; Taiichi Ohno, *Toyota seisan hōshiki* (The Toyota production system) (Tokyo: Daiyamondosha, 1978).

[58] In the harsh labor conflicts in Japanese companies, very often a moderate second union was formed by dissident workers out of an originally leftist union. Okochi and Matsuo, *Nihon rōdō kumiai monogatari*, vol. 2, pp. 136–40. AJAWU dissolved itself in December 1954.

[59] Totsuka and Hyodo, *Rōshikankei no tenkan to sentaku*.

been approved by the union he is officially promoted by the company."[60] The institutional bases of this union influence are the management council and collective bargaining. Without consent from the union through these institutions, the company could not transfer workers, direct overtime work, or promote workers. This does not mean the union has been antagonistic to management, but neither was it a passive subordinate. The union itself took pride in making the company prosperous. Although this relationship changed in 1986, and management regained its managerial power, it is important to note that the "domesticated" union retained a high level of influence in the company for a long period.

On the other hand, the Toyota union became much more cooperative after the 1953 strike, lacking the strength of the Nissan union. The Toyota union did not intrude into managerial decision making. Nevertheless, even in this case, workers were not exploited by management. Rather, management was very careful to preempt worker dissension through organizational and other informal activities, such as quality control circles and workers' voluntary associations. Management retained workers' solidarity by implementing a unique wage policy, which is one important component of Toyotaism. In principle, most of the wage is based on the output of workers, but collectively.[61] In other words, efficiency was measured by group performance. Furthermore, management used a calculation that would reflect fewer differences in efficiency in the actual payment. In other words, management tried to avoid treating workers as a commodity and tried to retain a notion of a solidaristic community. But this management practice was established without much consultation with labor.

Why did different labor-management relations emerge in these two companies, both of which broke the radical leftist union movement and ended up with cooperative enterprise unions? The orthodox understanding regards both unions as co-opted enterprise unions, ignoring the difference between them. Intra-company politics was an important determinant of this difference. In the case of Toyota, through the union election, radical leftist union leaders lost their power and authority to more cooperative leaders. Management implicitly and explicitly supported these cooperative leaders, but the process of leadership transformation occurred primarily as an internal and autonomous process within the union. The Nissan union, on the other hand, split itself into two

[60] Ichiro Saga, "Labour Relations in Japan: The Case of Nissan Motor Company," occasional paper no. 34, East Asian Institute, Free University of Berlin, Berlin, 1983, pp. 7–8. Similar findings are abundant in Totsuka and Hyodo, eds., *Rōshikankei no tenkan to sentaku*.

[61] Totsuka and Hyodo, *Rōshikankei no tenkan to sentaku*, p. 136.

unions, and the union, supported by management, fought harshly with the dominant leftist union. In due course management cooperated with the more moderate union and delegated extensive supervisory power to foremen who had been leaders in the radical union but later joined the second union. A semi-autonomous work peer group was union-based in Nissan, whereas it was incorporated into the company system in Toyota.

This management dependence on the union was consolidated in 1965, when Nissan Motor took over Prince Motor. Workers at Prince Motor were organized by the Sōhyō-affiliated leftist National Metal Workers' Union (*Zenkoku Kinzoku*), which was strongly critical of labor-management cooperation. The Prince Motor Union opposed this take-over, and the Nissan management needed to overcome this opposition. In due course, the Nissan union fought with the Prince union and succeeded in organizing a majority of the ex-Prince workers.[62] This incident made management more confident and dependent on the Nissan union. As a result, more autonomous discretion was placed in the hands of the union representatives at the shop floor and more influence was given to union leaders in company-wide decision making.

This comparison between Toyota and Nissan provides some lessons for understanding the place of the union within the Japanese company. First, it demonstrates that the enterprise union does not necessarily evolve into a powerless union, entirely subject to management dictates. As the Nissan case shows, political dynamics—that is, intra-company politics—could enable the union to exert substantial power over management by making management dependent upon the union. Second, the case of Toyota shows that even without a strong union like Nissan's, management might not be so exploitative. Rather, at Toyota, management tried to incorporate labor's demands into its company management system, partly because of management's paternalistic ideology and partly because management definitely needed labor's cooperation given its low capital resources and sense of vulnerability to foreign competition. In order to catch up with foreign companies as well as to compete with its domestic rivals, Toyota management believed it was necessary to preempt industrial conflict. This type of situation sometimes ended up in a management offensive against a militant labor movement, and sometimes it produced a conciliatory management that treated labor carefully.

The brief review of the institutionalization of micro-level labor accommodation shows that the enterprise union was not co-opted by manage-

---

[62] Ibid., p. 4.

ment. The union power within the company has been ignored by many orthodox labor scholars, who see the isolated union as a powerless company union. This chapter, however, shows that the enterprise union in Japan exerted substantial influence over management decisions, by exerting power based on skill formation and intra-company political dynamics. Thus, the union maintained its influence within the company and continued to affect company policy.

The management offensive from the top, led by the Nikkeiren, put the leftist national labor federation on the defensive at the macro level, but it could not dominate the micro-level labor-management relations. The labor offensive from below left important legacies in micro-level labor accommodation, and the enterprise unions in Japan developed their macro-level tactics on this micro-level achievement.

CHAPTER FOUR

Nationalizing Wage Negotiations

Labor nationalized and institutionalized wage negotiations to enable workers to enjoy substantial wage increases across industries. As described in chapter 1, wage increases were below productivity increases in the 1950s but caught up with productivity growth in the 1960s, and Japanese wages began catching up with those in the advanced industrial countries. The pattern of wage increases in relation to productivity increases was similar to that in Western European countries in the 1960s. The "politics of productivity," where labor and management adopted the principle of high wage increases based on high productivity increases, seems to have been institutionalized in Japan in the "postwar settlement" period.[1] In addition, in the 1960s wage differentials among Japanese wage-earners decreased substantially (fig. 7).[2] In this chapter, I argue that the institutionalization of the Shuntō wage bargaining contributed to this wage pattern.

Labor did not unilaterally succeed in institutionalizing national-level wage negotiations. Although Nikkeiren was willing to keep workers' wages low, the accommodationist Dōyūkai and the Japan Productivity Center (JPC) advocated a productivity increase as the best way to increase wages. Individual managers preferred the accommodationist line and offered higher wages to mobilize workers in the company production system. They wanted to support moderate and cooperative union leaders and also

[1] Charles Maier, *In Search of Stability;* Stephen Bornstein, "States and Unions."
[2] Income distribution in Japan measured in terms of the Gini coefficient (standard measure of equality of income distribution) also became more equal in the 1960s. Kuniaki Tanabe, "Social Policy in Japan," in Frieder Naschold and Michio Muramatsu, eds., *State and Administration in Japan and Germany* (Berlin: Walter de Gruyter, 1997), p. 124.

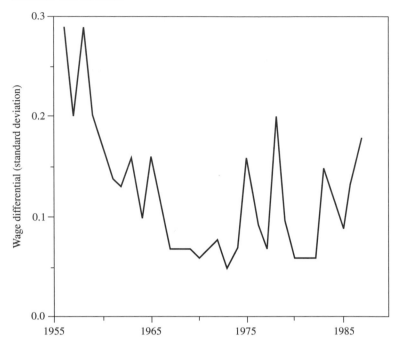

Figure 7. Wage differentials among Japanese companies. This graph plots the standard deviation of the wage increases among all Japanese companies in the Shuntō wage negotiations. From Shuntō Kenkyūkai, *Shuntō kawarunoka,* p. 31.

needed to maximize workers' commitment to the company. Labor exploited this situation by organizing nationally coordinated wage negotiations, Shuntō, which contributed to an egalitarian wage distribution. However, labor was not unified in establishing this new wage tactic. The political front line was not simply between labor and capital. Inter- and intra-class politics played a determining role in bringing about the Shuntō wage-negotiation system.

In this chapter I also analyze the economic impact of this Shuntō wage system and labor's response. The egalitarian wage structure brought by the Shuntō had an economic impact very similar to solidaristic wage bargaining in Sweden. Under the Shuntō system, the high growth sector paid lower wages with regard to its rapid productivity growth in comparison to the backward sector—including small and medium-sized companies—which had to pay wages higher than their productivity increases would warrant. The end result was that the growth sector had sufficient capital to reinvest, while the backward sector had to transform or rationalize its production to offset its relatively high labor costs. It is important to note that in both sectors the union was supposed to participate in management decision making as well as industrial policymaking. This is because in the former sector, as the union gave up some portion of a possible wage increase, it tried to ensure that investment would make the company or industry more competitive (and increase future wages and maintain secure employment), while in the latter sector, it needed to oversee the rationalization or transformation that would so strongly influence its members. I argue that the mainstream Sōhyō unions failed to realize this point and lost the potential opportunity to participate in decision making, while the private-sector unions within Dōmei (Japanese Confederation of Labor) and a few in Sōhyō eagerly pursued this path. This historical situation made it possible for the private manufacturing sector unions to gradually gain a strong position within the labor movement thereafter.

THE DEVELOPMENT OF SHUNTŌ WAGE BARGAINING

In the early 1950s when Shuntō started, there was a severe conflict between Nikkeiren and Sōhyō on how wages should be calculated. Sōhyō was organized in 1950 as a democratic union federation in opposition to the communist-led union movement and was welcomed by government and management as well as the GHQ. However, within a year, Sōhyō become a leftist federation driven by cold war politics. It began denouncing the capitalist world system under U.S. hegemony and opposed the presence of U.S. forces in Japan and Japanese rearmament.[3] This political reorientation of Sōhyō guided its wage policy. Under the leadership of Takano, Sōhyō established a new wage principle, the Market Basket Formula, in 1952, and demanded a radical wage raise, an immediate increase in average monthly wages from 10,000 yen to 25,000 yen with a subsequent 70,000-yen increase. It was almost impossible to achieve such wage increases given the economic downturn after the Korean War. Densan and Tanrō followed this wage principle and organized militant strikes in order to break through management's hard-line responses. But these

---

[3] In the Second Conference of 1951, Sōhyō adopted four principles for peace: 1) conclude peace treaties with all countries, 2) adopt a neutral foreign policy, 3) oppose the U.S. military bases in Japan, and 4) oppose rearmament. Furthermore, it rejected joining the International Confederation of Free Trade Unions. See Okochi and Matsuo, *Nihon rōdō kumiai monogatari*, vol. 2, pp. 47–49. In describing this transformation of Sōhyō, it is often said that a duck was born from a chicken egg.

efforts ended up in defeat. For moderate union leaders, it seemed obvious that Sōhyō's wage demands themselves were unrealistic. However, most Sōhyō leaders thought the difficulty in realizing their wage demands was political; they regarded the political regime as the cause of management's hardline policy.[4] Sōhyō leaders' understanding of the Japanese political economy of that period led the movement onto a political course.

They formulated their understanding of the Japanese political economy through a distinctive interpretation of contemporary economic and political events. The economic recession following the Korean War boom put labor on the defensive. Many workers were faced with rationalization efforts that led, in the worst case, to dismissals. In 1953, while manufacturing and mining output increased by 22.6 percent, employment increased by only 1.1 percent and nominal wages increased by 13.3 percent. The conservative government financially supported rationalization in various industries as an important means to prop up the Japanese economy. The first rationalization plan for the steel industry (1951–55) was a typical example.[5] This rationalization channeled money into the big steel makers and made them more competitive, so much so that the small and medium-sized steel makers could not but streamline their production. In due course, these companies dismissed many workers. The government was also trying to introduce several anti-union policies, such the Law to Regulate Strikes of 1953. With the support of some business leaders, the government concluded the Mutual Security Aid Agreement (MSA) with the U.S. government, which was expected to help Japanese economic growth by making economic aid available from the United States in exchange for Japan's commitment to rearm. Although the economic aid provided under the MSA Agreement was far below the original expectation, all these events convinced Sōhyō leaders that the Japanese government would try to develop the economy by rearming Japan under U.S. hegemony, and that in due course labor's interests would be sacrificed.

Sōhyō leaders as well as socialist politicians saw these events not as separate and economically motivated, but as systematic and politically motivated. In its Fourth Conference, Sōhyō declared that monopoly capitalists were trying to militarize the Japanese economy and make it dependent on U.S. hegemony in order to make profit at the expense of

[4] A recollection by Haruo Wada, the moderate union leader of the Japan Seamen's Union, is found in Takanashi, ed., *Shōgen: sengo rōdō undōshi*, pp. 178–79.

[5] Hideki Yamakawa, "Tekkōgyō" (The iron and steel industry), in Komiya, et al., *Nihon no sangyōseisaku*, pp. 255–76. Kume, "A Tale of Twin Industries," pp. 168–74.

workers, farmers, and small and medium-sized companies.[6] Sōhyō leaders, therefore, believed it necessary to resort to political tactics in order to protect workers' interests. The alternative path for Japanese economic growth was allegedly to enlarge the domestic market by increasing wages as well as to have market access in the communist countries by abandoning the existing pro-U.S. foreign policy. Tactically, they believed that because the unions in Japan were enterprise unions, and thus weak against the capitalists, they should mobilize a wider range of people. The tactic was initially promising because not only workers but also many ordinary people were suffering under monopoly capitalism and the "war economy" policy. This was the ideological basis of the Sōhyō movement in that period.

One notable but tragic outcome of this strategy was the Amagasaki Steel strike of 1954.[7] Amagasaki Steel was on the brink of bankruptcy with huge deficits. Management proposed emergency measures to restore business and asked for a 15 percent wage cut as well as a reduction in production. Management also asked for the union's immediate response to this proposal in three days, as this was a key part of the company's financing plan to meet the demands of creditors. The union rejected the proposal and was prepared to strike, as it believed management was bluffing. Tekkōrōren (the Japanese Federation of Iron and Steel Workers' Unions) and Sōhyō saw the proposal as a typical management offensive to rationalize business at the expense of workers, in line with the capitalist grand strategy described above. The Amagasaki union escalated its tactics, while management announced a plant closure for an unlimited term. The union mobilized its members' families and the local community against the plant closure. In June when the company finally could not meet its bills and was bankrupted, the union lost everything.

Despite this result, Sōhyō's mainstream leadership argued that the union had succeeded in demonstrating the potential power of labor by rallying a wide range of people against the capitalist offensive. They thought the strategy was effective. Sōhyō tried to establish an alternative political economy through political organizing. It claimed that this was the only way to prevent unemployment caused by rationalization.[8]

[6] Ministry of Labor, *Shiryō rōdō undōshi* (1953), p. 437.

[7] See Okochi and Matsuo, *Nihon rōdō kumiai monogatari*, vol. 2, pp. 192–96; Ministry of Labor, *Shiryō rōdō undōshi* (1954), pp. 349–70.

[8] Okochi and Matsuo, *Nihon rōdō kumiai monogatari*, vol. 2, p. 199. The struggle of the Muroran Plant of Nichikō (Japan Steel) is another similar example. Ministry of Labor, *Shiryō rōdō undōshi* (1954), pp. 370–421.

Sōhyō proudly called this a "family-wide/community-wide" mobilization struggle.

Nikkeiren, on the other hand, advocated a purely economic solution. It criticized Sōhyō's political movement as the cause of the tragedy at Amagasaki Steel and felt that the Amagasaki union should have cooperated with management.[9] Nikkeiren's basic view on wages drove their analysis. Although it had to accept the logic of a livelihood wage in the late 1940s, Nikkeiren began advocating a more economically rational wage system, especially after the Dodge Line brought about a surplus budget and subsequent deflation.[10] The Korean War boom, however, made individual management more conciliatory than Nikkeiren to labor's demands. The coal mining industry is a typical example, which showed that management—despite Nikkeiren's assertion—tended to be conciliatory to labor's wage demands, as long as it could transfer labor costs to user industries or the government.[11] In 1953, however, Nikkeiren found the economic recession after the Korean War to be a nice opportunity to propagate an economically rational wage system again. It proposed that labor conflicts should be solved only in the context of the national economy, which would be further constrained by the world economy. It criticized Sōhyō for demanding unrealistic high wages beyond the economic capacity of the economy in order to rally support for its political goal.[12] Nikkeiren substantiated this idea in the form of the Three Principles of Wages in 1954: (1) no wage increase should cause inflation, (2) no wage increase should be beyond the capability of the company to pay, and (3) no wage increase should be out of line with a productivity increase.[13]

These principles directly contradicted Sōhyō's political strategy, and Sōhyō denounced Nikkeiren.[14] Sōhyō's criticism that Nikkeiren merely sought to stop wage increases was not groundless, because although Nikkeiren advocated a productivity increase, it emphasized the necessity to suppress wage increases in order to make Japanese industries competitive in the world market: wage level had reached the prewar peak, so management should not allow further base-up type wage increases. While the ratio of wage earners to total job holders was 36 percent, the percent-

[9] *Nikkeiren taimuzu*, July 8, 1954.

[10] Nikkeiren, "Tōmen no chinginmondai ni taisuru keieisha no taido" (Management's view on wage issues), February 7, 1950, quoted in Nikkeiren, *110 nen no ayumi*, p. 141.

[11] See Kume, "A Tale of Twin Industries."

[12] Nikkeiren, "Kihonteki rōdōtaisaku ni kansuru iken" (Opinion on the basic labor policies), May 12, 1953, quoted in Ministry of Labor, *Shiryo rōdō undōshi* (1953), pp. 858–61.

[13] Ministry of Labor, *Shiryō rōdō undōshi* (1954), p. 779.

[14] *Shiryō sengo 20 nen-shi*, p. 261.

age of wage earners' income out of the national income was 49 percent in 1952,[15] and Japanese production costs and the price level for manufactured goods were allegedly higher than those in other industrial nations. Therefore, Nikkeiren concluded that it was necessary to suppress wage increases so as to reduce production costs and strengthen the competitiveness of Japanese industries. An increasing balance of payments deficit in 1953 further convinced Nikkeiren of the necessity of this wage policy, because it regarded a high wage/low productivity combination as the main cause of this deficit.[16]

The government apparently supported Nikkeiren's stance, although it tried to be a mediator between labor and management. In January 1954, Labor Minister Kosaka proposed a survey of the standard wage. He argued that as the government was implementing a surplus budget to control inflation and to solve the balance of payments deficit, it was necessary for the government to ask labor to refrain from demanding high nominal wage increases. He based his argument on the same data that Nikkeiren used, that labor's share was sufficiently large and consumer prices comparatively high. He also realized that government could not legally suppress wage increases, and thus he proposed a large-scale study on existing wage levels in order to find an economically sustainable wage level on which labor and management could agree.[17] This policy of the Ministry of Labor (MOL) convinced Sōhyō that the capitalists and government were working together to suppress wage increases. Furthermore, Labor Minister Kosaka was eager to introduce several antilabor policies. He proposed that the Labor Standard Law be revised to allow management more flexibility in its management practices. Moreover, he proposed that government revise several labor laws that had been introduced to promote the formation of labor unions in the occupation reform period.[18]

These proposals for a new labor policy were easily interpreted as an integral part of the government policy to reverse the democratization trend of the occupation era. The unions regarded legislation such as the Anti-Subversive Activities Law, the centralization of the police system, and the education reform that required teachers to be politically neutral as part of the government program to repress the labor movement, to sup-

[15] Ministry of Labor, *Shiryō rōdō undōshi* (1954), p. 859.

[16] Ibid., p. 778.

[17] Ministry of Labor, *Rōdō gyōsei yōran* (A survey of labor policy) (1955) (Tokyo: Rōdō Hōrei Kyōkai, annual), p. 26.

[18] Ohara Shakaimondai Kenkyusho, *Nihon rōdō nenkan* (Annual of Japanese labor) (1955) (Tokyo: Rōdō Junpō Sha), pp. 798–99.

press wage increases, and to transform the Japanese economy into a war economy.[19]

In sum, conflicts on wages among labor, management, and the government were harsh and highly political. Wage conflicts easily resulted in political conflict between Sōhyō, on the one hand, and Nikkeiren and the government, on the other.

While Sōhyō and Nikkeiren fought with each other, accommodationist moves began to appear within both labor and management. Views on how to determine wages converged. Earlier criticism against the politically oriented labor movement led by the communists had been a driving force in the establishment of Sōhyō. Sōhyō's founders criticized the leftist labor movement as being mobilized for the sake of revolution and for ignoring workers' concrete and immediate interests. Instead, Sōhyō initially advised that labor unions should set economic goals consistent with the level of the national economy.[20] However, when Sōhyō itself became political, this in turn revived arguments between leftist political unionism and economically driven business unionism.

While the left wing of Sōdōmei wholeheartedly supported the establishment of Sōhyō and dissolved, the right wing worried that public-sector unions would dominate the new organization.[21] This conflict became clear and deepened after the Densan-Tanrō disputes of 1952. Both unions followed Sōhyō's wage principle in organizing their industry-wide wage struggles, but they failed to achieve their wage goals in the face of management's hard-line response. Furthermore, the Densan union was defeated organizationally, and an enterprise union critical of Densan's tactics was organized within each company. Four member unions (textile, seamen, broadcasting, and movies) publicly criticized Sōhyō's strategy as being politically biased and ignoring the union members' interests. The Tanrō leaders rejected the mediation proposal by the Central Labor Relations Committee, which offered favorable wage increases, and went on strike, an event which was telling evidence that the leftist union leaders were exploiting union activities for political goals. These unions attacked

[19] Sōhyō, "Chingin sutoppu seisaku o uchiyaburu tōmen no chingintōsō hōshin" (Wage tactics to resist the policy to stop wage increases), June 10, 1954, quoted in *Shiryō sengo 20 nen-shi*, p. 261. A brief review of this "reverse course" is in J. A. A. Stockwin, *Japan: Divided Politics in a Growth Economy*, 2d ed. (London: W. W. Norton, 1982), pp. 68–69.

[20] Sōhyō, "Sōhyō kessei junbitaikai: Taikai sengen" (Preparatory conference for organizing Sōhyō: Manifesto), March 11, 1950, quoted in *Shiryō sengo 20 nen-shi*, p. 158; Sōhyō, "Sōhyō kihon kōryō" (Basic Principles), July 12, 1950, quoted in *Shiryō sengo 20 nen-shi*, p. 158.

[21] Okochi and Matsuo, *Nihon rōdō kumiai monogatari*, vol. 2, p. 30.

Sōhyō by appealing to the same logic Sōhyō used to denounce the communist-led unions.

In 1954 these four dissenting unions established the Zenrōkaigi (All Japan Labor Union Conference) in order to organize their own labor movement. In its constitution, Zenrōkaigi declared that labor unions should limit their goals to protect workers' economic interests and should refrain from political activities. It further proposed that unions should not try to maximize their immediate economic interests in a selfish way but rather pursue their interests in a way that would promote the welfare of the nation. This meant that Zenrōkaigi regarded productivity increase and industrial development as a basis for workers' long-term well being.[22]

Naturally, Nikkeiren welcomed these changes in the labor movement. It praised Zenrōkaigi for taking economic reality into consideration in demanding wage increases, while criticizing Sōhyō as a force to destroy the existing economic system.[23] However, these unions did not regard Nikkeiren as an ally. Instead they turned to the Japan Productivity Center (JPC) and Dōyūkai.

The JPC originated in the movement to increase productivity, which was originally supported by U.S. foreign economic aid and was run by a productivity promotion committee consisting of four national business associations (Nikkeiren, Dōyūkai, Keidanren [Federation of Economic Organizations], and Nisshō [Japan Chamber of Commerce]). The process of establishing the JPC in 1955, however, showed that the progressive management group within Dōyūkai took the initiative for the labor-management accommodation thereafter.[24] By increasing productivity and developing the national economy, it was thought that subsequently employment and real wages would increase. This policy was very different from Nikkeiren's blunt proposal to suppress wage increases and to legislate anti-union laws in order to make Japanese industries competitive. The JPC rather emphasized what it called an "expanding equilibrium," which was formed by increasing the size of the pie to be distributed.

In December 1953 the U.S. Embassy contacted Japanese business associations and recommended establishment of a bilateral commission to study managerial rationalization in order to help promote Japanese eco-

[22] Zenrōkaigi, "Kenshōzenbun" (A preface to the constitution), April 23, 1954, quoted in *Shiryō sengo 20 nen-shi*, p. 268.

[23] *Nikkeiren taimuzu*, January 1, 1954.

[24] The description below is based on Nihon Seisansei Honbu, *Seisansei undō 30 nen-shi* (Thirty years of the productivity movement) (Tokyo: Nihon Seisansei Honbu, 1985).

nomic development. The U.S. proposal was based upon successful experiences in West European countries and had its origins in the Marshall Plan. While Dōyūkai took this proposal seriously, Keidanren showed no interest in the beginning. MITI, which had already studied the European experience with this productivity movement and had already proposed establishment of the Japan Productivity Center in 1951, welcomed and supported this move.[25] Dōyūkai persuaded the other three national business associations to jointly establish the U.S.-Japan Productivity Promotion Committee. It was a management organization that had no labor union representatives, although the European productivity movement incorporated labor unions. Business groups worried that this movement would follow the path of the ill-fated Economic Recovery Conference with labor's participation. However, Dōyūkai, and especially one powerful advocate for this movement, Kohei Goshi, realized that it was inevitable to have labor cooperation in order to implement this movement for productivity increase.[26] When management reorganized the production committee into the Japan Productivity Center in 1955, it formally announced that the JPC would consist of management, labor, and men of learning and experience.

Labor was divided in its response to this move. Sōhyō criticized it as a conspiracy by Japanese and American capitalists to reduce the wage level, exploit workers, and rearm Japan under U.S. hegemony.[27] The moderate unions also did not accept this productivity movement in the beginning. Sōdōmei, which agreed to participate, nevertheless demanded two major conditions for its participation.[28] The first condition was that the movement not pursue industrial development at the expense of labor but provide labor with a fair share of the productivity increase. Second, in the course of efforts to increase productivity, labor unions should be full actors and fully consulted. The JPC immediately agreed to these points, and Sōdōmei decided to participate. Other moderate unions were not persuaded by the JPC's promise, however, and continued to withhold support. Zenrōkaigi moved cautiously, even though Sōdōmei was a major member of Zenrōkaigi. Within Zenrōkaigi, Zensen Dōmei (Japanese Fed-

[25] Ministry of International Trade and Industry, Kigyōkyoku Kigyō Dai 2 ka, "Seisansei o kōjō saseru michi" (A way to increase productivity), MITI internal document, 1955, quoted in *Seisansei undō 30 nen-shi*, p. 27.

[26] *Seisansei undō 30 nen-shi*, p. 99.

[27] Sōhyō, "Seisansei zōkyō ni taisuru kihontekitaido" (A basic attitude toward productivity increase), March 14, 1955, quoted in *Shiryō sengo 20 nen-shi*, pp. 306–8.

[28] *Seisansei undō 30 nen-shi*, p. 155. Technically, Sōdōmei demanded that the JPC formally endorse Sōdōmei's eight principles before it could participate, however, these principles can be roughly summarized in the two points discussed here.

eration of Textile Industry Workers' Unions) was the most cautious. The president of Zensen, Minoru Takida, argued as follows:

> The Zenrōkaigi took the productivity increase seriously. We are, however, concerned what this productivity movement will bring about, given the existing labor-management relation. . . . Although Dōyūkai has shown most for support this movement, Nikkeiren is now in front. We worry about Nikkeiren, which has been antagonistic to our movement on such issues as labor union regulation, wages, and collective bargaining.[29]

This was an understandable response from labor, because Nikkeiren aggressively led the management offensive, focusing on two issues, wages and managerial prerogatives. These two issues are directly related to the two concerns of Sōdōmei and the other unions. Nikkeiren had argued that wage increases should be suppressed to reduce production costs and increase the competitiveness of Japanese industries. Within Sōhyō, the private manufacturing sector unions, such as Tekkōrōren (an iron and steel union) and Gōkarōren (Japanese Federation of Synthetic Chemistry Workers' Unions), were opposed to the productivity movement based on the fact that productivity increases in the period 1950–54 did not result in parallel wage increases.[30] We should remember that wage increases were behind productivity increases in the 1950s (see fig. 5). It was reasonable for these unions to suspect that management, especially Nikkeiren, would exploit labor in the process of rationalizing for a productivity increase.

The JPC tried hard to find cooperation from the unions by arguing that the productivity movement was a totally new concept and very different from the traditional rationalization policies of the early 1950s. Kohei Goshi of the JPC emphasized this point:

> It is a perverted view that the productivity increase would result in an intensification of the labor process and suppression of wage increases. Our purpose is to increase employment opportunities and raise the level of real wages. The productivity movement is different from traditional rationalization and efficiency increases in that the benefits will be evenly distributed among labor, management, and consumers. . . . The chicken will stop laying eggs if we stop feeding it.[31]

---

[29] *Zenrō*, April 15, 1955, quoted in *Seisansei undō 30 nen-shi*, p. 165. Translated by the author.

[30] Ministry of Labor, *Shiryō rōdō undōshi* (1955), pp. 526–28.

[31] *Asahi shimbun*, February 21, 1955.

In sum, the JPC and Dōyūkai emphasized productivity increases, not wage suppression, as a means to reduce the production cost of Japanese manufactured products and to increase the competitiveness of the Japanese industries.

On the second issue—the status of labor—, Dōyūkai and the JPC were eager to incorporate the unions within the enterprise system as a legitimate partner, while Nikkeiren originally objected to this accommodationist approach. Nikkeiren, which had led the management counteroffensive of the early fifties, was not enthusiastic about labor-management consultation. It feared that such consultation advocated by the JPC and Dōyūkai might end up infringing on managerial authority again.[32] It regarded labor as a production factor and rejected the idea of the enterprise as a community, a position that was close to economic liberalism.[33] By contrast, Dōyūkai advocated a fair distribution of business profit. This view was based upon a different concept of the enterprise from that of Nikkeiren's. The JPC's first publication on management modernization clearly incorporated Dōyūkai's view. Management should not maximize capitalist gain, they argued but embrace a wider perspective, one that viewed enterprises as places of employment as well as institutions for social services.[34] This view of the enterprise as a place of employment matched the moderate unions' view that the enterprise is a community.

From the start, the JPC emphasized the need for the union and the management of an individual enterprise to cooperate and consult with each other in order to find an effective way to increase productivity. At the request of Zenkin Dōmei (Japanese Metal Industry Workers' Union), the JPC established a special committee to research this issue in 1956. The next year the JPC started efforts to help individual enterprises establish labor-management consultation mechanisms. The JPC's member unions organized their first official discussion meeting over the question of productivity increases in 1958 and began discussing their experiences about institutionalizing labor-management consultation.[35]

The labor policy of the LDP government was also changing at that time. The labor minister of the Yoshida cabinet had advocated anti-union policies, such as relaxation of the labor standard regulations, but the new labor minister Tadao Kuraishi of the Hatoyama cabinet argued that labor policy should aim to promote a reconciliation between labor and manage-

[32] Ministry of Labor, *Shiryō rōdō undōshi* (1954), p. 304.
[33] Hideo Otake, "The Zaikai under the Occupation."
[34] *Seisansei undō 30 nen-shi*, pp. 136–37.
[35] Ibid., pp. 304–16.

ment based on economic growth and flatly rejected the idea of deregulation of the Labor Standard Law.[36] Furthermore, the government began developing an intensive employment policy by incorporating the goal of employment maximization in its economic policies. This was partly a result of the Hatoyama cabinet formation. Anti-Yoshida conservatives, some of them reformists and some closer to the prewar national socialist tradition, had been critical of Yoshida's economic liberalism and advocated more economic planning and industrial policy, and it was they who set up the Hatoyama cabinet. They were more concerned with the employment issue than the Yoshida group, although they tended to be regarded as more hawkish in their foreign policy. Their plan to revise the postwar constitution contains a reformist orientation on economic issues alongside a rightist orientation on foreign and social issues: "The main goal of an enterprise should not be maximization of profits, but providing as many people as possible with decent jobs. . . . Labor and capital are indispensable components of the production activity, and thus they should be protected by the state. . . . Both labor and capital should cooperate with each other for production increases based on mutual understanding."[37] Here we find an accommodationist logic very similar to that of the JPC and Dōyūkai.

When the JPC and Dōyūkai as well as the LDP government made an accommodationist move toward labor, the moderate unions began responding. Zenrōkaigi and Shinsanbetsu, uneasy with Nikkeiren's membership in the JPC in the beginning, finally decided to cooperate. Inter-class politics, thus, played an important role in establishing a labor accommodation in the productivity movement.

Sōhyō, however, continued to oppose the movement. In 1956 while Zenrōkaigi (including Sōdōmei) organized 662,000 workers, Sōhyō boasted a membership of 3,138,000. Without Sōhyō's cooperation, the productivity movement could not have had any significant impact on labor. A closer look at Sōhyō's response to this movement reveals an important change in the organization. Although Sōhyō originally used a political rationale to oppose this movement, it later began emphasizing an economic one. It argued that productivity increases would not bring parallel wage increases.[38] This change of tactics was related to a change of leadership within Sōhyō. Criticism against the Sōhyō leadership of Takano

---

[36] *Nihon rōdō nenkan* (1957), p. 580.

[37] Jiyuminshutō, Kenpōkenkyūkai, "Kenpō kaisei sōan" (The plan to revise the constitution), quoted in *Nihon rōdō nenkan* (1958), p. 633.

[38] Akira Iwai, "Rōdōsha ni gisei o shiirumono" (At the expense of workers), *Nihon seisansei shimbun*, July 23, 1955, quoted in *Seisansei undō 30 nen-shi*, p. 145.

came not just from the outside moderate unions but also from within: Kaoru Ota, chairman of the Gōkarōren, criticized Takano's tactics. In December 1954 Ota advocated a joint wage struggle among Sōhyō unions in five major industries (coal mining, private railroads, synthetic chemistry, electric power, and paper and pulp manufacturing) instead of the family-wide/community-wide strategy of Takano. A month later, three more unions (metal, chemical, and electric appliances) joined this struggle. This was the origin of the Shuntō wage bargaining. While Takano argued that wider mobilization beyond individual industries was necessary for wage increases, Ota believed that the enterprise unions in the relatively prosperous industries should coordinate their wage struggles to achieve as large a wage increase as possible and should set the pattern for the remaining sectors.[39]

In the sixth Sōhyō convention in 1955, Ota took the leadership from Takano. Following this change, Sōhyō became more concerned with wage increases than with political struggles, although it still maintained a relatively strong political orientation.[40] While Takano objected to any efforts to increase productivity, Ota had no objection to it. What Ota did not want the union to do was to cooperate with management in increasing productivity. He thought that productivity increase was inevitable, but that the unions would have to fight to prevent the exploitation of labor. In other words, Sōhyō tried to exploit the productivity increase without being incorporated into the enterprise management system. On this point, Ota's strategy was similar to American business unionism, which allows productivity increases but maintains an arm's-length relationship with management based on job-control unionism. So Shuntō started as a combination of a conciliatory management move and Sōhyō's partial turn to business unionism.

In this process, Nikkeiren failed to realize its original plan for economic growth. It argued that as capital investment in production facilities was the main cause for productivity increases in the 1950s, management should be entitled to most of the fruit.[41] However, the fruit of the productivity increases was distributed fairly to labor. Nikkeiren's opposition to wage increases did not succeed. Nikkeiren also criticized the base-up practice in

[39] Okochi and Matsuo, *Nihon rōdō kumiai monogatari*, vol. 2, p. 219.

[40] This is partly because despite his victory, Ota still had to make concessions to Takano's group. Another reason is that public-sector unions were forced to politicize their movements once they tried to demand higher wage increases, because their right to strike was prohibited by law. In the public sector, any economic struggles tend easily to become political.

[41] Nikkeiren, "Tōmen no chinginmondai ni kansuru wareware no kenkai" (Opinion on the wage issues), March 4, 1955, quoted in Ministry of Labor, *Shiryō rōdō undōshi* (1955), pp. 675–77.

wage negotiations because it was economically irrational. Nikkeiren, instead, advocated a rational wage determination based on job category and worker efficiency. The point of Nikkeiren's job-based wage was to make it clear that a wage is the price for the workers' contribution. This Nikkeiren plan also did not succeed and the base-up practice continues to this day.

Why did Nikkeiren fail on these two points? Enterprise unionism alone can explain the failure. In the management offensive led by Nikkeiren, labor-management relations became isolated within the enterprise. The management offensive did not centralize the power of management under Nikkeiren; individual managements had their own goals and retained complete discretion to maintain a peaceful relationship with labor.[42] Within the enterprise labor had its own power resources and management was often forced to seek cooperation from it. The power of labor within the company, from time to time, made individual managements offer larger wage increases than what Nikkeiren deemed rational.[43] Given the necessity for labor-management accommodation, it was impossible for management to suppress the wage level within an enterprise and to introduce a rational job-based wage system. Individual managements thus followed the accommodationist JPC line rather than Nikkeiren hard line and chose to form a productivity coalition with labor. The micro-level accommodation constrained the national-level wage bargaining. This micro-level accommodation, although favorable to Sōhyō's Shuntō strategy, eroded the other half of Ota's strategy, the establishment of an arm's-length relationship with management in the negotiation of productivity increases.

THE FUNCTIONING OF SHUNTŌ

Shuntō is a concerted, interindustry union action devoted to gaining an annual wage increase. Sōhyō used it as a way to overcome the weakness of enterprise unionism by coordinating wage struggles across industries at one time in the year, and thereby setting the pattern of wage increases for

---

[42] Otake, "The Zaikai under the Occupation."

[43] For instance, Nikkeiren complained that management in the coal mining industry tended to compromise with the union on wage issues as well as management issues. Kume, "A Tale of Twin Industries." It also criticized management in capital intensive industries, such as the chemical industry, for tending to offer higher wage increases. Nikkeiren, "Tōmen no chinginmondai ni kansuru wareware no kenkai" (1955). For concrete criticism against wage increases in the ammonium sulfate industry, see *Nikkeiren taimuzu*, April 21, 1955.

the rest of the year and standardizing wage increases across industries, even in the unorganized sectors.[44]

Since the start of the Shountō wage struggle in 1955, the number of workers participating in Shuntō has steadily increased from 3,000,000 in 1956 to 10,080,000 in 1984.[45] This development is attributable to the sequential participation of unions in this struggle: The public-sector unions in 1956, iron and steel and shipbuilding unions in 1959, and one national federation, Chūritsurōren (Federation of Independent Unions of Japan), in 1959. Sōhyō and Chūritsurōren established the Shuntō Joint Struggle Committee. Furthermore, in 1963 the other two national federations, Dōmeikaigi (the later Dōmei) and Shinsanbetsu, decided to have their wage negotiations at the same time as Shuntō, although separately from the Shuntō Joint Struggle Committee.

In Shuntō wage negotiations, deciding which unions will set the pattern for wage increases has been a central issue. Before Shuntō started, electric power workers, coal miners, and public-enterprise employees were the driving force for wage increases. From 1955 to 1965, private railway workers and steel workers dominated, and since then, a coalition of the four metal industry unions (IMF-JC, consisting of the unions in the iron and steel, electric appliances, automobile, and shipbuilding industries) has gradually become dominant. According to Kazutoshi Koshiro, five factors explain the changes in wage leadership: (1) the maturity of labor-management relations, (2) business fluctuations, (3) the organizational strength of unions, (4) social circumstances, and (5) the ups and downs of a particular industry.[46]

For this analysis, the basic trend of wage leadership was a move from public-sector unions to private manufacturing sector unions. In the immediate postwar era, private manufacturing industries suffered from the losses of wartime defeat and were not a significant economic force in the Japanese economy. It was thus natural that unions in the public sectors and in industries subsidized by the government (such as coal mining and electric power) took the leadership in wage bargaining. As the private sector recovered from economic hardship, those unions became more important in wage negotiations. But this was not just a functional change in response to the market, it was also a political one.

[44] Seiichiro Hayakawa, "Shuntō no tenkai to henbō" (Development and transformation of Shuntō) in Hoseidaigaku Ohara Shakaimondai Kenkyūsho, ed., *Rengōjidai no rōdōundō* (The labor movement in the era of Rengō) (Tokyo: Sōgō Rōdō Kenkyūsho, 1992), p. 245. Cf. Sōhyō, "Teikitaikai kakukyoku hōkokusho," 42nd annual convention, 1971.

[45] Shuntō Kenkyūkai, *Shuntō kawarunoka*, p. 31.

[46] Kazutoshi Koshiro, *Nihon no chingin kettei kikō* (The structure of wage determination in Japan) (Tokyo: Nihon Hyōronsha, 1973), pp. 90–99.

In 1964, Prime Minister Ikeda and Sōhyō's Secretary-General Ota agreed on the pay compatibility principle between public and private sectors. This enabled public sector workers, who are restricted in their union activity, to achieve compatible levels of wages and working conditions in the private sector.[47] At the same time, this political deal set an institutional foundation for private-sector leadership in wage negotiations. In addition, the labor-management accommodation based on the idea of the productivity increase presumed the leadership of the manufacturing sector. The JPC felt that productivity increases in the private manufacturing sector would become the key for Japanese economic development by reducing the production costs of Japanese industries and increasing their competitiveness. It was also in private enterprises that profits from the productivity increase could easily be distributed to workers. For this accommodation to be maintained, wage negotiations must not be interrupted by an outside force, in this case, the public-sector union, because public sector union leadership might upset the cycle of productivity increases and wage increases.[48]

Labor enjoyed rapid, real wage increases in the period from the start of Shuntō to the first oil crisis. From 1956 to 1974, the annual average nominal wage increase was 13.08 percent and the annual average real wage increase was 7.18 percent. As figure 5 shows, wage increases in the 1960s caught up with productivity increases, although in the 1950s, they were behind productivity increases. Moreover, as Shuntō developed more fully after 1965, wage increases became even higher. These data easily lead us to the conclusion that the Shuntō development contributed to wage increases. We should be careful in making this conclusion, however, because many labor economists argue that wage variation is a function of the unemployment rate, profit rate, and consumer prices. In the Japanese context, many scholars attribute the large wage increases to a tight labor market in the high economic growth period. However, some Japanese labor economists attribute those increases to the role of unions. And according to one study, the Japanese wage increase can be explained more by the profit rate than that in other countries.[49] This seems to show

[47] Kazutoshi Koshiro, "Labor Relations in Public Enterprises," in Shirai, ed., *Contemporary Industrial Relations in Japan*, p. 279.

[48] This is what happened in Sweden in the 1970s in a slightly different way. The white-collar unions did not follow the blue-collar unions lead but instead pursued wage drifts. This caused a chain reaction among many unions, which resulted in further wage drifts. The end result was a breakdown of the well-elaborated solidaristic wage policy. Anders S. Olsson, *The Swedish Wage Negotiation System* (Aldershot: Dartmouth, 1991), pp. 32–35.

[49] A. W. Phillips, "The Relation between Unemployment and the Rate of Change of

that unions succeeded in realizing the Shuntō goal of winning labor's fair share of productivity gains.

Labor also enjoyed a standardization of wage increases across all sectors in this period of high economic growth. The pay structure within the company became egalitarian. The pre-tax compensation for the president was 23.6 times of that of the newly employed male, college graduate in 1963, while that ratio had been reduced to only 14.5 by 1980.[50] Wage increase rates in small and medium-sized companies were higher than in large companies, so the differences in wages between small and medium-sized companies and larger ones became smaller.[51] If we control for factors such as educational background and age, we find the wage difference to be even smaller. Figure 7 demonstrates that the variation in wage increases across industries declined substantially in that period. This was also true for individual industries. Wage increases among companies within the same industry became very much the same. Koshiro found the following factors contributing to the standardization:

> First, the increasing pressure of a labor shortage in the 1960s and early 1970s contributed to a decrease in the wage differentials among companies and industries. The starting wage rates for new school graduates increased rapidly and then leveled off. Second, the follow-the-leader practice among major companies has been reinforced by two other factors: (1) competing companies preferred to accept the same actual amount (or the same percentage rate) of wage increase, and (2) the desire to maintain industrial peace tended to compel the less profitable companies to pay the same (or similar) wage as the more prosperous companies.[52]

As Koshiro argues, one important precondition for this standardization was the tight labor market. But other factors outside the market played an important role, too. Several studies show that wage increases are not just

Money Wage Rates in the United Kingdom, 1861–1957," *Economica* (November 1958); Richard B. Freeman, *Labor Economics*, 2d ed. (Englewood Cliffs, N.J.: Prentice-Hall, 1978); Toshimitsu Shinkawa, *Nihongata fukushi no seijikeizaigaku* (Political economy of the Japanese welfare system) (Tokyo: Sanichi Shobō, 1993), p. 229; Ono, *Sengo Nihon no chinginkettei*; Sano, *Chingin kettei no keiryōbunseki*; Nakamura, Sato, and Kamiya, *Rōdōkumiai wa hontoni yakunitatteirunoka*, chap. 1; and OECD, "Prices and Incomes Policies and Collective Bargaining," working paper no. 4 of the Economic Policy Committee, February 1972, quoted in Yoko Sano, *Chingin to koyō no keizaigaku* (Economics of wage and employment) (Tokyo: Chuō Keizaisha, 1981), p. 44. Sano confirms the positive effect of the profit rate on wage increases (pp. 68–92).

[50] Abegglen and Stalk, *Kaisha*, p. 192.

[51] Koike, *Shigoto no keizaigaku*, chap. 8.

[52] Koshiro, "Development of Collective Bargaining in Postwar Japan," in Shirai, *Contemporary Industrial Relations in Japan*, pp. 223–24.

Table 4. Wage comparison during wage negotiations (Manufacturing industry survey results)

	Nature of comparison			
	Within same industry		Across industries	
Action	Management's views (%)	Labor's views (%)	Management's views (%)	Labor's views (%)
No comparisons made	4.7	5.3	17.4	12.8
Comparions used as reference	31.9	30.7	68.7	63.2
Comparisons had substantial influence	53.4	52.8	13.5	22.3
Comparisons resulted in attempts to match wages	5.2	5.7	0.0	0.0
Comparisons resulted in negotiating for higher than average wages	4.7	5.5	1.4	1.6

SOURCE: Adapted from Sano, Koike, and Ishida, eds., *Chinginkōshō no kōdōkagaku*, pp. 98–99.

determined by market forces but also by social considerations. According to a 1970 Ministry of Labor survey of 3,000 companies asking what factor contributed the most to wage determination, 41.2 percent picked company profits, 32.5 percent picked the average wage increase of other companies, and 15.6 percent picked maintenance of their work force. Although the profit consideration increased to 64.9 percent in 1979, pay rates of other companies were still considered the most influential by 18.2 percent of the surveyed companies.[53] Another survey showed that unions as well as management took wage comparisons into account in negotiating wages (table 4).[54]

This was the behavioral basis for wage standardization. Shuntō facilitated this behavior by setting wage negotiations at one time in the year, making it easier and sometimes inevitable for management and labor to compare their wages with others.

At what level were wage increases standardized? At the start of Shuntō there were two contradictory predictions for its future. Takano predicted

[53] Ministry of Labor, Rōseikyoku Rōdōkeizaika, "Chinginhikiage nado no jittai ni kansuru chōsakekka" (Report on the reality of the wage increase), annual, quoted in Goro Mori, ed., *Nihon no rōshikankei shisutemu* (The labor-management system in Japan) (Tokyo: Nihon Rōdō Kyōkai, 1981), p. 349.

[54] Yoko Sano, Kazuo Koike, and Hideo Ishida, eds., *Chinginkōshō no kōdōkagaku* (Behavioral study of wage negotiations) (Tokyo: Tōyō Keizai Shinpōsha, 1969), pp. 98–99.

that because Shuntō's interindustry wage struggle was based on enterprise unions, its strategy would not lend enough force to unions to increase wages, given the tough stance of the monopoly capitalists. He argued that, in the course of Shuntō, individual unions would depend on each other and would not strengthen the bargaining power of the working class as a whole.[55] The end result was seen to be a wage freeze at a low level. On the other hand, Nikkeiren worried that Shuntō would result in unbearable wage increases. In that scenario, Shuntō would bring about wage hikes in the competitive sectors that would squeeze reinvestment capital and result in social unrest due to huge wage differentials between the competitive and backward sectors. If the standardization mechanism worked, the scenario would be even worse, because standardization at too high a level would weaken Japanese industries' competitiveness. In short, Nikkeiren expected that Shuntō could actually achieve extreme wage hikes.[56]

The actual result was wage standardization at a middle level. Yoko Sano's analysis of the relation between the profit rate and wage increases shows this point clearly. The profit rate, according to her, would influence wage increases in Japan. But this is a macro-level phenomenon, which means that a positive correlation exits between the average profit rate and the average wage increase rate in Japanese industries as a whole. This correlation would disappear, however, by disaggregating the data at the industry and firm levels. She concluded that this phenomenon was a result of the pattern-setting practice of Shuntō, in which the pattern-setter did not try to maximize its share of profits, but rather tried to demand reasonable wage increases from the perspective of the national economy.[57] The implication is that wage standardization would occur at the middle point of the profit variation across industries.

The analysis of the relation between productivity and wage increases in several industries leads us to a similar conclusion. Wage and productivity increases in coal mining, textile, steel, automobile, and electric equipment industries in the United States and Japan are plotted in figures 8, 9, 10, 11, and 12. In the declining industries, such as coal mining and

[55] Nobuhiro Hiwatari, *Sengo Nihon no shijō to seiji* (Market and politics in postwar Japan) (Tokyo: Tokyo Daigaku Shuppankai, 1991), pp. 120–21.

[56] Nikkeiren, "Tōmen no chinginmondai ni kansuru wareware no kenkai" (1955). Hajime Maeda, an executive director of Nikkeiren, commented in 1957 that it should realize that Sōhyō strengthened its bargaining power by adopting the Shuntō strategy. Shuntō Kenkyukai, *Shuntō kawarunoka*, p. 24.

[57] Sano, *Chingin to koyō no keizaigaku*, chap. 4. Analysis of the pattern-setter function is in Atsushi Nakamura, "Chinginkettei no Yōinbubseki (2)" (An analysis of the determinants of wage), *Chingin fōramu* (Spring 1976).

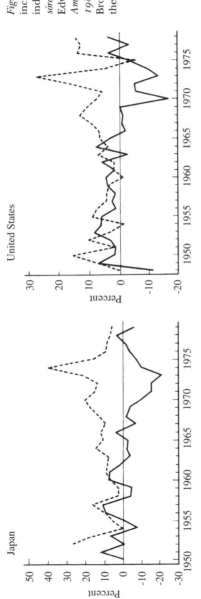

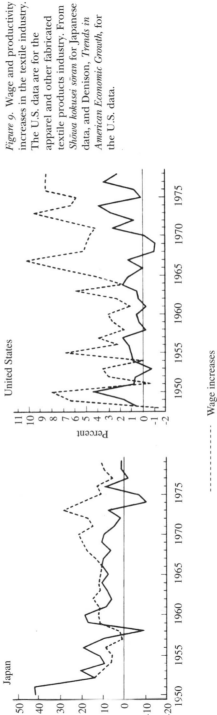

Figure 8. Wage and productivity increases in the coal mining industry. From *Shōwa kokusei sōran* for the Japanese data, and Edward F. Denison, *Trends in American Economic Growth, 1929–1982* (Washington, D.C.: Brookings Institute, 1985), for the U.S. data.

Figure 9. Wage and productivity increases in the textile industry. The U.S. data are for the apparel and other fabricated textile products industry. From *Shōwa kokusei sōran* for Japanese data, and Denison, *Trends in American Economic Growth*, for the U.S. data.

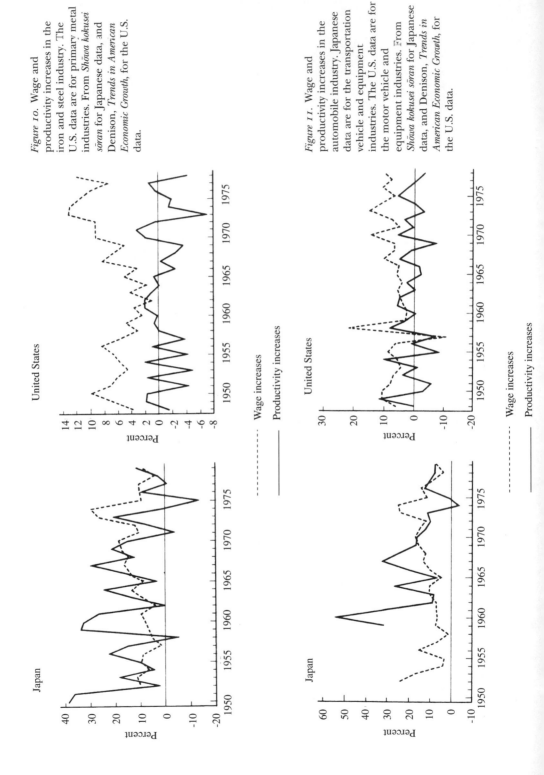

Figure 10. Wage and productivity increases in the iron and steel industry. The U.S. data are for primary metal industries. From *Shōwa kokusei sōran* for Japanese data, and Denison, *Trends in American Economic Growth,* for the U.S. data.

Figure 11. Wage and productivity increases in the automobile industry. Japanese data are for the transportation vehicle and equipment industries. The U.S. data are for the motor vehicle and equipment industries. From *Shōwa kokusei sōran* for Japanese data, and Denison, *Trends in American Economic Growth,* for the U.S. data.

---- Wage increases
—— Productivity increases

---- Wage increases
—— Productivity increases

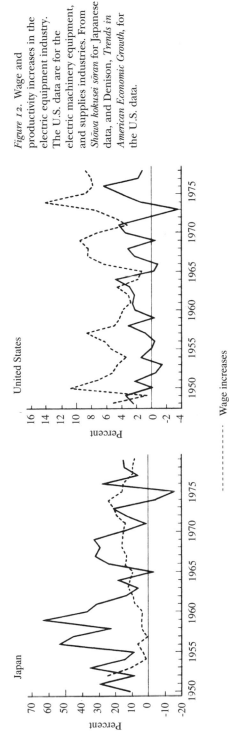

Figure 12. Wage and productivity increases in the electric equipment industry. The U.S. data are for the electric machinery equipment, and supplies industries. From *Shōwa kokusei sōran* for Japanese data, and Denison, *Trends in American Economic Growth*, for the U.S. data.

textiles, both countries show similar wage increase patterns: wage increases exceed productivity increases in both. But American and Japanese wage increase patterns were different in the then-growing industries of steel, automobile, and electric equipment. In Japan, productivity increases exceeded wage increases, and vice versa in the United States. In Japan in the period of economic growth, Japanese workers as a whole enjoyed wage increases as high as those in the OECD countries in relation to productivity. But taken separately workers in declining industries received wage increases that were higher than productivity increases, while those in the booming industries received wage increases that were lower than productivity increases.

The economic outcome is clear: there was a transformation of industrial structure toward a more internationally competitive one. Management in a booming industry can use more profit for reinvestment as a result of relatively lower wage increases than productivity increases, while management in a declining industry does not have such a reinvestment advantage. This transformation of industrial structure contributed to Japan's economic growth.

POLITICS AND WAGE STANDARDIZATION

The Shuntō wage negotiations functionally resembled the Swedish solidaristic wage policy, in that both achieved the standardization of wages at a middle level. The solidaristic wage policy was a key in the Rehn-Meidner model, which tried to reconcile full employment with price stability and promote the international competitiveness of Swedish industries. The basic idea is as follows:

> On the one hand, a concerted union effort to increase wages for the low paid (beyond what market forces dictate) would squeeze the profit margins of less efficient sectors or firms and force them either to rationalize production or to go out of business. And the wage restraint of the well paid implied by the principle of wage solidarity would promote the expansion of more efficient sectors or firms. The effect would be to raise average productivity in the economy and thereby make it possible for average wages to rise without threatening macroeconomic stability.[58]

This policy mix contains several inherent difficulties. Let us focus on labor's problems with this policy. First, because workers in efficient sectors

[58] Jonas Pontusson, *The Limits of Social Democracy: Investment Politics in Sweden* (Ithaca: Cornell University Press, 1992), p. 60.

have to restrain their wage increases, they tend to oppose this policy. Second, workers in the less efficient sectors would be hurt by industrial restructuring. Third, workers, if they agree on this policy, cannot be confident that management in efficient sectors will invest excess profits in a way to increase the prosperity of the given industry or firm. In order to solve these problems, the Social Democratic government in Sweden introduced several policies. The government first put pressure on the confederation of blue-collar unions, LO (Landsorganisationen), to restrain wage increases to prevent inflation, as price instability would harm industrial competitiveness.[59] LO, faced with this pressure, tried to introduce wage restraints voluntarily. But in due course, the low-paid workers demanded a solidaristic wage policy to accept the wage restraint. This meant that a solidaristic wage policy was not just a product of egalitarianism among workers, but also a political creation.[60]

The active labor market policy to help redundant workers adjust to changes in the demand for labor is another important building block of the Rehn-Meidner model. The tax on corporate profits is also important in encouraging management to reinvest profit to promote economic growth. The Rehn-Meidner model did not work politically without these government policies. In addition, the sheer existence of the Social Democratic government seems to have been conducive to the implementation of the solidaristic wage policy. Comparatively speaking, the existence of the hegemonic Social Democratic government in Sweden seemed to make it easier for LO leaders to persuade workers to comply with this policy in order to achieve a long-term benefit for labor.[61]

By comparison with Sweden, how has Japan's functionally similar wage practice, Shuntō, been consolidated under the conservative LDP government? In order to answer this question, we must consider three aspects of this activity: symbolic politics, public policies, and labor-management consultation.

Symbolic Politics

One way to consolidate the Shuntō wage practice is to make workers confident of future economic growth. Both the relatively low-paid workers

---

[59] Ibid., p. 63.

[60] Swenson, *Fair Shares*, p. 132.

[61] Heclo and Madsen argued that after the solidaristic wage policy was fully introduced, the unions and workers began legitimizing it as an expression of concern for equality that lay at the heart of the labor movement. Hugh Heclo and Henrik Madsen, *Policy and Politics in Sweden: Principled Pragmatism* (Philadelphia: Temple University Press, 1987), p. 117.

in the efficient sectors as well as the higher-paid workers in the inefficient sectors who feared rationalization would have to be convinced that they would be better off as a result of economic growth. Prime Minister Ikeda's Income Doubling Plan of 1960 convinced the Japanese of future economic growth and subsequently supported the development of this wage practice. Ikeda came to power after the political turmoil in 1960 over the issue of revising the U.S.-Japan Security Treaty. The previous Hatoyama and Kishi cabinets had faced severe political conflict with the socialists on issues such as revision of the constitution and rearmament. Ikeda put these political issues aside and focused on economic policy as a way to stabilize LDP rule.[62] His main policy was the Income Doubling Plan, in which he proposed that wages should be doubled in ten years. Labor minister Ishida of the Ikeda cabinet refocused labor policy on economic issues as well, on wages and employment issues rather than on strikes and labor movements.[63] Although the Income Doubling Plan itself was not a substantial policy but just a prediction of economic growth, it changed people's perception of politics and the Japanese economy. People began realizing they were living in a growing economy. This was the start of the Japanese version of the politics of productivity. Kiichi Miyazawa, then cabinet secretary general, recollected, "It was Ikeda's wisdom to sell 'income doubling' as a political agenda, not just as an economic prediction." Masaya Ito, advisor to Ikeda, said, "I found that it is important in politics to convince people of some good future. . . . The experience of selling the 'Income Doubling Plan' taught me this."[64]

Let us analyze how people accepted Ikeda's new economic policy, using the Jiji Press monthly poll data.[65] Figure 13 shows that the Ikeda cabinet (1960–64) entertained one of the highest average support rates among population at large as well as workers in the last thirty years. Furthermore, in 1960, when Ikeda became prime minister, the policy-based support was more than 10 percent, which is the highest score in the postwar period (fig. 14). These data imply that Ikeda succeeded in boosting up popular support by selling his main policy, the "Income Doubling Plan." Political discourse in the 1960s became more economic in nature and thus created a favorable environment for the accommodationist, business-oriented

---

[62] Michio Muramatsu and Ellis S. Krauss, "The Conservative Policy Line and the Development of Patterned Pluralism," in Kozo Yamamura and Yasukichi Yasuba, eds., *Political Economy of Japan*, vol. 1.

[63] *Nihon rōdō nenkan* (1961), p. 369.

[64] Ekonomisuto, *Shōgen kōdoseichōki no Nihon*, vol. 1, pp. 42 and 66.

[65] Since 1960, the Jiji Press has conducted a monthly survey using similar questionnaires. In this and the following chapters I have used the Jiji Press Monthly Survey data extensively.

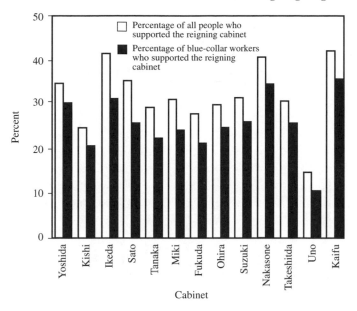

Figure 13. Average cabinet support rate among the population at large and blue-collar workers. Support rate for the Kaifu cabinet covers until March 1990. From the Jiji Press Monthly Survey.

unions. This symbolic politics evidently helped consolidate the Shuntō wage practice.

Public Policies

In Japan, as in Sweden, the government introduced an active labor market policy to solve problems emerging from industrial restructuring. Management efforts to rationalize the production system in the early 1950s had often ended up with the dismissal of redundant workers and caused harsh labor-management conflicts especially in inefficient sectors. The Shuntō wage practice sped up industrial restructuring and could have potentially created a labor surplus in the declining industries more quickly. This could have brought about the same labor problem that existed in the early 1950s. However, this wage practice and the sped-up investment could also increase a labor shortage in the booming industries.[66] Therefore, the Ministry of Labor tried to introduce an "active labor market policy" in place of a public job-creation program for the unem-

[66] This view was held by the Japan Productivity Center. *Seisansei undō 30 nen-shi,* p. 127.

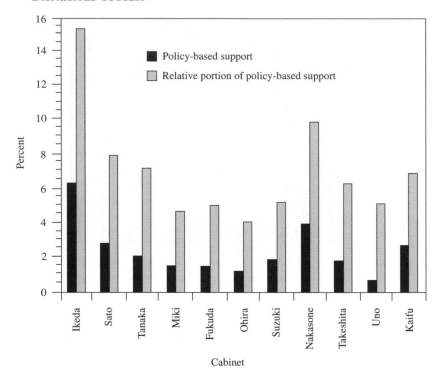

Figure 14. Percentage of people who supported the cabinet because of its policy intiatives. *Policy-based support* is the average percentage of people who support the reigning cabinet because they like the policy intiatives of the cabinet in the monthly Jiji poll. *Relative portion of policy-based support* refers to the percentage of the policy-based support within the total rate of support for the reigning cabinet.

ployed in the early 1960s. This policy was designed to alleviate the imbalance between labor supply and demand across industries, regions, and occupations, by introducing a vocational training program, financial aid to increase labor mobility, a job market information system, and so forth.

However, this new policy was not formulated by MOL as an economic reaction to these problems; the process was more political. Labor won this new policy after its defeat in the Miike Strike of 1960, in which the union in the declining coal mining industry attacked rationalization in the industry. Chapter 6 shows how the union changed its strategy after the defeat and began demanding an intensive employment policy to compensate workers hurt by restructuring. Management supported this strategy as did the government. The active labor market policy was fully developed in the labor movement.

Industrial policy also played an important role. For my argument, it is convenient to make a distinction between policy for an efficient sector and one for an inefficient sector. The purpose of the latter policy is to help rationalize inefficiency (for example, the policy for shipbuilding in the 1970s) or to alleviate the industry's decline (for example, the policy for coal mining in the 1960s). On the other hand, the purpose of industrial policy for the efficient or would-be efficient sectors is to speed up the process of development. One of the important policy tools was tax incentives for rationalization investment.[67] Japanese policies regarding deductions and depreciation have been favorable to large firms in the period of high economic growth. Although these policies extended in the late 1950s to small business, which was regarded as inefficient, it is important to emphasize that these policies also encouraged capital reinvestment in order to rationalize business.[68]

Many studies also explore how Japanese political institutions contributed to high economic growth and have claimed various policies, such as rationalization cartels and low-interest loans for targeted industries, as causes. Although there exist different views on the real effect of these governmental policies on Japanese economic growth, it is sufficient here to note that these policies drove management to invest energetically to rationalize business by providing various incentives, or by decreasing uncertainty in management investment decision making through a dense information exchange among public and private actors.[69] The 1961 edition of the Economic Planning Agency's *Economic White Paper* said, "Investment invites more investment." Given these industrial policies and the actual investment behavior of management, Japanese labor did not have to worry so much about the possibility that management in the efficient sectors would unfairly and unproductively consume the excessive profits coming out of the Shuntō wage practice.

In sum, these public policies were important foundations of the Shuntō wage practice. However, the management commitment to productive investment could not automatically buy labor's support. This was because management investment for rationalization might result in not just labor redundancy but also an intensification of work. Labor unions have to

---

[67] Johnson, *MITI and the Japanese Miracle*, pp. 233–36.

[68] Calder, *Crisis and Compensation*; Ikuo Kume, "Party Politics and Industrial Policy: A Case of Japan," paper presented to an international conference, the Economic and Social Research Council Research Initiative on Government-Industry Relations, May 20–22, 1992, Exeter, U.K.

[69] Friedman, *Misunderstood Miracle*; Noble, "The Japanese Industrial Policy Debate"; Komiya et al., *Nihon no sangyōseisaku*; Kume, "Party Politics and Industrial Policy"; Imai, "Komento."

influence investment decision making. Because Japan's unions were enterprise unions, they had to accomplish this task within the firm. As a
result, the firm-level labor-management consultation forms, developed in
the postwar period, naturally took this role.

Labor-Management Consultation within the Firm

Chapter 3 argues that Japanese unions succeeded in maintaining their
status as a legitimate participant in running the firm even after the management counter-offensive. The main institution was the labor management consultation mechanism. The moderate unions, Sōdōmei and
Zenrōkaigi, argued that labor-management consultation should be a key
component of the productivity increase movement. They supported the
idea that a productivity increase could be potentially beneficial to labor,
but they also believed that, without labor's participation in that process,
management would rationalize the business at the expense of labor and
reap the profit. The JPC agreed and introduced various policies to advance the labor-management consultation mechanism. Although both
Nikkeiren and Sōhyō, for different reasons, were reluctant to develop such
a mechanism, labor and management at the firm-level began establishing
them. Unions in the private sector began cooperating with or at least
stopped opposing management in increasing productivity, while at the
same time, beginning to use labor-management consultation to influence
management. Most commonly while the union agreed to cooperate with
management for productivity increases, management agreed to not dismiss any workers as a result of rationalization, to consult with the union on
work reorganization prior to rationalization, and to reward workers with a
fair share of productivity increases.[70] This micro-level labor participation,
in turn, helped the unions to further cooperate with management in the
productivity increase.

LABOR POLITICS AT THE DIVIDE

The productivity increase movement was a good opportunity for the
unions to establish the Shuntō wage practice and to achieve a high wage
increase in line with the productivity increase. The enterprise unions
nationalized wage bargaining and standardized the wage structure. In this

---

[70] Nihon Seisansei Honbu, *Rōshikyōgisei no jujitsu o motomete* (For the development of labor-
management consultation) (Tokyo: Nihon Seisansei Honbu, 1990), p. 12.

sense, Ota's strategy adopted by Sōhyō was successful. The union developed its movement from the micro-distributive arena (wage bargaining in the firm) to the macro-distributive arena. Under Ota's leadership, Sōhyō achieved a high wage increase by adopting the Shuntō wage strategy, despite the fact that Nikkeiren advocated a wage freeze. This success was possible partly because management became conciliatory and organized the productivity increase movement through the JPC. The management in individual firms sought labor's cooperation in planning the rationalization and tended to offer higher wages than what Nikkeiren had proposed in order to form the productivity coalition. The coordinated wage demands by the unions under Shuntō forced management in relatively inefficient companies to offer wage increases as high as those in efficient ones, if they wanted to catch up with the leading company by maximizing workers' commitment. The decentralized labor-management system prevented Nikkeiren from realizing its hard-line plan for industrial development based on a wage-freeze policy, because Nikkeiren's power was bounded by micro-level labor politics. It could not force individual companies to comply with its wage policy.

On the other hand, Sōhyō's success was not complete. Sōhyō avoided the micro-productive arena, that is, labor-management consultation within the firm. It advocated an arm's-length relationship with management, because it feared that the enterprise union would be easily coopted by management within the firm and would consequently become a docile company union.[71] Sōhyō's policy worked for a time. But once the union demanded a wage increase as a fair share of a productivity increase, it was natural for the union to try to increase productivity by cooperating more actively with management. Hiroki Sato and Takashi Umezawa, based on their extensive survey research, found that enterprise unions in the 1970s began participating more in the process of increasing profits which would then be distributed between management and labor. Case studies from the same research project supported this finding.[72] Despite Sōhyō's hesitation, individual unions especially in the private sector began developing their activities in the micro-productive arena.

This development gradually eroded the Sōhyō-led labor movement. The fact that the private-sector unions affiliated with Sōhyō participated in the productivity increase movement as early as 1958, despite Sōhyō's

---

[71] Ota argued that the enterprise union is not capable of achieving any gains by participating in managerial decision making through labor-management consultation. *Kikan rōdōhō*, no. 92 (Summer 1974).

[72] Sato and Umezawa, "Rōdōkumiai no 'hatsugen' to kumiairuikei," and other case studies in Nihon Rōdō Kyōkai, ed., *80 nendai no rōshikankei*.

opposition to the JPC, shows how unrealistic Sōhyō's strategy was. Even within the Ota-led Gōkarōren, several enterprise unions began criticizing Gōkarōren's policy toward the productivity increase. The Shin'etsu Chemical and the Kanegafuchi Chemical unions withdrew from Gōkarōren in 1967 and 1968, respectively, claiming that Gōkarōren, obsessed with the zero-sum class struggle concept, ignored the possibility that the union could achieve a larger gain by contributing to productivity increases.[73] Gōkarōren gradually lost its member unions and its leading position within the labor movement, it finally abandoned Ota's strategy in 1986 when an anti-Ota group became dominant.

The failure of Sōhyō's anti-rationalization strategy is attributable to micro-level labor politics, too. It ignored what labor had achieved during the postwar labor offensive, that is, labor's legitimate position as a participant in running the firm. The idea that labor is not just a production factor, but an active partner in the firm is deeply embedded in the labor-management institutions in postwar Japan.[74] Sōhyō did not choose to develop its movement on this foundation. It was the private-sector unions affiliated with Dōmei and the IMF-JC who did so.

This was not just a result of Sōhyō's rejection of accommodationism. We should remember that this idea, in a more radical form, prevailed everywhere in the immediate postwar period, as the production control movement shows. The private-sector unions developed their movement based on accommodationism. Two other conditions were important for this development: market competition and labor's micro-level power. First, these unions were organized in the sectors where market competition, either domestically or internationally, was harsh, and thus they had a strong sense of vulnerability to competition. Therefore, once they realized the possibility that their companies might lose in this competition, they become eager to cooperate with management to increase the productivity of their firms. This is not management co-optation, but rather a rational and autonomous response based on calculation of their interest. The findings by many Japanese labor scholars that the union tended to vitalize its activity in the micro-productive arena when the company was faced with economic difficulties supports this interpretation.[75]

[73] Hiroshi Fujii, "Shinetsukagaku no Gōkarōren dattai riyū" (Reasons for the withdrawal from the Gōkarōren), *Gekkan rōdōmondai* (August 1967). Sei'ichi Tsukumo, "Seisansei kōjō to rōso no shisei" (Productivity increase and unions' attitudes), *Gekkan rōdōmondai* (November 1968).

[74] Abegglen and Stalk, *Kaisha*.

[75] Yasusuke Murakami argued that the decreasing average cost situation in most export-oriented industries enhanced market competition. Murakami, "The Japanese Model of Political Economy," in Yamamura and Yasuba, eds., *Political Economy of Japan*, vol. 1. Kume,

Second, labor's power at the micro-level also matters. The fact that Gōkarōren was against participation in the productivity increase movement is very telling. Harsh market competition did exist in the synthetic chemical industry. Then why did Gōkarōren resist pursuing possible economic gain through more positive cooperation with management? In my view as labor's power within the firm was not strong in this industry, the unions were less confident in developing labor-management cooperation. In this highly capital-intensive industry, management did not depend so much on workers for increasing productivity as it did in other manufacturing industries.[76] The chemical unions had less power than other manufacturing unions. On the other hand, unions could easily disturb the production process by organizing partial strikes, because the companies had adopted the continuous production method. Management was forced to buy labor's quiescence in order to continue production. This situation favored Ota's strategy, keeping arm's-length relations with management and demanding as much benefit as possible out of productivity increases. The difference in the nature of the power in the chemical industry compared to other manufacturing inductries would explain their policy toward rationalization.[77]

This process of the development of Shuntō thus demonstrates that labor can work on both the micro level and the macro level, and that enterprise unionism is not dead-end unionism. However, the development of labor politics is constrained by achievements in the past. In the case of Japan, the micro-level labor management accommodation was sticky enough to channelize labor politics at the macro level. Sōhyō successfully developed its labor movement at the macro-distributive level

---

"A Tale of Twin Industries." See the case studies in Nihon Rōdō Kyōkai, ed., *80 nendai no rōshikankei.*

[76] Noriyuki Itami, *Nihon no kagakusangyō: Naze sekai ni tachiokuretanoka* (The Japanese chemical industry: Why it could not catch up) (Tokyo: NTT Shuppan, 1991), pp. 12–17.

[77] We still need to answer why an increasing number of unions ran away from Gōkarōren, despite the common nature of the production system. One possible explanation seems to be that the companies of the splinter unions were introducing a new technology, which provided the unions with a new opportunity to assert their role in the micro-productive arena. The leaders of the two splinter unions, Shinetsukagaku and Kanegafuchikagaku, both claimed that technological changes required union cooperation for productivity increases. See Fujii, "Shinetsukagaku no Gōkarōren dattai riyū" and Tsukumo, "Seisanseikōjō to rōso no shisei." However, the fact that the Dōmei-affiliated chemical union has been more active in the micro-productive arena may show that the nature of the production process is not the determining condition for the union's anti-rationalization policy, but rather that the union's ideology and political tactics have more autonomous influence on their policy toward rationalization. Cf. Mitsuhide Shiraki, "Kumiai no sanka e no shiko to shokuba" (The union's attitude toward participation and the shopfloor), in Nihon Rōdō Kyōkai, ed., *80 nendai no rōshikankei*, pp. 301–37.

(Shuntō), but it ignored labor accommodation at the micro level. This resulted in two related outcomes: First, as Shuntō developed, Sōhyō gradually lost its leadership in the field of wage negotiations. The private-sector unions affiliated with the IMF-JC and Dōmei, which were more active in the micro-productive arena, became dominant in this field. Second, the Shuntō wage practice was so successful in achieving workers' economic interests that the private-sector unions remained relatively apolitical.[78] On the other hand, Sōhyō developed its political movement on a more ideological front, cooperating with the Japan Socialist Party. As long as private-sector unions were not interested in using national politics to protect their economic interests, Sōhyō and the Socialist party could be a leading force in national labor politics. But without having their effective and active movement in the micro-productive arena, their foundation was shaky. This point will become clearer as we examine the process in which the unions developed their movement in the macro-productive arena, that is, the politics of industrial adjustment at the national level. The following chapters will focus on this macro-level development.

[78] Hiwatari, *Sengo nihon no shijō to seiji*, p. 137.

CHAPTER FIVE

Back into Politics:
Labor in the 1970s

Throughout the 1970s and 1980s, Japanese labor politics changed as a result of dynamic interaction among labor, business, and government in response to changes in the Japanese political economy and domestic politics. Changes in the political economy—emerging political demands (such as environmental concerns), high inflation, and internationalization of the Japanese economy—all drove unions into political activity. Led by Sōhyō, unions politicized their movement in order to respond to these new changes based on social-democratic ideology. By contrast, changes in domestic politics, the LDP's electoral decline and its subsequent strategy to expand its support base, provided labor with favorable political opportunities. For the time being, this new situation worked well for the Sōhyō-led union movement. It achieved various policy victories, such as social welfare and anti-pollution policies. However, the first oil crisis of 1973 further transformed labor politics. Private-sector labor became more aware of and responsive to either the national economy or to productivity issues within individual firms. The apolitical labor accommodation in the private-sector that had flourished in the 1960s was challenged in the early 1970s. The private-sector unions also politicized their movement and began organizing their political activities around the issues of employment security and inflation. However, their political strategy was very different from that of Sōhyō, and gradually eroded Sōhyō's hegemony in the labor movement at the national level.

THE CHANGING POLITICAL ECONOMY

In the late 1960s, labor accommodation gradually became faced with new challenges, owing to the changing political economy of Japan. I focus here on three important changes: political demands; the wage-productivity relationship, which brought about inflation; and internationalization of the Japanese economy.

In the late 1960s and early 1970s, people were becoming more vocal in their political demands. This change was attributable to a demographic change in society as well as to economic growth. As economic growth proceeded in the 1960s, more and more people were moving from rural areas into urban areas. This urbanization liberated people from the traditional social institutions and drove them to make more political demands. For instance, as the traditional large family was transformed into a nuclear family consisting of parents and their children alone, the cry for a social welfare system increased. Japanese voters became more concerned with expected material gains from their voting than with their social relations with candidates' organizations.[1] In the late 1960s and early 1970s, the governing Liberal Democratic Party continuously lost support to the opposition parties in both national and local elections as welfare and pollution became important issues.

This change influenced workers' preferences and consequently transformed union activities. In the 1960s unions in the private sector did not pursue political goals eagerly because they were satisfied with a labor accommodation in which they could achieve economic benefits. Labor politics at the national level was thus dominated mainly by leftist unions appealing to ideological issues such as the U.S.-Japan Security Treaty. However, in the late 1960s and early 1970s, unions as a whole became more concerned about national policies directly related to their own interests, such as social welfare and pollution control. According to surveys of union members, workers in the early 1960s were more optimistic about the future of the national economy and their personal future than workers in the early 1970s.[2] In the early 1970s nominal wages were increasing at a higher rate than in the 1960s, and the pessimistic view of the future held by workers can be attributed to the emergence of the new issues of welfare and pollution. This change in perception propelled unions to undertake more political activity in the 1970s than in the 1960s.

---

[1] Ichiro Miyake, *Tōhyō kōdō* (Voting behavior) (Tokyo: Tokyo Daigaku Shuppankai, 1989), pp. 56–62.

[2] Akihiro Ishikawa, *Shakaihendō to rōdōsha ishiki* (Social changes and workers' consciousness) (Nihon Rōdō Kyōkai, 1975), p. 114.

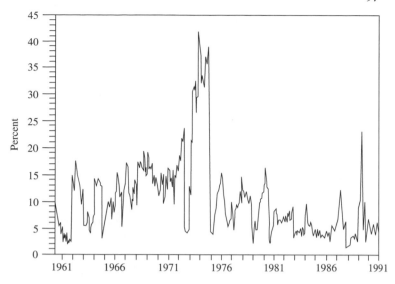

Figure 15. Percentage of those surveyed who did not support the cabinet because of inflation. From the Jiji Press Monthly Survey.

The changes described above occurred outside labor-management relations, but relations between labor and management also changed. In the first half of the high economic growth period (1960–68), productivity and nominal wage increases were well balanced, in that the latter exceeded the former by only 2.2 percent, while between 1969 and 1973 that gap rose to 7.0 percent. On the other hand, in the latter period, management continued to eagerly invest in production facilities. This naturally resulted in higher inflation. While in the former period inflation averaged 5.7 percent, it averaged 7.0 percent in the latter period.

This change seemed to influence the political perception of voters. The monthly Jiji Press survey showed that in the late 1960s and early 1970s an increasing number of people opposed the LDP government because of its failure to control inflation (fig. 15). More interestingly, among occupational groups, white collar officials, blue collar workers, and wives were more concerned about inflation than other categories of people in that election.[3] Faced with this new situation, unions began demanding that the government control inflation and so entered into political activities.

The third change was the internationalization of the Japanese political

[3] Kōmei Senkyo Renmei, *Dai 33 kai shūgiin sōsenkyo no jittai II* (The 33rd Lower House election, part 2), pp. 142–49, quoted in Masao Soma, ed., *Kokuseisenkyo to seitōseiji*, p. 145.

Table 5. Exports of goods and services as a percentage of GDP

Country	1960–67 (%)	1968–73 (%)	1974–79 (%)	1980–83 (%)
Japan	9.9	10.6	12.7	14.5
West Germany	18.5	21.4	25.9	29.6
France	13.8	16.2	21.0	23.1
Great Britain	20.0	22.8	28.5	27.1
Italy	15.0	18.1	25.1	26.1
Canada	19.2	22.7	24.8	27.1
United States	5.1	5.7	8.4	9.0

SOURCE: OECD, *Historical Statistics.*

economy. In the period of postwar reconstruction, Japanese industries were fairly well protected from foreign competition. However, in 1960 Prime Minister Ikeda established a policy to open up the Japanese economy. The Japanese government started liberalizing trade in 1961 and achieved 90 percent liberalization in 1964. Liberalization of direct investment by foreign companies began in 1967, although the process was slow. These changes forced Japanese industries to compete with foreign firms within the domestic market.

In the late 1960s this competition became more intensified as the export dependence of Japanese manufacturing industries increased. Competition became internationalized; Japanese manufacturing industries began competing with foreign companies in the international market. Japan's export of goods and services as a percentage of GDP had been lower than that of most OECD countries (table 5). However, as figure 16 shows, the manufacturing industries (steel, automobiles, electric equipment, and so forth) became heavily dependent on exports. The appearance of the newly industrialized economies (NIEs), such as South Korea, showed another change in a similar direction. In the early 1970s textile companies began to face severe competition from companies in the NIEs, which paid their workers lower wages.

While leading the liberalization, the government, especially the Ministry of International Trade and Industry (MITI), introduced various policies to alleviate the costs of liberalization and to make Japanese industries competitive against foreign companies. The basic goal was to restructure Japanese industries to make them more competitive. In due course, MITI tried to use intensive consultation between industries and itself. The most important development was MITI's establishment of an Investigatory Council on Industrial Structure in 1961, which was reorganized as the Deliberation Council on Industrial Structure in 1964. Using this institu-

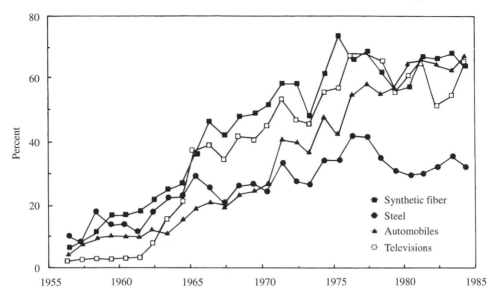

Figure 16. Export dependence of Japanese industries. Calculated by the author from *Japan Statistical Yearbook.*

tion, MITI tried to regulate excessive competition among the companies within each industry and to pursue optimal resource allocation across industries. Although MITI failed in its attempt to get a law passed—the Temporary Law to Promote Designated Industries—that would help it guide the development of targeted industries, it continued to intervene in industries by helping promote their competitiveness. Scholars differ in their evaluations of the effectiveness of MITI's intervention, but internationalization of the Japanese economy certainly intensified the political interaction between business and the government in the 1960s.[4]

These changes gradually made unions in the private manufacturing sector conscious of their companies' and industries' competitiveness, a condition that would provide their members with increasing wages and secure employment. In the late 1960s, these unions began advocating union participation in industrial policy formation.

These three changes in the Japanese political economy drove unions

[4] Among many scholars interested in this matter, Chalmers Johnson argues that MITI's intervention was essential to Japanese economic success, while many economists argue that MITI's intervention was potentially harmful but, due to its failure to implement its policies, Japanese economic success was achieved after all. See Johnson, *MITI and the Japanese Miracle*; Komiya et al., *Nihon no sangyōseisaku.*

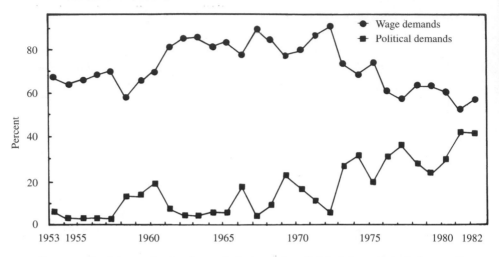

Figure 17. Breakdown of union demands during strikes. Political demands include a small number of demands in sympathy strikes. Calculated by the author from *Nihon rōdō nenkan.*

to political activities. Figure 17 shows that the percentage of political demands made by unions on strike increased since the late 1960s. Unions demanded political solutions to new problems in the late 1960s because these problems would have been difficult to solve within the wage negotiation framework. This repoliticization of the Japanese labor movement occurred not just in the public sector but also in the private sector.

However, a union's increasing political demands are one thing, and its actual participation in policymaking is another. In other words, these changes were a necessary condition for union participation in national policymaking, but not a sufficient condition. Unions had been mostly excluded from national policymaking by the governing coalition of business, bureaucracy, farmers, small industrialists, and merchants, all of whom had been supporting the LDP government. Labor unions had not been powerless as political actors; from time to time unions cooperating with the opposition parties restrained the LDP government from moving too far right, as for instance, when the anti-rearmament movement constrained the LDP's own defense policy efforts. However, unions were not inside actors in national policymaking. As Japan was continuously governed by the LDP since 1955, it is necessary to analyze the LDP's relations with labor in order to understand the political opportunity structure for labor.

POLITICAL OPPORTUNITY STRUCTURE: CHANGING LDP STRATEGY
TOWARD LABOR

Although the LDP is a conservative party, it has had a tendency to cater to some of labor's concerns. In its first national conference, the LDP proclaimed that it would pursue a policy to enable workers to have a stable standard of living, while at the same time criticizing the leftist unions' class struggle agenda.[5] In 1957 the LDP admitted that it was worried about leftist groups joining with labor unions and claimed that it planned to approach unions. This kind of statement can be found recurrently since then.

This idea of incorporating labor in the LDP's camp was based on the LDP's own perception of labor in a capitalist society. In the plan of the revised constitution proposed by an LDP study group in 1956, there was some pro-labor language: "Firms must not pursue maximization of their economic interests, but rather try to provide as many people as possible with decently paid jobs. Capital and labor should be protected by the state, because they are both fundamental factors for economic activity."[6]

Although the LDP's effort to revise the constitution was criticized severely by opposition parties, it is noteworthy that this pro-labor phase was formulated by members of the LDP. This was partly because the LDP was formed by two conservative groups, one of which adhered to economic liberalism and took a less conciliatory attitude toward labor (Shigeru Yoshida's faction), while the other group, consisting of Bismarckian paternalists and reformists, advocated some kind of a pro-labor policy.[7] Among the latter group were prewar reform bureaucrats (such as Shinsuke Kishi) and a group of capitalist revisionists including Keynesians (such as Tanzan Ishibashi). The latter group manifest the LDP's "pro-labor" tradition, and prevented the LDP from becoming a truly liberal party.[8] It is well known

---

[5] LDP, "Ippanseisaku" (General policy), 1st Conference, 1955, quoted in *Jiyuminshutō tōshi: Shiryō-hen* (Tokyo: Jiyuminshutō, 1987), pp. 93–97.

[6] LDP, Kenpōkenkyūkai, "Kenpō kaisei sōan" (The plan to revise the constitution), quoted in *Nihon rōdō nenkan* (1957), p. 633.

[7] Hideo Otake, *Adenauer to Yoshida Shigeru* (Adenauer and Yoshida Shigeru) (Tokyo: Chuōkōronsha, 1986).

[8] This characteristic of the LDP can be partly explained by the fact that the two groups, the Yoshida group and the anti-Yoshida group, competed with each other before the 1955 merger. In the course of this competition, the Yoshida group had been mostly in power and pursued a policy of economic recovery following the surplus budget policy and a policy of capital accummulation for big business with less state intervention after 1949. On the other hand, the anti-Yoshida group had to rally popular support against the Yoshida policy; they pursued a more populist welfare policy and a plan-oriented industrial policy. In due course,

that this latter group was a strong advocate of welfare policy within the LDP. Using Esping-Andersen's terms, the LDP has included both a liberal welfare-state orientation and a conservative welfare orientation.[9]

This pro-labor orientation was consolidated in the LDP's Charter on Labor in 1966. It proclaimed that human beings should not be regarded as an instrument for any purpose but as an end in and of themselves, and thus it is a fundamental responsibility of government to provide everyone with jobs based on will and ability. Further the government should work toward the goals of full employment, the improvement of working conditions, and the promotion of social welfare. The LDP now officially admitted that labor unions were legitimate organizations to protect workers' economic interests and also asserted that labor and management should cooperate to develop the national economy. This charter was criticized by rightist politicians within the LDP as too pro-union, but it was an epochmaking achievement for the LDP.[10]

Although the LDP has expressed this position on labor from its birth, its popular base of support was always small and medium-sized industrialists, self-employed merchants, and farmers (fig. 18). In 1964 Nakasone's report on the party's principle stated that small and medium-sized industrialists and merchants, farmers, fishermen, youths and wives were the fundamental supporters of the party, and that it should execute policies to support their well being.[11] However, the LDP began pursuing the expansion of its popular support, being faced with electoral decline. Figure 19 shows that the LDP's support declined from 1960 until the mid-1970s. Given that the LDP was a party of farmers and the self-employed, its decline from the early 1960s on was inevitable because the number of farmers decreased drastically, while the employee population increased (fig. 20). This situation worried the LDP, and as early as 1961, one prominent politician within the LDP, Hirohide Ishida, published an article proclaiming that as this demographic change continued and the number of workers increased, the LDP would lose power and the JSP would gain power.[12] In the 1960s as a result of industrialization employed

---

the anti-Yoshida group incorporated a pro-labor stance within its policies. Cf. Kume, "Party Politics and Industrial Policy."

[9] Gøsta Esping-Andersen, *Three Worlds of Welfare Capitalism* (Princeton: Princeton University Press, 1990).

[10] Yasuhiro Nakasone and Tokusaburo Kosaka, "Hoshutō wa shisei wo tadase" (Straighten up the conservative party), *Ekonomisuto*, January 7, 1964, p. 68.

[11] LDP, "Tō undōhōshin hōkoku" (Report on the party's tactic), 13th conference, 1964, quoted in *Jiyuminshutō tō-shi: Shiryō-hen*, p. 199.

[12] Hirohide Ishida, "Hoshu seitō no vision" (Vision of a conservative party), *Chuōkōron* (January 1963).

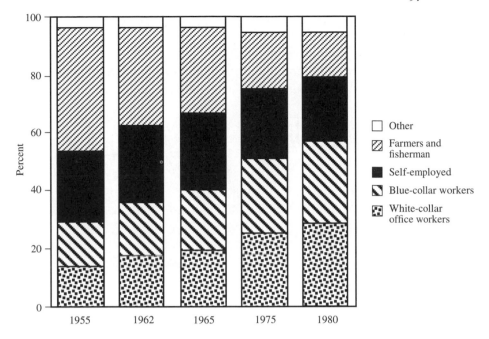

Figure 18. Breakdown of support for the LDP by occupation. From Asahi Shimbunsha, *Survey* (Tokyo: Respective years).

workers became a majority within the population. Industrialization and its subsequent demographic changes were important factors conducive to the birth of the labor movement and socialism in European countries in the early twentieth century. Ishida predicted that Japan would follow this European path.

In order to adapt to this new situation, the LDP gradually began trying to expand its popular support among workers. It wanted Japan to follow a different path from Europe. Initially, this new LDP strategy did not work, and the LDP continued to lose worker support until the mid-1970s (fig. 21). Despite a new intensive employment policy, the Employment Measure Law of 1966, that endorsed full employment, the LDP did not attract workers.[13]

So the LDP accelerated its efforts. Further decline in LDP support, especially in urban areas and, more importantly, the emergence of many leftist local governments advocating welfare and antipollution policies shocked the LDP. At its twenty-second conference in 1969 the LDP first

[13] Ikuo Kume, "Institutionalizing the Active Labor Market Policy in Japan: A Comparative View," in Kim et al., The Japanese Civil Service.

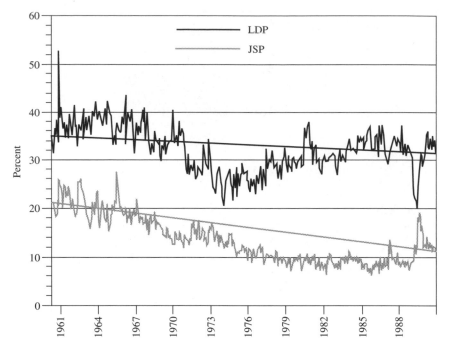

Figure 19. Support rates for the LDP and the Japan Socialist Party (JSP). From the Jiji Press Monthly Survey.

announced a response to this new situation. Kakuei Tanaka, then secretary-general, presented "A Report on the Circumstances of the LDP" in which he stated, "It is evident that our party is now faced with difficulties in the urban area, where various opposition parties are gaining support. We have to develop our own urban policies to solve the problems of housing, transportation, pollution, etc."[14] Furthermore, it was proposed that as unions are not opponents but partners, the LDP would have to engage them in dialogue.[15] Despite Ishida's grim prediction of a JSP victory over the LDP, the popularity of the JSP also declined among employed workers. Other small opposition parties had begun gaining their support in the late 1960s, but in the early 1970s they also lost support (figs. 22 and 23). There appeared an increasing number of independent voters among both white- and blue-collar workers. The LDP targeted these independent voters. One 1973 LDP report proclaimed that

[14] LDP, "Tō undōhōshin hōkoku," 22nd conference, 1969, quoted in *Jiyuminshutō tō-shi: Shiryō-hen*, pp. 265–68.
[15] Ibid.

116

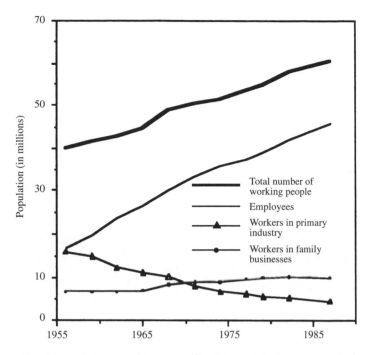

Figure 20. Employment demographics, 1955–87. *Primary industry* means agriculture, forestry, and fishery. From *Shōwa kokusei sōran.*

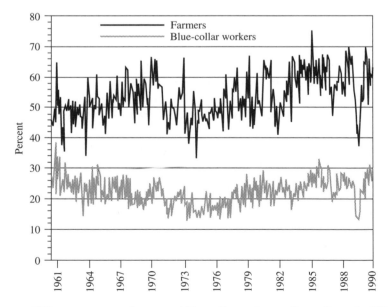

Figure 21. LDP support among farmers and blue-collar workers, 1960–90. From the Jiji Press Monthly Survey.

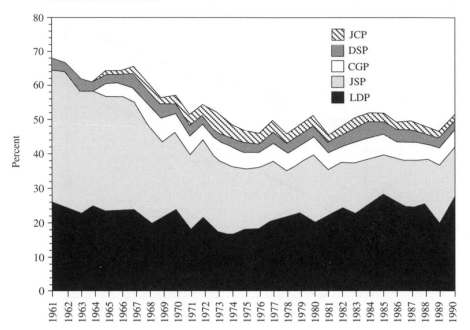

Figure 22. Party support among blue-collar workers, 1960–90. JCP (Communist Party), DSP (Democratic Socialist Party), CGP (Clean Government Party), JSP (Japan Socialist Party), and LDP (Liberal Democratic Party). From the Jiji Press Monthly Survey.

"The employed workers and their family members consist of 80 percent of the nation, and only 30 percent of the employed workers are organized. Furthermore, because organized workers do not necessarily support leftist parties, the LDP should try to reach out to these people by introducing new policies, e.g., policies to facilitate the increase of workers' wealth and to reduce work hours."[16]

The LDP was eager to open the political process to labor and incorporate workers into the party. This changing political opportunity structure in combination with increasing political demands from labor resulted in increasing labor's participation in policymaking in the 1970s. However, union policy achievements changed from social democratic welfare policies to economic policies that is, to employment and industrial concerns. The openness of the political opportunity structure alone cannot explain this change. We also need to analyze inter- and intra-class politics in this period to understand a significant change in Japanese labor politics after

[16] LDP, "Tō undōhōshin hōkoku," 28th conference, 1973, quoted in *Jiyuminshutō tō-shi: Shiryō-hen,* pp. 310–13.

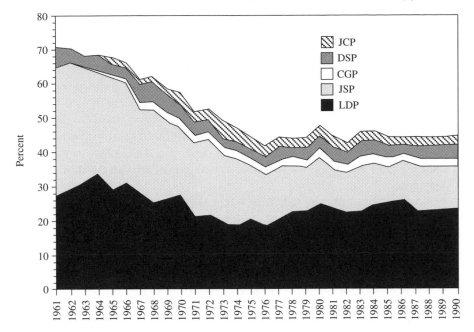

Figure 23. Party support among white-collar workers, 1960–90. JCP (Communist Party), DSP (Democratic Socialist Party), CGP (Clean Government Party), JSP (Japan Socialist Party), and LDP (Liberal Democratic Party). From the Jiji Press Monthly Survey.

the oil crisis. Let me turn to an analysis of two phases of politicization of the union movement since the end of 1960s, 1969–74 and 1975–80.

PHASE ONE: 1969–74

In this period, labor unions began pursuing political goals in national policymaking. Sōhyō led the politicization of the movement in this phase. After the unexpected defeat of the JSP in the general election in 1967, Sōhyō decided to appeal to a wider range of people by advocating an anti-inflation policy, pollution control, tax cuts, and such.[17] In due course, it tried to propose an alternative to the existing political economy. At its 1969 conference, Sōhyō emphasized that transforming the Japanese political economy would be the only way to solve the new problems of the

---

[17] Ministry of Labor, *Shiryō rōdō undōshi* (1970), p. 630. Sōhyō Seisaku-kyoku, ed., *Sōhyō chōsa nenpō 1989: Sengo rōdōundō no tōtatsuten* (Sōhyō annual study report 1989: Achievements of the Sōhyō movement) (Tokyo: Rōdōkeizaisha, 1989), pp. 34–35.

day. It advocated a totally new policy package for economic growth for the sake of the Japanese people, criticizing existing policies as protecting monopoly capitalism, pursuing further militarization, and maintaining the U.S.-Japan Security Treaty.[18] In 1971 Sōhyō declared that Shuntō should be a struggle to protect people's livelihoods and decided to negotiate with national and local governments as well as management to achieve this goal.[19] For instance, Sōhyō demanded free medical care for the elderly and an allowance for dependent children. In 1973, faced with unprecedented inflation caused by the first oil crisis, Sōhyō organized what it called the "People's Shuntō", in which it fully integrated its policy demands.[20]

To cope with inflation, Sōhyō as well as Dōmei originally put priority on higher wage demands to compensate for price increases. Unions successfully demanded higher wage increases given high inflation. As inflation rose in this period, wages rose at a higher rate. Since 1969 wages had increased by more than 15 percent annually and in 1974 they rose by 32.9 percent. It is true that consumer prices increased at a high rate (7.0 percent in the period 1968–73), but wage increases surpassed price increases by a large margin. Unions also demanded that government control consumer price increases, but they, especially Sōhyō, were very cautious in the introduction of an incomes policy that would require unions to heed wage restraints in exchange for price controls by government. This was a major reason why Sōhyō was originally reluctant to participate in the regular MOL Sanrōkon meeting among business, labor, "men of learning and experience," and the government.[21] Sōhyō was afraid that Sanrōkon's national meeting might be used to introduce an incomes policy. Sōhyō was committed to a fight for higher wages to cope with inflation and was not ready to deal with the government, although it did unilaterally demand a national policy to stabilize consumer prices. As long as Dōmei and the IMF-JC unions did not begin pursuing some form of political exchange with the government, Sōhyō was not faced with losing its leadership in the labor movement.

On the issue of internationalization of the Japanese economy and its subsequent industrial adjustment, unions also politicized their movement in order to protect their members' working conditions, especially employment. As I will analyze in the next chapter, in the late 1960s unions in

---

[18] Sōhyō, "Undō Hōshin" (Tactics), 1969 annual conference, quoted in Ministry of Labor, *Shiryō rōdō undōshi* (1969), pp. 847–50.
[19] Ministry of Labor, *Shiryō rōdō undōshi* (1971), pp. 31–35.
[20] Sōhyō Seisaku-kyoku, *Sōhyō chōsa nenpō 1989*, pp. 36–37.
[21] *Mainichi shimbun*, December 28, 1969.

the private sector began arguing that they should have their own industrial policy to solve new problems caused by internationalization, technological change, and subsequent industrial restructuring, and that they should force the government to incorporate their views into policy. Furthermore, they established industry-wide labor-management consultation councils. Here again Sōhyō was reluctant about the unions' industrial policy proposal because it feared that such a proposal might make labor unions accept the existing economy of monopoly capitalism as a given and might domesticate the unions' anti-rationalization movement.

There subsequently appeared a clear division on this issue between Sōhyō's mainstream public-sector unions and the private unions affiliated with Dōmei and the IMF-JC. This was a potentially serious problem for Sōhyō's leadership in the labor movement. The number of private-sector unions affiliated with Sōhyō became fewer than those with Dōmei in 1967; thus, the schism between Sōhyō and Dōmei could be regarded as a conflict between the private and public sectors. This meant that Sōhyō might lose its leading position in the labor movement as a whole and come to represent only the public-sector unions. This schism did not do immediate harm to Sōhyō's leadership, however, although the private-sector unions began realigning. This was because the internationalization of the Japanese economy was not yet perceived as threatening by unions in much of the private sector.

In this phase, therefore, Sōhyō maintained its leadership in the labor movement, even though it was faced with the rise of trade unionism in the mid-1960s led by the IMF-JC. New political issues such as welfare and pollution control were appealing to union members as well as the general public, and Sōhyō could rally its unions around these new issues. Furthermore, Dōmei and other private-sector unions were not so different from Sōhyō in their demands for welfare policy. Dōmei published its Welfare Vision in 1972, and its policy proposals were almost the same as Sōhyō's. In 1973 Sōhyō joined with three other national union federations to struggle for political goals, like welfare and anti-inflation and anti-pollution measures. Given these situations, Sōhyō could lead the politicization of the labor movement in the first phase.

THE REFORM OF EMPLOYEES' PENSIONS (1973)

Except for health insurance, introduced in 1922, Japanese welfare policy development in the 1960s was far behind that in the advanced industrial democracies. However, in 1973 the Japanese government introduced a series of welfare policies and declared it the beginning of the Japanese welfare state. Among the new welfare policies, free medical service for the elderly over age seventy, 70 percent coverage of medical costs for dependent family members, and public pension reform were the major policy innovations in that year. The labor unions played an important role in the policymaking process of this welfare legislation.

The Japanese government introduced the employees' pension program in the prewar period as part of the war mobilization policy, but it was suspended after the war due to economic turbulence. However, since the employee pension reform of 1954, the Ministry of Welfare had gradually developed its own welfare policies, although Nikkeiren was opposed to this policy development, arguing that the Japanese economy could not afford public pensions.[22] In the 1960s the employee pensions were reformed repeatedly to increase the benefit level. "From 1965 to 1969, the model EPS [Employee Pension System] benefit was raised from ¥3,500 to ¥20,000 a month, more than a fivefold increase in nominal terms, and a jump from under 20 percent of average wages in the early 1960s to 36 percent in 1965 and 45 percent in 1969."[23] Although it increased rapidly, the level of pension benefits was still regarded as low in the 1960s even by officials in the Ministry of Welfare. They were obsessed with the International Labor Organization's standard of 60 percent of average wages, which was achieved in the 1973 pension reform.[24]

Another problem of the pension system was its lack of indexation. As John Campbell explained, the government was constantly having to adjust the review schedule to deal with inflation.

> Under the old method, pension benefits were supposed to be adjusted in the scheduled Fiscal Review every five years "in case of extreme fluctuations in national living standards or other conditions." In inflationary times considerable purchasing power can be lost over five years. In practice, to deal with this problem, the Fiscal Review had routinely been moved up a year or two, benefit hikes had gone well beyond the amounts of price or wage increases, and in 1971 adjustments were made between reviews. However, pension

[22] Hiroaki Yamazaki, "Nihon ni okeru rōrei nenkinseido no tenkai katei" (The developmental process of the pension system for the elderly in Japan), in Tokyo Daigaku Shakaikagaku Kenkyūsho, ed., *Fukushikokka* (Welfare state), vol. 5 (Tokyo: Tokyo Daigaku Shuppankai, 1985), p. 181.

[23] John C. Campbell, *How Policies Change* (Princeton: Princeton University Press, 1992), p. 101.

[24] Ibid., p. 156.

experts had long been bothered by the delays as well as the administrative vagueness and political uncertainty of this procedure.[25]

Pension benefits were actually adjusted to inflation and wage increases, and the LDP in the late 1960s found this adjustment policy beneficial during election time. But the adjustment was not institutionalized, and this institutionalization was made in the 1973 reform.

Although several unions started a movement for old-age security (*rōgo hoshō tōsō*) in the mid-1960s, this agenda was not unified and got little attention.[26] A main driving force in those days was the radical Zennichijirō, because it organized the beneficiaries of the public job creation program, who were mainly the elderly.[27] In the 1970s labor unions became eager for employee pension reform as the ratio of elderly increased. In the early 1970s, the old-age security movement was coordinated at the national level by unions and the issue of public pensions became part of the political agenda. During its fortieth conference in 1970, Sōhyō, as a part of its political demands described earlier, claimed that the government should introduce a public pension that could sufficiently support retired workers.[28] Sōhyō then strengthened its attempts to improve the public pension program by organizing a National Old People Rally and a series of demonstrations, and it put pressure on the Ministry of Welfare (MOW).[29] On February 25, 1971, Sōhyō presented its agenda to increase pension benefits and introduce indexation in its negotiations with the government. At the same time, based on the report of its overseas study group sent to France, Italy, West Germany, and Great Britain, Sōhyō criticized the Japanese pension system for being far behind the European system—still at the stage Europe was at before World War I.[30] This argument was effective, because MOW itself was obsessed with the ILO (International Labor Organization) standard.

Labor unions continued to put priority on the pension issue. On September 15 (Respect the Elderly National Holiday), 1971, over 10,000 participants gathered in Tokyo for the National Old People Rally, and in due course Sōhyō met with the Ministers of Welfare and Labor and the Cabinet Secretary General to demand pension reform as well as free medical care for the elderly. Establishment of the Employee Pension

---

[25] Ibid., p. 160.
[26] Ibid., p. 157.
[27] *Nihon rōdō nenkan* (1972), p. 398.
[28] Ministry of Labor, *Shiryō rōdō undōshi* (1971), p. 593.
[29] Ibid. The first rally was organized in 1967, and this was the fourth rally since then.
[30] Ibid., p. 594.

Reform Committee during the 1972 Shuntō preparations in October 1971 also shows union prioritization of this issue. At that time Sōhyō announced that it would prepare for strikes in each industry to keep pressure on the government to reform the pension system, while arranging meetings with the government and organizing a petition movement targeted at the Diet.[31] In 1972 Sōhyō, cooperating with Chūritsurōren, kept up the pressure by organizing rallies and demonstrations. On November 9, the National Association of Retirees was established on Sōhyō's initiative, and on the same day 21,000 people rallied for a "Pension May Day" organized by Sōhyō and Chūritsurōren, which was followed by negotiation on the issue of pension reform with the Ministries of Welfare and Finance. The Shuntō Joint Struggle Committee led a further series of rallies and demonstrations and finally organized a pension strike on April 17, 1973, in which 1,433,583 workers participated. Unions appealed to this strike in order to put pressure on the Diet at the final stage of legislation.

While unions kept pushing the government to reform the pension system, the political opportunity structure for unions became very favorable. First, as described before, the LDP government, faced with decline in electoral support, began opening the policymaking process to labor. In addition, Kakuei Tanaka became prime minister on July 7, 1972, after competition with Takeo Fukuda. Tanaka won this competition, successfully selling himself as an innovative political leader who could bring about changes after seven years of the Sato administration. For instance, on October 12, Vice Prime Minister Takeo Miki met with leaders of four national labor union federations (Sōhyō, Dōmei, Chūritsu, Shinsanbetsu). Miki emphasized that the new administration would pursue consultation instead of confrontation, and that it was important for the government to consult with unions, because they were influential social forces. In this meeting, union leaders demanded increases in pension benefits, and Miki responded that the government would develop a welfare policy.[32]

Second, Tanaka's new administration actually sought a set of new policies. For Tanaka, this policy change was not just an attempt to buy out labor. He tried to introduce a new policy mix to transform the Japanese economy so as to solve several emerging problems simultaneously. Welfare policy was a key component of this new policy mix. In the twenty-seventh party conference in 1973, Tanaka argued that as the Japanese economy advanced, they would use this economic power to increase

[31] Ibid., p. 595; Campbell, *How Policies Change*, p. 157; Ministry of Labor, *Shiryō rōdō undōshi* (1971), pp. 596–97.
[32] Ministry of Labor, *Shiryō rōdō undōshi* (1972), p. 485.

people's standard of living by shifting resources to social welfare and social capital formation, which would increase Japanese domestic consumption and solve trade friction with the United States.[33] The Tanaka administration considered it necessary to improve the standard of living of employees, who constituted 70 percent of the Japanese work force, in order to build a welfare state. This action consequently might boost workers' support for the LDP.[34] This policy change was a good opportunity for labor to realize its goals. For instance, Dōmei alleged that as the Tanaka administration was destined to transform the LDP's old policy, Dōmei should be able to realize its policy demands.[35]

Third, unions gained significant allies to realize their demand for pension reform. As Campbell noted, in the early 1970s, the media and public awoke to the problem of the elderly. Media coverage of and public interest in this issue surged.[36] Unions could count on the media as a significant ally in demanding welfare policies. However, what was more important was that unions had allies within the governing coalition, that is Nikkeiren and the Ministry of Welfare. As described before, MOW was obsessed with the ILO's 60 percent standard and had continuously pursued the development of welfare policy. For instance, in November 1971 a discussion group within the Employee Pension Division of the Social Insurance Deliberation Council (the advisory committee to MOW) proposed that the next fiscal review (scheduled for 1974) should be executed as soon as possible, so as to bring about a large increase in the benefit level. It was actually MOW that cautiously guided this discussion. MOW could be a potential ally for labor, although its weak position among national bureaucracies disappointed unions from time to time.

Nikkeiren was also an important ally for unions in the pension reform of 1973. Until the mid-1960s, Nikkeiren was opposed to the public pension program for employees because it liked the intra-firm welfare programs. It argued that workers were entitled to receive a retirement bonus (fifty to one hundred times their monthly payments), and this should be regarded as a kind of private welfare scheme for employees. Nikkeiren did

[33] *Jiyuminshutō tō-shi: Shiryō-hen*, pp. 307–9.

[34] LDP, "Seisaku hōkoku" (Policy report), 28th conference, 1974, quoted in ibid., p. 324. An integrated policy package with this policy orientation can be found in Tanaka's famous "Nihon rettō kaizōron" (Plan to reform the Japanese Archipelago).

[35] "Dōmei rondan: Shinseiken no tōjō to seisakutenkan tōsō" (Domei opinion: New administration and the policy transformation struggle), *Dōmei* (August 1972).

[36] Campbell, *How Policies Change*, pp. 140–42. This situation is very similar to ones in which American labor succeeded in achieving progressive public policies in the era of the Kennedy and Johnson administrations.

not want management to pay additional costs for the development of a public pension program for employees. Meanwhile, as a single-payment retirement bonus became burdensome for companies because of wage increases, many companies began introducing a company pension paid over an extended period in place of the retirement bonus. In the mid-1960s, Nikkeiren changed its attitude toward the public pension and began supporting a benefit increase as long as some coordination was made between public pensions and company pensions. In 1963 management proposed that large companies with company pension programs should be allowed to contract out the income-proportional part of the employee pensions. Unions strongly opposed this proposal, arguing that the retirement bonus was a deferred wage and not part of a welfare scheme.[37] The Social Insurance Deliberation Council was deadlocked, and MOW led the process of the 1966 pension reform, proposing a compromise between management and labor.

MOW's plan was to allow management to choose to contract out on the conditions that 1) it would not reduce the retirement bonus, 2) coordination between public and private pensions would be executed with the union's approval, and 3) pension reserve funds would be deposited in a trust bank or insurance company rather than invested by the employer. In return, MOW introduced a triple increase in the pension benefit.[38] This process was important in bringing about a deal between labor and management that would allow benefit increases to be easily made thereafter. In the 1973 reform, labor could count on Nikkeiren to support the benefit increase.

Nikkeiren made it clear it would demand a welfare policy for the elderly. In September 1972 Nikkeiren met with four national union federations and exchanged opinions on welfare reform and related issues. After reaching agreement on a large rise in pension benefits, reducing the tax on the retirement bonus, and health insurance reform, Nikkeiren presented these demands to the prime minister and other ministers, saying that these demands were supported by unions. On September 18, Nikkeiren further endorsed the introduction of indexation into the pension programs.[39]

Finally, unions were unified in their demand for pension reform, which enabled Sōhyō to lead this movement. Although Dōmei and private-sector

---

[37] Yamazaki, "Nihon no rōrei nenkinseido," p. 192, note 33.

[38] Ibid., p. 188; Campbell, *How Policies Change*, pp. 90–91.

[39] Yamazaki, "Nihon no rōrei nenkinseido," p. 198; Ministry of Labor, *Shiryō rōdō undōshi* (1972), p. 485.

unions were somewhat skeptical of Sōhyō's leftist strategy, their views did not differ on this issue of pension reform.[40]

Although unions succeeded in forming a strong alliance with management, MOW, and top LDP leaders for an increase in pension benefits and introduction of indexation, this did not mean the process was unanimous and automatic. First, the Ministry of Finance resisted a large rise in pension benefits. However, Prime Minister Tanaka after his inauguration effectively supported the ¥50,000 pension and overrode MOF's resistance.[41] Second, unions wanted to change the contribution ratio from 50:50 between labor and management to 30:70. They sought to index pension benefits to wages rather than consumer price increases. MOW's plan was to raise the benefit level automatically, if consumer prices increased by more than 5 percent. But unions wanted the benefit rise to be linked to wage negotiations directly. And they desired a pay-as-you-go financing system. In the existing system, each generation's contributions plus interest would cover all its estimated future benefit.[42] Unions preferred the pay-as-you-go system. As the pension account was running a surplus because of the still-young population, unions could expect easier benefit hikes in that new financing system.

On these points, labor and management representatives disagreed during the Social Insurance Deliberation Council held on October 17, 1972. This is why unions kept pressure on the government even though they succeeded in making allies with management, MOW, and top LDP leaders for a large rise in pension benefits and the introduction of indexation. After the pension strike, unions obtained some positive responses to their demands from the Minister of Welfare: (1) The government would consult with unions for future pension reform. (2) Fiscal review would be done flexibly in order for pension benefits to catch up with wage increases. (3) Although it was difficult to immediately introduce the pay-as-you-go system, given the rapidly aging society, the government would consider it in a positive way. These points were written into a resolution attached to the Pension Reform Law of 1973.

After this reform, fiscal review was done in 1976 and 1980, and benefit levels increased to 64 percent in 1976 and 68 percent in 1980. On the other hand, the level of contributions was kept lower than what was necessary to keep pension financing sound for the future, which made it

---

[40] "Zadankai: Kenpo-nenkin tōsō o kaerimite" (Discussion: Retrospecting on the process of health care/pension struggles), *Dōmei* (October 1973).

[41] Shinkawa, *Nihongata fukushi no seijikeizaigaku*, p. 109.

[42] Campbell, *How Policies Change*, p. 163.

necessary to rationalize the pension system again in 1984.[43] Although the pay-as-you-go system was not introduced, unions got de facto indexation to wage. It is also noteworthy that although the contribution ratio was kept at 50:50 between management and labor, the contribution level was kept lower. All in all, unions achieved a policy victory in pension program development.

PHASE TWO: AFTER THE FIRST OIL CRISIS

The social democratic labor movement led by Sōhyō was faced with a challenge after the first oil crisis. Private-sector unions affiliated with Dōmei and the IMF-JC began taking leadership in the labor movement. They began restraining wage demands, while demanding public policies to maintain or improve their living standards and industrial/employment policies to protect their jobs. This was very different from the Sōhyō-led social democratic movement. I will now turn to this transformation, that is, politicization under the private-sector union leadership.

Since 1975, the total pattern of the Japanese economy changed. The increase in real GDP dropped to around 4 percent, the nominal wage increase fell to single digits, and the real wage increase went down to around 2 percent; meanwhile, the unemployment rate increased to more than 2 percent. Table 6, which summarizes my regression analysis of wage determination, indicates that before the oil crisis, the tightness of the labor market was less of an explanation for wage increases than after the oil crisis. In the period from 1956 to 1973, the R-squared of unemployment in the regression analysis of wage increase is 0.258, but it is 0.721 in the period after 1974. In addition to labor market conditions, the consumer price increases, productivity increases, and corporate profits have come to have substantial explanatory power. The R-squared of the multiple regression analysis increases from 0.687 (1956–73) to 0.963 (1974–83). These data suggest that during the pre–oil crisis period, owing to the tight labor market, labor was largely unaffected by threats of unemployment; during the post–oil crisis period, however, labor became concerned about unemployment. As these aggregate data eloquently show, the patterns of industrial relations have changed since 1975, which in turn challenged the Sōhyō-led social democratic labor movement.

[43] Hiroaki Yamazaki, "Kōsei nenkin seido no 'bapponkaisei' katei" (The reform process of the employee pension system) in Tokyo Daigaku Shakaikagaku Kenkyusho, ed., *Tenkanki no fukushikokka ge* (Welfare state in transition, vol. 2) (Tokyo: Tokyo Daigaku Shuppankai, 1988).

Table 6. Regression analysis of wage determination

Years	R-squared	Regression coefficients			
		CPI	Productivity	Profit rate	Unemployment rate
1956–73					
Unemployment (Simple regression)	0.258	—	—	—	—
All variables (Multiple regression)	0.687	0.642	0.509	−1.998	−4.667
1974–83					
Unemployment (Simple regression)	0.721	—	—	—	—
All variables (Multiple regression)	0.963	1.68	0.154	1.389	9.444

SOURCES: Calculated by the author from *Japan Statistical Yearbook* (Tokyo: Sōrifu Tōkeikyoku, annual) and *Asahi nenkan* (Tokyo: Asahi Shimbunsha, annual).

NOTE: The dependent variable is wage increase; independent variables are consumer price increase (CPI), productivity increase, profit rate change, and unemployment rate change.

Wage Restraint—The 1975 Shuntō

The 1974 Shuntō seemed to be the time of labor's greatest strength. A 32.9 percent nominal wage increase was achieved along with a 4–5 percent increase in labor's relative share of corporate profits. In contrast, the average profit rate of individual firms decreased drastically. At first glance, this decrease might seem to be the result of labor's strategic success. But consumer prices and the unemployment rate also increased, confronting Japanese workers with the typical trade-off between wage increases, on the one hand, and unemployment and inflation, on the other. In addition, in 1974 and 1975, the productivity improvement measurement and firms' investment increase became negative: the real GDP increase dropped to −1.0 and 2.0, respectively. Of course, this economic downturn cannot be attributed only to the labor offensive. The biggest immediate cause was the oil crisis itself. But the critical impact of labor unions on inflation was recognized in late 1974, because by then oil prices had stabilized and the government's strict policy to shrink total demand had lowered demand-pull inflation.[44] Subsequently, the cost-push inflation caused by wage increases came to be considered most problematic by government and business. Based on this understanding, the government and the employ-

[44] *Ekonomisuto*, February 17, 1976.

ers' organization started making efforts to change the existing pattern of wage bargaining.

On the basis of Haruo Shimada and Toshimitsu Shinkawa's excellent case studies of the 1975 Shuntō, I shall briefly review that process.[45] In the midst of the 1974 Shuntō, Nikkeiren organized a task force to investigate the impact of the large wage increase of 1974. This task force was designated to formulate management's strategy for the 1975 Shuntō, and it later played an important role in setting up the agenda of that Shuntō. Immediately after the 1974 Shuntō, Minister of Finance Takeo Fukuda also proposed an investigation of the impact of the large wage hike. In response to his proposal, the Economic Planning Agency analyzed the impact of wage drift, and the LDP's Labor Problem Research Group started a study of a Japanese incomes policy. In May the EPA (Economic Planning Agency) reported that the 32 percent wage increase in 1974 caused the consumer price index to increase by 10 percent. According to the EPA report, a 16–20 percent wage increase in 1975 would be better for the national economy than a 30 percent increase.[46] With this report as a basis, in a meeting of the Accounting Committee of the House of Representatives, Fukuda advocated setting up wage guidelines in a "democratic way."[47]

At this stage, MOL was not convinced by this argument, and in June it reported to the Sanrōkon tripartite meeting that the wage drift in 1974 should be attributed to the tremendous consumer price increases and high profit rate in 1973; moreover, the impacts of a wage increase could be absorbed by individual firms' efforts. This optimistic view grew in part out of the pro-labor tradition in MOL. This dissension within the government might have weakened its ability to set up a new pattern of wage determination and industrial relations. Prime Minister Tanaka and Chief Cabinet Secretary Nikaido eventually persuaded Minister of Labor Hasegawa to exert strong influence over MOL bureaucrats to follow the leadership of Fukuda in August. Once MOL bureaucrats started falling into line with the other government agencies and the cabinet, the government was able to achieve a unified approach to the 1975 Shuntō.[48]

On the labor side, some labor union leaders took significant steps

[45] Shimada, "Wage Determination and Information Sharing" and Toshimitsu Shinkawa, "1975-nen Shuntō to keizaikiki kanri" (The 1975 Shuntō and economic crisis management), in Hideo Otake, ed., *Nihonseiji no sōten* (Issues in Japanese politics) (Tokyo: Sanichi Shobō, 1985).

[46] *Asahi shimbun*, May 23, 1974. Hereafter *Asahi*.

[47] *Asahi*, May 24, 1974. Shimada, "Wage Determination and Information Sharing."

[48] *Asahi*, June 4 and August 8, 1974; Shinkawa, "1975-nen Shuntō."

toward accommodating the new policies. On August 28, Yoshiji Miyata, the Chairman of the Federation of Steel Workers' Unions, declared that, as a result of the economic slowdown, it had become impossible to rely on pre–oil crisis wage-bargaining tactics (namely, a pattern of demanding sizable increments to wage increases attained in the previous year). On September 5, the chairman of Dōmei, Amaike commented in support of Miyata's view that if management would commit itself to reducing inflation and to pursuing some social welfare policies, Dōmei would consider moderating its wage demands in the 1975 Shuntō. In contrast, many Sōhyō unions criticized Miyata and Amaike's approach for its "social contract" characteristics. The split within labor lasted until the 1976 Shuntō.[49]

In contrast, management consolidated its national strategy at the 1975 Shuntō. On September 11, Keidanren and Kankeiren (Keidanren's western district counterpart) announced that they would cooperate with Nikkeiren in setting up a new pattern of industrial relations and would continue to support government's effort to restrain wages and stabilize inflation by tightening money policies.[50]

On November 5, explicit wage increase guidelines were established by Nikkeiren's task force investigating the impact of large wage hikes. Its recommendations that wage increases in 1975 be under 15 percent, and in 1976 and thereafter less than 10 percent, were adopted.[51] On December 9, 1974, the new cabinet headed by Prime Minister Miki was formed. In this cabinet, Fukuda, who was by now vice chairman of the LDP and minister of the EPA, continued to hold a leadership position in economic policy, and Hasegawa continued as Minister of Labor. Therefore, the government's economic policies and its approach to industrial relations remained unchanged; furthermore, Miki's public image as a reformer contributed to success in later negotiations with labor. Anyway, Fukuda supported Nikkeiren's position that a 15 percent wage increase was preferable for the national economy. Consequently, the government and the national centers of employers became strongly committed to a wage increase of no more than 15 percent.

But strong commitment alone would not ensure wage restraint. By November, each national federation of labor had already decided on a wage increase goal. The Shuntō Joint Commission (Sōhyō and Chūritsurōren) called for 30 percent, Dōmei for 27 percent, and the IMF-

---

[49] *Asahi*, August 29, September 6, and September 13, 1974; Shimada, "Wage Determination and Information Sharing."

[50] *Nikkei shimbun*, September 11, 1974. Hereafter *Nikkei*.

[51] *Nikkei*, November 6, 1974.

JC for 25 percent. Their demands were far beyond the government's guidelines, although some leaders of Domei and IMF-JC were privately open to more moderate increases.[52] Interestingly, employers at individual firms expected average increases of 20 percent. (These data were collected in November 1974.) The individual firms were afraid of the possible conflicts with their labor unions that might result from low wage increases and were more cautious about labor relations within their own firms than in the national economy as a whole.

To ensure that guidelines for a wage increase of no more than 15 percent were followed, the government first tried to create favorable economic circumstances. It publicly committed itself to reducing consumer price increases to less than 15 percent by March 1975, just before the Shuntō wage bargaining. In order to achieve that goal, it continued the tight money policy, the effect of which was to reduce total demand. Furthermore, the government decided not to increase the cost of public utilities in the 1974 fiscal year.

Second, high government officials met with labor union leaders to persuade them of the need to restrain wages. Prime Minister Miki met with leaders of four major labor organizations and requested reasonable wage settlements in return for the government's promise to work toward favorable economic circumstances.[53] EPA Minister Fukuda repeatedly attended Sanrōkon and emphasized that the wage increase would have a deleterious impact on the national economy. In addition to the formal meeting with labor leaders (such as Sanrōkon), there were meetings in which individual union leaders of the IMF-JC met separately with business leaders and with ministers of the EPA and MOL.[54] In sum, the government tried hard to reduce inflation and to foster common understanding in order to appeal to labor unions. The private-sector union leaders were convinced of government's sincerity.

Finally, government and business leaders tried to influence individual employers to comply with the 15 percent wage increase. Actually, the government's tight money policy so depressed most industries that they could not offer high wage increases. Furthermore, in the most depressed industries, the wages of supervisors and senior managers were cut in order to prevent sizable layoffs. Faced with the trade-off between employment

---

[52] Some leaders in Dōmei and the IMF-JC did not seem seriously committed to high wage demands and informally aimed at a 17 percent wage increase. These were tactical goals for some private-sector union leaders. Cf. Shinkawa, "1975-nen Shuntō."

[53] *Asahi*, December 26, 1974.

[54] Shimada, "Wage Determination and Information Sharing."

and wage increases, the labor unions as enterprise unions had few options but to opt for continued employment, thus easing management's fears about potential industrial conflicts.

Firms in the then-booming steel industry felt direct pressure from Nikkeiren to restrain wage increases. In a special meeting of the presidents of ten major companies held by Nikkeiren on March 18, presidents from the depressed industries, such as automobile and shipbuilding, which are also big purchasers of steel, demanded that the steel industry restrain wage increases. Consequently, the presidents from the steel industry were forced to promise to hold down wage increases.[55]

On April 9, 1975, wage offers were made by five major steel companies and eight shipbuilding companies. In both industries, the increase accepted was the same across companies and slightly lower than the 15 percent guideline. This pattern was followed by the other industries, keeping the average wage increase in 1975 under 15 percent.[56] In subsequent years, this new pattern was consolidated. Wage demands were no longer too far from the settled wage increase, which suggests that labor also started thinking in terms of the national economy or their companies' overall needs. Leading forces on the side of labor to introduce this epochal change (Dōmei, the IMF-JC, and private company labor unions) have become increasingly powerful within the Japanese labor movement.

Many criticisms of this change, especially from the left, have been made. Critics argue that low or negative real wage increases after 1975 are clear evidence of labor's defeat and that such defeat occurred partly because of the rational economism of Dōmei and the IMF-JC. If we evaluate this change only in terms of wage bargaining, these criticisms might be correct, although it should not be forgotten that the average real wage increase after 1975 has been about 2 percent and labor's relative share has at least remained constant. However, wage bargaining alone does not explain the changes that took place after the oil crisis. Even before the oil crisis, Dōmei and the IMF-JC had begun to participate in the politics of the insider. Since then, they have committed themselves much more eagerly to the politics of the insider. In other words, the new pattern of wage bargaining has coincided with labor's increasing entry into the policymaking process.[57] In order to understand the change in the labor

---

[55] Shinkawa, "1975-nen Shuntō"; *Nikkei*, March 18, 1975.

[56] Shimada, "Wage Determination and Information Sharing."

[57] Peter Lange demonstrates the possibility that wage regulation will not result in a loss to labor but in a clear benefit to it. Peter Lange, "Unions, Workers and Wage Regulation: The

movement, we have to analyze labor's activities in the policymaking process as well as in the narrow wage bargaining process.

Anti-inflation Policy and Tax Reduction

In a formal incomes policy setting, the government would control consumer price increases below some level in exchange for wage restraint. Although in Japan a formal incomes policy was never implemented, there appeared a strong consensus among private-sector unions, management, and the government that lower inflation should be achieved in exchange for unions' restrained wage demands. The basic idea was that this political exchange would provide workers with higher real wage increases, and management and the government with lower inflation. In the middle of the 1975 Shuntō, union leaders seeking wage restraint demanded that the inflation rate be kept low. For instance, Yoshiji Miyata (of the Steel Workers' Union and the IMF-JC) argued in his meeting with Vice Prime Minister Fukuda in March that as unions were trying to be cautious about the impact of wage increases on inflation, the government in return should be responsible in lowering inflation. He also added that wage negotiations were closely linked to the inflation rate.

It is true that unions' demand for lower inflation was not new, but the fact that unions linked their wage demands directly to consumer price increases was new. Faced with economic turmoil caused by the first oil crisis, private-sector unions became more concerned with real wage increases. This concern drove the private-sector unions, which had been depoliticized in the 1960s, into the policymaking process, demanding an anti-inflation policy.

Unions at the same time resorted to another means to maintain and increase the real wage level: tax reduction tied with wage increases. Because the progressive tax system in Japan is very rigid, tax rates must be revised every few years in response to inflation. Although tax reduction itself was not a new phenomenon after the oil crisis, the process of tax reduction changed considerably afterwards. Before the crisis, the amount of reduction was decided mainly among the members of the governing coalition, especially the Ministry of Finance and the LDP in a more or less economically rational way; after the crisis, the issue of tax reduction became more political and attracted more participants, including labor.

Rational Bases of Consent," in Goldthorpe, ed., *Order and Conflict.* Cf. Adam Przeworski and Michael Wallerstein, "The Structure of Class Conflict in Democratic Capitalist Societies," *American Political Science Review* 76 (1982).

On November 2, 1974, four national union federations proposed a ¥20 billion tax reduction in order to maintain the level of real wages against inflation. In 1977, Japan's Chamber of Commerce (consisting of small and medium-sized businesses) and Kankeiren supported labor's demand, although Keidanren did not.[58] On January 12, 1977, union leaders met with Prime Minister Fukuda to demand tax reduction. Despite growing budget deficits, Fukuda had begun to think tax cuts might be necessary.[59] At the same time, the newly formed Council for Policy Promotion Unions (the CPPU; later the Private-Sector Unions Association and the main force behind Rengō), consisting of the big private-enterprise unions from all the national organizations, consulted with high government officials to persuade them of the need for tax cuts. Also, in the Diet, labor persuaded all opposition parties, including members of the conservative New-Liberal Club, to support their demand. On March 9, the LDP added ¥360 billion to the original ¥350 billion reduction. This was the first substantial amendment to the national budget since 1955 and is regarded as a victory for the opposition parties.[60]

Labor's success was in part the result of a close power balance in the Diet at that time. However, if we take into account the business groups' sympathetic attitudes to the tax reduction, we can see that the reduction was not just the result of intraparliamentary politics but also of changes in the relations between labor and business. While the labor unions, especially Dōmei and the IMF-JC, agreed to restrain wages, they began to seek tax cuts in order to maintain real wages. In response to the unions' new position, some business groups started supporting their demands. We can see the prototype of this pattern in 1972 when Nikkeiren and the four national union federations cooperated in order to reduce the tax on retirement bonuses.[61] After the oil crisis, this labor-management cooperation for tax cuts became common, although in the 1980s it became more difficult for labor to achieve actual tax cuts because of the heavy budget deficits: in 1975 and 1976, for example, the issue of inflation-adjustment tax cuts caused conflicts among labor, business, MITI, all opposition parties, and some LDP members, on the one hand, and the Ministry of Finance and other LDP members, on the other; in 1984 the issue of tax reduction for persons taking up posts without their families caused conflicts between the Private-Sector Unions Association, Keidanren, and the Ministry of Labor, on the one hand, and the Ministry of Finance, on the

[58] *Asahi*, November 2 and November 4, 1977.
[59] *Asahi*, December 31, 1976.
[60] *Asahi nenkan* (1978), p. 501; *Asahi*, January 22 and March 10, 1977.
[61] Ministry of Labor, *Shiryō rōdō undōshi* (1972), p. 511.

other. These cases show that labor has become an important actor in the policy process of tax reductions.

The 1980 Shuntō clearly demonstrated unions' strategy to increase the real wage level by combining wage demands with demands for inflation control and tax reduction. Worried about the possibility of high inflation due to the second oil crisis, all union federations decided to demand a modest 8 percent wage increase. The unions' wage demands were based on the government's inflation prediction for the 1980 fiscal year, 6.4 percent. As unions demanded a strong anti-inflation policy, the government publicly committed itself to keeping the inflation rate below 6.4 percent in the 1980 fiscal year. Unions further backed the opposition parties in the budget-making process within the Diet and won some concessions from the government, such as lowering the original plans to increase electricity and gas fees and adding ¥50 billion to the original budget bill for measures to control inflation.[62] The average wage increase was eventually 6.74 percent for that year. This pattern was very similar to the 1975 Shuntō.

But while unions restrained wage increases, consumer prices began increasing steadily after the Shuntō. Unions thus decided that if the inflation rate exceeded the 6.4 percent mark the government had predicted, they would demand tax reductions to compensate for inflation. At the same time, they began demanding that the government make more efforts to keep the inflation rate below 6.4 percent. On November 26, Chairman of Dōmei, Tadanobu Usami, claimed that if the government could not keep inflation below 6.4 percent, unions would have to increase their wage demands for next year, which would result in higher inflation. Prime Minister Suzuki replied that the government appreciated sound industrial relations as a basis for Japanese economic success and would do its best to keep inflation below 6.4 percent.[63] In spite of government efforts, the inflation rate reached around 8 percent at its worst point in 1980. Faced with this situation, union federations set a 10 percent wage increase as their unified goal for the 1981 Shuntō, and won a 7.68 percent increase. But in 1981, the inflation rate shrank rapidly to 3.9 percent in November, which enabled unions to boast of real wage increases.

As unions became more concerned about the real wage, it became necessary for them to participate in policymaking to demand anti-inflation policies and tax reduction. This drove labor into political activities. Wage negotiations became closely linked with the unions' policy

---

[62] Ministry of Labor, *Shiryō rōdō undōshi* (1985), p. 405.
[63] Ibid., pp. 412–13.

demands, but in a different way than was the case during the Sōhyō-led movement in the early 1970s.

Employment Policy—Securing Jobs

Labor became active in policy formation concerning employment security, as exemplified by its role in legislating new policies such as the Revision of the Employment Insurance Law (1974), the Special Measures for Laid-off Workers in the Targeted Depressed Industries (1977), and the Employment Stabilization Funds (1977). Each of these laws, designed to deal with employment problems, favored labor. Let me review the policy formation process of the first law briefly. (The formulation of the second law and the significance of the employment policy development are analyzed in detail in the next chapter.) In 1974 the Ministry of Labor proposed the Employment Insurance Law as a revision of the Unemployment Insurance Law in order to adjust the law to the anticipated recession and the increase in unemployment. Originally, MOL planned to reduce the compensation period for younger workers from ninety days to fifty days in order to shift its fund toward older and more disadvantaged workers and also to introduce incentives to companies that would implement the employee retraining program. Furthermore, MOL intended to decrease the payments for migrant workers from agricultural districts in order to increase payments for full-time workers.[64] At first, Sōhyō opposed this plan, on the ground that it would help private companies rationalize production at the expense of younger, female, and part-time workers. Dōmei, on the other hand, favored the revision, because it included the Employment Adjustment Grants Program, which Dōmei had been demanding. The purpose of this program was to "grant substantial subsidies to private business to prevent them from laying off workers. In particular, it provided money to employers who kept employees on paid furloughs rather than discharging them."[65] As the recession became increasingly serious, Sōhyō also decided to support this revision. On November 20, Sanrōkon achieved unanimous agreement concerning this bill, and eventually, on December 25, 1974, the new Employment Insurance Law passed. This case and the other two cases discussed in the next chapter show that the labor unions participated in the policymaking process to a considerable degree.[66]

[64] *Asahi*, November 26, 1974.

[65] T. J. Pempel, *Policy and Politics in Japan: Creative Conservatism* (Philadelphia: Temple University Press, 1982), p. 105.

[66] *Asahi*, November 22 and November 26, 1974; *Asahi nenkan* (1978), p. 501; and Kume, "Changing Relations among the Government, Labor, and Business."

An Analysis of Intra- and Inter-Class Politics

As discussed above, unions in the first phase began to participate in the policymaking process. The new political opportunity structure for labor, that is, the LDP's opening of political institutions to participation by unions, is an important condition that enabled labor to realize its political demands. This condition continued to exist in the 1970s, however, it could not explain why labor politics changed in the second phase. One possible explanation is that the labor movement was co-opted by management and the conservative government. Selling the crisis and encouraging right-wing union leaders, management and the government might have domesticated the labor movement.[67] This explanation, however, cannot explain why workers continued to gain higher welfare benefits (pension benefits, for example, continuously increased in the 1970s) and how unions achieved employment security policies. The domesticated-labor thesis is too simple.

We should focus instead on another aspect of the political opportunity structure, that is, the formation of labor alliances. In other words, we need to analyze inter- and intra-class relations to understand labor politics in the 1970s. In the first phase, Sōhyō led labor politics, advocating high wage increases and demanding public policies to solve the new problems of welfare. Before the oil crisis, there were few significant differences in concrete policy demands among the four union federations, although their ideological stances differed greatly. Sōhyō's radical goal to totally transform the Japanese political economy can be contrasted with Dōmei's moderate reformist goals.

In the second phase, after the oil crisis, Sōhyō's leadership in the labor movement was taken over by the private manufacturing sector unions, Dōmei, the IMF-JC, and the CPPU. They began pursuing a new set of goals through the labor movement, economically rational wage increases, tax cuts, and public policies to control inflation and secure employment. These unions in the private manufacturing industries were the central forces transforming labor politics. An official in MOL stated retrospectively that, without the cooperation of most union leaders in the private sector, such as those in the steel, auto, electric equipment, textile, shipbuilding, and engineering industries (that is, Dōmei and IMF-JC leaders), it would have been impossible to introduce the new pattern of wage determination.[68] Generally speaking, it was natural that the economic

---

[67] Shinkawa, *Nihongata fukushi no seijikeizaigaku*, p. 201.

[68] Ibid., p. 214. Cf. Yosuke Ashimura, *Daikigyō rōshi no kenka matsuri* (Extravaganza among

recession, increasing unemployment, and inflation compelled union leaders to reconsider their tactics concerning wage increases. But there were vastly different attitudes among the union leaders. Leaders in Dōmei and the IMF-JC were willing to restrain their wage demands, while most leaders of Sōhyō were strongly opposed to such restraint. Did this difference result only from their different ideological standpoints? The answer is partly yes. But what conditions produced those ideological differences? It is notable that such differences exist between industries rather than within each industry. As I mentioned before, the left wing of Sōhyō consists of unions in the public sectors and service industries such as private railroads, while Dōmei and the IMF-JC are composed largely of private-sector unions, especially big manufacturing enterprise unions.

The concerted wage demands of the Shuntō relieved union worries about the domestic competitiveness of their own companies. Nor did they have to worry about the international competitiveness of their companies before the 1970s because wages in Japanese industries at that time were still lower than those in competing foreign companies. However, in the 1970s, Japan's wage level exceeded Britain's, and after 1974, the improvement in productivity that had absorbed the wage drift before 1974 was reduced by half. In other words, wage increases began threatening the competitiveness of Japan's industries in the 1970s.

In that decade two more important changes in the economic system occurred. One was the country's increasing dependence on exports of the Japanese manufacturing industries. Japan's exports of goods and services as a percentage of GDP has been lower than those of most OECD countries (table 5). However, as figure 16 shows, the manufacturing industries in which Dōmei and the IMF-JC are dominant (steel, automobile, electric equipment, and so forth) became heavily dependent on exports. Unions in these industries became more aware of their companies' international competitiveness. The second change was the rise of the newly industrialized economies (NIEs), such as Korea. In the 1970s, textile companies began to face severe competition from companies in the NIEs, which paid their workers lower wages.

Because of these changes, unions in export-oriented manufacturing industries have become conscious of the tradeoff between wage increases and their companies' competitiveness, which ultimately provides a guarantee of secure employment.[69] The oil crisis and its impacts on the

---

management and labor leaders in big business) (Tokyo: Nihon Rōdō Kyōkai, 1982), pp. 149–50.

[69] Cf. George Ross, "What Is Progressive about Unions?" in *Theory and Society* 10 (1981).

Japanese national economy have finally actualized these concerns of union leaders in the export-oriented industries. While these union leaders were willing to restrain wage increases, the union leaders in the public sector and the service sector did not share such concerns. Because public- and service-sector union leaders did not face the issue of international competitiveness in their own wage and employment conditions, they continued to demand much higher wage increases until 1977. Even after the oil crisis, unions in some service industries gained relatively high wage increases.[70]

Why have the export-oriented industry unions become active in the policymaking process? As shown above, Dōmei, the IMF-JC, and the CPPU actively participated in the policymaking process. For example, as the case of employment security policies discussed in the next chapter shows, Sōhyō was interested in attacking the conservative government, while Dōmei, the IMF-JC, and the CPPU were more concerned with the introduction of new employment policies per se.

First, as the export-oriented industry unions could no longer depend on high wage increases as a means to improve or maintain the real wage, they had to turn to national policymaking to demand tax reductions and anti-inflation policies. Furthermore, because these policies did not undermine companies' competitiveness but did contribute to expansion of the domestic market, unions could mobilize employers' cooperation. Success in this field further reinforced the unions' commitment to a political strategy.

Second, the micro-level labor-management accommodation, the productivity coalition, drove the unions in these industries to such policy demands. Once the basis of the coalition—the increasing growth of the company—was in danger, the union became more eager to cooperate with management to protect the company. As described in chapter 4, the economic crisis of the company further consolidated the labor-management collaboration within the company. However, because the firms' capacity to ensure employment was limited, unions had to seek sufficient guarantees for full employment or, at least, compensation for unemployment from the government. Because employees in the public sector are less vulnerable to layoffs resulting from international competition than those in the private sector, Sōhyō was less eager to achieve concrete employment policy gains. Thus, Dōmei, the IMF-JC, and the

[70] After 1977, Sōhyō reduced its wage demands. This was because it wanted to cooperate with the private-sector unions in Shuntō. In 1986, the Joint Commission of the Service-Sector Unions was set up to seek higher wage increases than those for the IMF-JC member unions.

CPPU became more active in this policy process. These private unions can expect employers to support policies that maintain full employment, because they strongly commit themselves to the "life-time" employment system.[71] In addition, they also have their own interest in demanding a government employment policy, because such a policy would help management get union cooperation in reorganizing the production system. Private-sector labor could join with management in demanding policies for employment security.

In addition, the private-sector unions, which were concerned about the company's and/or industry's competitiveness as a member of the enterprise, restrained their wage demands. However, they did want to maintain or increase the real wage level by other means, that is, by tax cuts and an anti-inflation policy. Management was happy to support unions on these issues too, because these policies would help management satisfy workers without increasing labor costs. Here emerged a new inter-class alliance at the national level between management and labor in the private manufacturing sector. Micro-level labor accommodation helped this nationalization of the productivity coalition.

Why then did the once-strong leftist union movement wither away? First, the forces that supported leftist goals lost power. The prospect of setting up a leftist government lost its promise as the centrist parties began gaining power in the mid-1970s. Furthermore, the disillusionment with socialism might have been reinforced by international events, such as the Soviet invasion of Afganistan and the Sino-Vietnam War. Although analysis of changes in the public attitude toward leftist goals is beyond the scope of this study, such goals have undoubtedly lost their appeal. Even unions in Sōhyō, such as the private railroad unions, have lost their militancy.

However, the reason is not just exogenous to the labor movement. The new issues of structurally depressed industries, tax cuts, and the like require unions to participate in political negotiations with the conservative government. However, Sōhyō cannot bargain with the government without receiving criticism from the leftist unions. The next chapter shows that coal miners and some manufacturing industry unions within Sōhyō failed to set up the union's industrial policy because of internal opposition against this policy. Dōmei, the IMF-JC, and the CPPU have not had such leftist unions, and their members are more willing to work toward

---

[71] The problem of whether management will reinvest the profit in the domestic area has not become serious in Japan until recently, partly because big business has been relatively reluctant to invest in foreign countries. But, this issue is becoming serious recently as the strong yen makes Japanese goods expensive in foreign markets.

policy victories within the existing political system. These groups, mainly composed of private-sector unions, developed this strategy relatively easily based on the practice of the participation of labor in the management decision making within the company. They exploited this opportunity in order to reunite unions nationally under private-sector leadership.[72] As a result of considerable policy victories since 1974, these private-sector unions succeeded in strengthening their position in the labor movement. Because the private-sector unions are now achieving their policy goals within the existing political system, it is understandable that leftist political goals have lost their attractiveness and the leftist influence in the labor movement has been weakened.

In sum, a combination of the changing domestic political alignment, especially the LDP's strategy toward labor, and repoliticization of the Japanese labor movement contributed to labor's participation in the policymaking process. Politicized unions found favorable political opportunity structures for them. This first facilitated the success of the social democratic labor movement led by Sōhyō in the early 1970s. However, internationalization of the Japanese economy and the first oil crisis drove the private-sector unions to participate in the policymaking process to maintain their employment and real wage standard, while restraining their nominal wage increases. This new union movement, criticizing Sōhyō's leadership as insensitive to the interests of private-sector workers, began cooperating with management to realize their policy goals. Intra-class politics within labor as well as inter-class politics changed, and this change supported a new labor politics in the 1970s.

[72] Yutaka Tsujinaka, "Kyuchi ni tatsu rōdō no seisakukettei" (Policy decision by labor in crisis), in Minoru Nakano, *Nihongata seisakukettei no henyō* (Transformation of Japanese policymaking) (Tokyo: Tōyō Keizai Shinpōsha, 1986), p. 289.

CHAPTER SIX

Defending Employment Security

Employment security has proven to be one of the most important issues in the study of Japanese political economy. For our purposes, the question, How did labor respond to industrial restructuring in order to protect jobs?, opens the door to some revealing insights. Simply, the answer is that labor realized its policy demands by exploiting new, favorable political opportunity structures. The widely acknowledged commitment of Japanese companies to employment security is not just a phenomenon at the company level, but can be found at the national level, too. Since the end of World War II the Japanese government has developed an extensive employment policy. Many scholars who study labor's influence overlook the inter- and intra-class politics that supported this employment commitment. Those scholars who believe that Japanese enterprise unionism is weak depict the significant achievements of employment policy as a token reward for co-opted unions. This view neglects labor's actual influence. In this chapter, I show that Japanese labor made impressive policy achievements to protect jobs. In the cases of the industrial restructuring of coal mining in the early 1960s and of manufacturing in the early 1970s, unions enjoyed intensive employment policy benefits after their supposed defeat in the former case and the demobilization of their resources in the latter. Here we see one of the paradoxes of Japanese labor politics. How could the allegedly weak labor movement achieve these policy victories? I will explain this paradox by focusing on inter- and intra-class politics instead of the unions' unilateral resource mobilization.

EMPLOYMENT POLICY DEVELOPMENT IN POSTWAR JAPAN

Japan's new constitution, formulated under the auspices of the occupational force, has strong pro-labor clauses. The rights to organize unions and to bargain collectively with employers are, for instance, described as fundamental rights of the people and legislated into the Labor Union Law of 1945. Furthermore, the constitution has an employment right clause that requires government commitment to full employment, although not to its immediate realization. Consequently, in the field of labor policy, major institutional and policy developments were made after World War II. In 1947 the socialist Katayama cabinet established a separate Ministry of Labor out of the labor policy and safety bureaus which were part of the Ministry of Welfare, and it legislated the Public Employment Security, Unemployment Insurance, and Labor Standards Laws. To implement these laws, MOL set up its own network of local branches, the public employment security offices in charge of unemployment insurance and public occupational placement, and 334 labor standards offices to regulate working conditions.

This constitutional right and those policy developments did not promise the automatic achievement of full employment. The economy was destroyed, and it would be a long time before that goal could be reached. In 1946, while the number of fully unemployed people was 1,590,000, there were many under-employed or potentially unemployed persons. There were 965,000 people who worked less than one week per month, while 995,000 people worked in a family enterprise without pay, and 2,448,000 people worked eight to nineteen days a month.[1] Faced with this economic situation and increasing unemployment as a result of postwar demobilization, the government decided to implement public works projects in order to reconstruct the economy and to provide the unemployed with jobs. However, the public works projects did not absorb all the targeted unemployed people. In 1948 only 20 percent of those working in these projects were the people targeted by the public employment security offices. This was partly because the location of public works projects was often far from the urban high unemployment areas. In 1946 almost 70 percent of public works projects were implemented in rural areas, although some urban public works were established.[2] This was because

[1] Ministry of Labor, *Shitsugyō taisaku nenkan* (Annual of unemployment relief public works projects) (Tokyo: Rōdōshō, 1951), p. 3.
[2] Yoshitaka Imaki, "Shittaijigyō hōsei no enkaku" (History of the legal framework of the unemployment relief public works projects), in Sōgō Rōdō Kenkyūsho, ed., *Gendai rōdōhō*

such projects aimed more to reconstruct the infrastructure of the economy than to create public relief jobs, as explained in the Cabinet Decision on Urgent Public Employment Measures of February 15, 1946. This document stated that the public works projects should not degenerate into poor relief but should contribute to reconstruction of the Japanese economy.[3]

Until 1949, however, when the Dodge Line's disinflation policy was implemented, real unemployment was thought to have been covered up to a great degree in the heavily subsidized economy.[4] The members of the policy community predicted that the Dodge Line would change the situation dramatically and inevitably increase the unemployment rate. Administrative reform and rationalization in the private sector in those days resulted in a substantial unemployment increase. The number of fully unemployed people increased from 240,000 in 1948 to 440,000 in 1950.[5]

Predicting increasing unemployment and its subsequent sociopolitical costs, the government, following the cabinet decision of March 4, 1949, quickly submitted the Urgent Relief Measure for the Unemployed to the Diet, which passed it immediately. The basic idea of the cabinet decision was that although the unemployment problem should be solved by developing the national economy, it would be necessary to create public jobs for the unemployed, given the economic difficulties of the times. Consequently, the government started the Unemployment Relief Public Works Program (URPW) as a project separate from the existing public works project. The goal of this new program shifted from economic reconstruction to temporary creation of jobs for the unemployed. The cabinet decision of 1949 described this new category of public works as a relief

---

kōza (Lecture on modern labor law), vol. 13 (Tokyo: Sōgō Rōdō Kenkyūsho, 1984), pp. 253–54.

[3] *Shiryō sengo 20 nen-shi*, vol. 5: *Rōdō*, p. 3.

[4] In 1945 and 1946, it was very difficult to recruit workers in the coal mining and textile industries. This was because, with hyper-inflation and the extent of the underground economy, people just did not have enough motivation to work in the productive sectors. Yasutsuna Nakajima, *Shokugyō antei gyōsei shi* (Administrative history of employment security) (Tokyo: Koyōmondai Kenkyūkai, 1988), pp. 165–68. In 1946 the Ministry of Welfare conducted a survey of 400,000 unemployed workers and found only 23,000 people wanted to be employed. Also in 1946 only 68 percent of job openings were filled. Keizai Antei Honbu, "Keizai jissou houkokusho" (Report on economic reality) (1947), quoted in *Shiryō sengo 20 nen-shi*, vol. 5: *Rōdō*, p. 1.

[5] Sōrifu Tōkeikyoku, "Rōdōryoku chōsa" (Labor power survey), quoted in *Shiryō sengo 20 nen-shi*, vol. 5: *Rōdō*, p. 530.

measure for the unemployed.[6] This program was quickly developed in the following years and created many public jobs.

The number of fully unemployed, however, did not increase as predicted. This was partly because of the economic boom caused by the Korean War of 1950. Under-employment instead became regarded as a more important problem by members of the policy community. In 1953 MOL's Deliberation Committee on the URPW published a report on under-employment. The report defined under-employment as a situation in which workers were employed in unreasonably bad conditions of very low wages and/or short and volatile terms. It thus proposed that MOL should target not only the fully unemployed but also the under-employed, by developing a comprehensive employment policy to make all workers better off.

The issue of under-employment in this context requires an employment policy to be integrated in the economic policy as a whole. There was, however, no consensus on a way to solve the unemployment problem in a broader economic policy in the early 1950s, either among the party politicians or within the policy community. Roughly speaking, we can find three types of solutions, although advocates of all of them agreed upon the necessity of the URPW program. The first was the socialist idea of emphasizing the state's responsibility to ensure employment of everyone. State ownership was often proposed as a means to deal with unemployment. The nationalization of the coal mining industry was a typical example of their policy orientation. The second was an economic liberal idea that emphasized the market mechanism as a fundamental tool for the unemployment problem. These liberals regarded public job creation for the unemployed as a necessary but temporary or exceptional measure. For them, unemployment was to be solved through economic development, which only market competition could realize. Third, there was a democratic idea, which proposed more planning and state intervention. For the advocates of this idea, an integrated industrial policy was necessary in order to develop the Japanese economy with the lowest cost of unemployment.

After the demise of the Katayama and Ashida Socialist-Democrat coalition governments and as the leftists within the Japan Socialist Party gained power, socialist ideas could no longer be realized. Thereafter, significant political discourse on employment policy occurred between liberals and democrats. Parliamentary discussion in the early 1950s demonstrated a typical difference between these two groups on employment policy. Labor

[6] *Nihon rōdō nenkan* (1950), p. 793.

minister Hori of the Yoshida Liberal government stated that although everyone wanted full employment, this should not be the first political goal. He argued that an increase in employment should come after economic development. At that time, the government supported management's rationalizing efforts within private companies. Unions were, on the other hand, militantly opposed to any rationalization and subsequent unemployment. For the liberals, it seemed necessary to have "frictional" (i.e., short-term transitional) unemployment, which the future rationalized economy could absorb. For this purpose, union power to resist rationalization was regarded as the most serious problem by the liberals. In 1954, Labor Minister Kosaka of the Yoshida cabinet bluntly proposed an anti-labor policy. He proclaimed that the government should reduce protection for unions and advocated deregulation of the labor standard policy—although he did propose new legislation to control lay-offs at the same time. His idea was somewhat similar to the neo-liberal ideas of the 1980s because it presumed that if the market functioned freely and the economy developed, the unemployment problem (not unemployment per se) would eventually disappear.

The democrats criticized this liberal idea as laissez-faire capitalism insensitive to the economic problems of workers as well as small and medium-sized companies. For instance, Shuji Kawasaki of the Democratic Party, criticizing the labor policy of the Yoshida cabinet, advocated integration of the full employment goal into the economic development plan.[7] It is noticeable that politicians in the democratic camp, criticizing Yoshida's liberal government, were eager to make full employment a goal of industrial policy.[8]

This democratic idea was introduced into the Hatoyama cabinet's labor policy, especially under labor minister Kuraishi, after the merger of the Liberal and Democratic Parties in 1955. In the Diet, Kuraishi proposed that labor policy should be integrated in a broader economic policy.[9] Against the economic-growth-comes-first idea, he argued that economic development and employment increases should be pursued simultaneously in the economic development plan. Then he flatly denied the necessity of reducing protection of workers by reforming the Labor Standards Law to increase employment. For the first time, the labor minister

---

[7] *Nihon rōdō nenkan* (1952), pp. 638–39.

[8] Shinsuke Kishi and Tanzan Ishibashi are among those politicians who advocated full employment and industrial policy against Yoshida's laissez-faire capitalism. Kume, "Party Politics and Industrial Policy." See also Shinsuke Kishi, *Kishi Shinsuke kaikoroku* (The autobiography of Kishi Shinsuke) (Tokyo: Kōseido, 1983).

[9] *Nihon rōdō nenkan* (1956), p. 640.

proposed government intervention to make the labor market function efficiently and absorb as many unemployed people as possible. This was a start toward a new market-oriented employment policy.

In the next year, Kuraishi proposed a more comprehensive policy package consisting of three proposals to solve the unemployment problem. First, he urged support of the productivity increase movement of the Japan Productivity Center. Second, he proposed new legislation—the Basic Employment Law, the objective of which was to require the government to consider maximizing employment in its formulation of every economic policy.[10] Third, he wanted a new Minimum Wage Law. The common goal of these three policies was to develop the economy with maximum employment and better working conditions. The logic behind them was straight forward. Increasing productivity through rationalization might result in a marginal increase in unemployment, at which point the government should intervene and introduce policies to facilitate economic development, which would in turn provide better jobs in the prospering industries to the unemployed workers. In this policy package, MOL tried to transform its employment policy into a market-oriented policy. It emphasized expansion of the economy as a major mechanism to achieve maximum employment rather than direct government creation of jobs for the unemployed.

This market-oriented employment policy was further consolidated by labor minister Ishida in the Ikeda cabinet. In July 1960, when he was reappointed as minister of labor, Ishida said, "The labor policy hereafter will focus more on the labor economy such as wages and employment than on policy toward labor unions."[11] At that time MOL recognized three problems as main challenges to the Japanese labor economy: (1) an increase in young job seekers, (2) difficulty in finding jobs for middle-aged people, in spite of the existing labor shortage of skilled workers, and (3) severe unemployment lingering in some regions. Therefore MOL advocated an active labor market policy (originally called the developmental employment policy). It consisted of two specific policy goals: to increase labor mobility across the nation to solve regional unemployment, and to help workers acquire necessary skills in the prospering manufacturing industries.

This new employment policy finally resulted in legislation of the Employment Measure Law in 1966. This new law prescribed that the government should pursue the goal of full employment in formulating and

---

[10] This was finally legislated as the Employment Measure Law in 1966, as described below.
[11] *Nihon rōdō nenkan* (1961), p. 369.

implementing public policies. This was not the first legislation to state a commitment to full employment; such a commitment was also made in the Law to Establish the Deliberation Committee on Employment in 1957. However, the 1966 law was very important in employment policy development, in that it was the basic law requiring the government to coordinate its policies to maintain full employment. It required the government to set up the Basic Plan to Facilitate Employment at the cabinet level, in which economic and industrial policies could be coordinated with employment policies, such as the occupational placement service and skill formation measures.

Among other programs, the Subsidies for the Change of Jobs Program, which the Employment Measure Law introduced, shows the characteristic nature of active labor market policy. This program was targeted at two categories of persons: those who could not find jobs easily, such as the handicapped and the elderly, and those who had lost their jobs in the restructuring industries targeted by the government. Those people, after receiving their unemployment insurance compensation, could now receive additional allowances for living, training, and job search trips. Moreover, this program provided employers of the targeted people with subsidies to hire and train them. The basic idea of this program was that the government would try to increase the value of unemployed people in the labor market and to help them to find appropriate jobs. This so-called active labor market policy differs from the policy mix of public job creation and unemployment insurance. The latter presumes a clear demarcation between market and government, with the government playing the role of an emergency shelter outside the labor market. The former seeks active government intervention in the functioning of the market. It requires the employment policy to be a part of economic policy. Here we can find changes in the nature of the employment policy from state-centered to market-oriented. These two policies also differ on another important point. The latter explicitly facilitates labor mobility across the nation, while the former tends to be indifferent to such a move. The URPW legislation was enacted to reduce serious unemployment in some regions by creating jobs in those areas rather than forcing the unemployed move to a different area. A market-oriented active employment policy also creates a nation-wide labor market.

The high economic growth period of the 1960s and the early 1970s enabled Japan to have a full employment economy. This was good news for MOL. The bad news was that business leaders and politicians now began talking about the end of the employment policy and of MOL as an organization. The special budget for labor insurance (including unemployment insurance and labor accident insurance) now produced a huge surplus. MOL could not but start seeking a new *raison d'etre*, and it eventually formulated a new policy goal, increasing workers' welfare and preempting unemployment. As described in chapter 5, private-sector unions supported this new policy development and the new policy idea resulted in the Employment Insurance Law in 1974.

This law set up three programs besides unemployment insurance, using the insurance account: the Employment Improvement Program, the Developing Worker's Ability Program, and the Employment Welfare Program. The former two arose out of the active labor market policy of the Employment Measure Law of 1966 as part of its emphasis on training and labor mobility. The Employment Insurance Law is important for two reasons. First, it emphasizes preventing unemployment.[12] The programs in this law introduced many subsidies for employers to prevent unemployment, such as subsidies for extending the retirement age, for employing workers from targeted declining industries, and for training employees. Since then, similar but more intensive programs for this purpose, such as the Employment Stability Fund, were developed.[13] These policies played a positive role in helping many industries to restructure production and maintain employment. What is more important is that this law further incorporated the employment policy in an overall economic agenda. Industrial policy and employment policy were closely coordinated in this new agenda.

Second, this law established a stable fund for implementing the employment policy. It transformed the special account for labor insurance, which had been creating a huge surplus, into an employment insurance special account and enabled MOL to use this account. This account is independent of the general account, because it is based on contributions from labor and management as well as transfers from the general budget.

Comparatively speaking, Japan's employment policy development is closer to that of Sweden's than the United States'.[14] We find very similar employment policy development in Japan and Sweden. This is surprising, given the difference in these two regimes: one is social democratic and the

---

[12] This is why this law is called the Employment, not Unemployment, Insurance Law.

[13] See Akira Takanashi, *Aratana koyōeisaku no tenkai* (Development of a new employment policy) (Tokyo: Rōmu Gyōsei Kenkyūsho, 1989).

[14] Margaret Weir, *Politics and Jobs: The Boundaries of Employment Policy in the United States* (Princeton: Princeton University Press, 1992). Cf. Gary Mucciaroni, *The Political Failure of Employment Policy, 1945–1982* (Pittsburgh: University of Pittsburgh Press, 1992). Helen Ginsburg, *Full Employment and Public Policy: The United States and Sweden* (Lexington: Lexington Books, 1983); Heclo and Madsen, *Policy and Politics in Sweden*. Kume, "Institutionalizing the Active Labor Market Policy."

other is conservative. In Sweden, the strong centralized labor union, LO, and the hegemonic Social Democratic Party played an important role in maintaining the full employment goal, while Japan's decentralized enterprise unions and "life-time" employment practices contributed to maintenance of the goal of full employment. Japanese enterprise unions benefited from a well-developed employment policy. The question here is how the supposedly weak enterprise unions could attain this.

I will analyze two employment security movements in the 1960s and 1970s. The first is the coal miners' movement to protect their jobs, faced with the decline of the coal mining industry. Coal mining was the first industry to face industrial restructuring in postwar Japan. The second case is the employment protection movement after the first oil crisis, led mainly by unions in private manufacturing industries. We will find similarities and differences between these two cases. In both cases, unions achieved some significant policy benefits out of their movements. But unions achieved their benefits with more ease in the second case than in the first. These outcomes can be explained by focusing on the emergence of new inter- and intra-class politics.

THE CASE OF THE COAL-MINING INDUSTRY

Labor-Management Accommodation in the Coal Industry until 1960

The occupation force quickly realized that shortages of coal and steel in the immediate postwar period were the main causes of a downward spiral of production shortfalls. Therefore, the GHQ ordered maximum coal production as early as September 1945, and the cabinet also adopted new emergency measures for coal production.[15] In November, the government decided to increase state-controlled coal prices in order to increase coal miners' wages, expecting that labor shortages in the coal industry would be solved by such increases. In June 1946, the government decided to give priority to miners in food rationing and to support housing construction for them. In 1946 priority production (*keisha seisan*) was also begun in order to increase coal and steel output. The Reconstruction Finance Bank was established in 1947 to better finance these industries, and the Coal Distribution Public Corporation (Haitan Kodan) was set up in 1947 to purchase, sell, and distribute coal under the direction of the Economic Stabilization Board.

In 1948, the state took over control of the coal mines under the first

[15] Samuels, *Business of the Japanese State*, p. 91.

socialist cabinet of Katayama, although state control was weakened by many compromises during the legislative process. The small and medium-sized companies did not want state control, for fear that their inefficient mines would be scrapped to set up rationally planned coal production. In due course, they succeeded in transforming the law into a state support system for the coal industry rather than a system of state ownership.

In 1946, after a number of union movements at the local level, two national federations of coal miners' unions were set up. One was the leftist Zentan, consisting of workers in large mines. The other was the reformist Nichikō, consisting mainly of small and medium-sized unions. Originally both were industrial unions rather than groups of enterprise unions. But in 1947 these two national organizations and the other independent coal miners' unions established a single national organization, Tankyō, in order to achieve the principle of equal pay for equal work across the coal industry.[16] This move was also supported by the coal companies and the government, because coal prices were controlled nationally and it was easy for management to negotiate wages with labor at the national level. Militant union movements, especially wage strikes, enabled coal miners to earn higher wages than other workers. However, the relations between labor and management in the coal industry were not as antagonistic as is often believed. Rather, in the 1940s labor and management were on good terms.

During reconstruction, coal sold itself as a result of widespread short-ages. Thus the only concern for management in the coal industry was how to produce as much coal as possible. The companies preferred stable production to low-cost or low-wage production which might result in strikes that would disturb stability. The coal companies solved a high labor cost problem by selling coal at a higher price and transferring their labor costs to the coal users. Coal users would in turn receive government grants—price differential subsidies—to buy coal. Thus, government grants subsidized high labor costs. In addition, the coal industry acquired special government financing from the Reconstruction Finance (*fukkin yūshi*) program. Generally speaking, these were the bases of the labor-management coalition in the early postwar coal industry. Even though the revolutionary demands to control production advocated by radical union members caused severe conflicts, such demands were easily moderated because of the nature of the system.[17]

[16] Yoshihisa Tokida, "Tanrō" (Coal Miners Union), in Saburo Okazaki, ed., *Nihon no sangyōbetsu kumiai* (Industrial unions in Japan) (Tokyo: Sōgō Rōdō Kenkyūsho, 1977) .

[17] Mitsui Kōzan Kabushiki Kaisha, ed., *Shiryō Miike sōgi* (Documents of the Miike strike) (Tokyo: Nihon Keieisha Renmei, 1963), pp. 8, 30.

This cooperative system was institutionalized in several organizational forms. Each company set up a management council, later called a "production council," consisting of representatives from the union and management. In addition, parallel organizations arose at the national level. In February 1947, labor and management set up a voluntary cooperative organization to increase coal production, the National Council for Reconstructuring Coal Production. This council also issued various demands concerning the well-being of miners.[18] During this period, management and labor in the coal industry enjoyed enormous economic benefits, owing to government support.

However, this situation changed in 1949, when GHQ forced the Japanese government to adopt a series of strong anti-inflationary policies called the Dodge Line. Reconstruction Finance was abolished. State control of the coal industry was eliminated. This was an effort to bring the market mechanism into the coal industry. The ensuing liberalization of the coal industry undermined the cooperative alignment of labor, management, and the government by reducing state support and by stirring conflict between labor and management.

Without government grants, the coal-using industries, such as steel, had to pay higher costs, which made them complain about coal prices. The coal companies started rationalizing production in response to this new situation. However, conflict arose between the small and medium-sized companies and the large ones, because severe competition soon concentrated coal production in the hands of the larger companies. Within only one year of liberalization, the market share of the smaller companies decreased from 29 percent to 26 percent.[19] The companies in March 1951 formed different coal mining associations, the Nihon Sekitan Kōgyō Rengōkai for smaller companies and the Nihon Sekitan Kyōkai for the larger ones. Large companies were eager to rationalize their production in a capital-intensive way (for instance, with the introduction of Kappe mining technology), while the small, labor-intensive mines were not able to. Instead, they tried to decrease labor costs by work-force reductions and wage cuts. As a result, in 1949, the unions in the small mining companies started organizing strong strikes against massive dismissals. However, the main goal for Tankyō's successor, Tanrō, in 1949–50 was not to organize anti-dismissal strikes, but to demand wage increases. Tanrō's major concern reflected the interests of miners in large coal companies.

[18] Nihon Tankō Rōdōkumiai, *Tanrō 10 nen-shi* (Ten years of the coal miners union) (Tokyo: Rōdō Junpōsha, 1963), p. 118.
[19] *Nihon rōdō nenkan* (1951), p. 238.

This situation exemplified the split in the coal industry. The coal union movement changed substantially after liberalization. During the reconstruction era, coal miners' unions tried to introduce the principle of equal pay for equal work. This movement was mainly led by the national center of coal unions. But thereafter, unions began to pursue their individual interests within the company system, rather than on an industry-wide basis. The labor movement became decentralized, and enterprise unions became the main actors in labor disputes. In other words, unions in the large companies, which dominated Tanrō, gave up the concept of equal pay for equal work, and sought high wages from their own companies. Conflict grew between the large and small enterprise unions. And in 1949, Nichikō, consisting mainly of unions in small companies, left Tanrō. After this, the coal miners' movement was mainly led by the unions at large companies.

In the 1950 spring wage negotiation, the first one after liberalization, Tanrō demanded an increase of ¥730 per day per miner in the standard wage without increasing standard job obligations. However, owing to the economic downturn, management offered only ¥363 coupled with new standard job obligations. Management's offer would actually have reduced the pay per output ratio. After a series of strikes, the unions failed to realize their demands; in several companies, they won no increase in the standard wage. Management had committed itself to a rationalizing effort to deal with the economic downturn and a more competitive market. This might seem to imply that the basically cooperative alignment among labor, management, and the government was dissolving in a new environment. But this negotiation did not set a new pattern because the economic boom caused by the Korean War brought enormous benefits to the coal industry. In the fall wage negotiation of 1951, the unions in eight big coal companies, after two forty-eight hour-strikes, gained a wage increase of 20 percent.

Labor unions also succeeded in achieving a substantial wage increase after a sixty-three-day strike (Densan-Tanrō Sogi) in 1952. The government finally had to mediate the dispute. It directed management to increase wages by 7 percent without increasing standard job obligations and to pay a special bonus. This sixty-three-day strike is often characterized as a defeat for the union. It is true that union demands were not fully met and that the struggle was stopped by government order. For Sōhyō, which tried to use this strike as a means to transform the Japanese political economy, this was an evident defeat. But it is also true that the workers enjoyed a substantial wage increase. Therefore, I believe that the basic alignment among labor, management, and the government continued.

During this time, large companies began to rationalize production, and in due course they planned to reduce the work force in order to improve production efficiency. In August 1953, Mitsui Mining Company dismissed 3,464 workers as a part of a rationalization plan. Unions at Mitsui immediately organized in strong opposition and mobilized miners' wives and families to keep their solidarity. Eventually, after 113 days, the union succeeded in forcing management to cancel the dismissal of 1,815 workers.

Significantly, large coal companies did not pursue a vigorous program of job reduction and rationalization, in contrast to other firms such as Nissan Motors, where company management strongly committed itself to rationalizing its production and drastically strengthened its managerial power following a strike in 1953.[20] This difference is attributable to the strength of the coal miners' union, and also to the spoiled capitalist spirit of coal company management. As long as costs could be transferred to someone else, coal management did not mind compromising with labor and destroying its own rationalization plans. This tendency can also be found in the relation between coal firms and the government. In 1955, in response to the recession in the coal industry after the end of the Korean War, the Coal Mining Rationalization Special Measures Law was passed. The Coal Mining Rationalizing Public Corporation was set up to purchase a number of inefficient mines and to restrict the opening of new ones. However, the second postwar boom and the Suez crisis of 1956 stimulated domestic coal demand. Coal companies, faced with this opportunity, chose not to use profits to streamline production. Instead, they expanded production to take advantage of government subsidies and to reap handsome short-term profits.[21] Labor unions still tried to achieve high wage increases, while opposing management's rationalization efforts. Coal companies still tried to pass labor costs on to their customers and the government. They also succeeded in having the government maintain import restrictions on foreign fuel and in winning reductions on interest payments for government loans. They definitely lacked a long-term strategy, probably because market competition among coal mining companies was not high. Thus the basic alignment among labor, management, and government persisted into the mid-1950s.

Coal, however, began to lose its competitive edge against oil in the late 1950s. In 1957 many people began to realize that the decline of the coal industry was inevitable. The industry was faced with a continuous business

[20] Okochi and Matsuo, *Nihon rōdō kumiai monogatari*, vol. 2, pp. 136–39.
[21] Samuels, *Business of the Japanese State*, pp. 111–12.

downturn, while other industries were booming. A shift in energy usage was taking place. Eventually, coal company management started wholeheartedly rationalizaing its practices.

In 1959 the government advised that coal companies should cut back their operation by 20 percent of 1957's output, following the procedure stipulated in the Coal Mining Rationalization Special Measures Law. Each company took this advice and started efforts to streamline operations. In its meeting with the unions, on September 18, 1959, the Coal Association (Nihon Sekitan Kyōkai) stated that "As the coal industry crisis was caused by the energy revolution, we must reduce our work force by 100,000 workers in order to adjust to this crisis and rationalize our production by 1963."[22] Earlier that year, on February 27, cabinet members had agreed on measures to deal with the unemployment caused by rationalization in the coal-mining industry. It proclaimed that while unemployment should be avoided as much as possible by job transfers within a given company, the government should implement both job placement services to facilitate labor mobility and urgent relief public works. In October, following this cabinet agreement, the government submitted a bill which would establish the Association to Help Laid-Off Coal Miners and place it in charge of these employment policies for miners.[23] This bill passed the Diet in March 1960.

Labor criticized this government policy from the beginning. Tanrō responded to the situation by organizing an anti-rationalization movement. At its twentyth regular conference in July 1958, it decided that its member unions should flatly reject any plans to rationalize production and cut back operations, and should organize struggles to turn down those plans immediately after company management proposed them. In cooperation with Sōhyō in October 1959, it further established a plan to deal with the coal industry crisis. This plan called for organizing a struggle to solve this crisis, to develop the coal industry, and to protect employment in it.[24]

They had four concrete demands, although not entirely consistent. (1) The rationalization plan at the expense of coal miners should be abandoned, and lay-offs should be banned. Government relief measures targeted only at coal miners should not be introduced; rather all laid-off miners should receive unemployment allowances until they can find new jobs. (2) The government should invest in the coal-mining industry to

---

[22] Mitsui Kōzan Kabushiki Kaisha, *Shiryō Miike sōgi*, p. 398.
[23] Ministry of Labor, *Shiryō rōdō undōshi* (1959), pp. 1316–17.
[24] Sōhyō, *Gekkan Sōhyō*, Special Issue (October 1959).

find new coal mines deeper underground. (3) The government should increase the tax on oil to promote consumption of coal. And (4) a comprehensive economic plan to help regions that would suffer from the rationalization and subsequent operations cut-backs should be introduced by the local governments as well as the national government.[25]

Management, on the other hand, supported the government policy. Criticizing the unions' demands, Keidanren's task force on fuel issues published its opinion on the measures for the coal industry on December 8, 1959. It argued that the government should not help the coal industry at the expense of other industries nor distort the fuel market by protecting coal, but rather it should help the coal industry become more competitive by enabling it to reduce the price of coal. Nikkeiren also published its proposal on "The Future of the Coal Industry and Measures for Laid-Off Miners." It proposed the following actions: (1) As miners would be laid off massively due to the restructuring of the coal industry, the existing temporary relief public job program was not adequate. The government should introduce a new policy to transfer redundant miners to new job openings in other industries by retraining them. (2) Business should support an urgent and adequate social welfare policy for the laid-off miners in small and medium-sized companies. (3) The government should introduce a comprehensive employment policy for laid-off miners by establishing a headquarters in charge of measures to help them.[26]

Here we see a big difference in attitudes toward the coal crisis between labor and management. Although it demanded some measures to help the laid-off miners, Tanrō's main goal was to maintain employment for all miners within the coal industry even at the expense of other industries. On the other hand, management demanded that its crisis be solved in a wider national economic framework, that is, rationalization of the coal industry and reallocation of redundant workers from coal to other growth industries. The government was on management's side.

The coal companies simultaneously announced their rationalization plans in April 1959, following the government's advice based on the Coal Mining Rationalization Special Measures Law. They began asking employees to take voluntary retirement. Unions resisted these rationalization efforts, but the disputes were mainly settled by July 1959, as company management offered better compensation for early retirees. The Mitsui Mining Company was not among them, however. In 1959 the Mitsui

[25] Ministry of Labor, *Shiryō rōdō undōshi* (1959), p. 526.
[26] Ibid., p. 500.

Mining Company announced the voluntary retirement of 5,000 workers, but the union immediately refused to cooperate in choosing volunteers for early retirement. Management dismissed 1,277 workers, including 300 union activists. In January 1960, the union escalated its struggle, and went on strike for an indefinite period. This was the beginning of the fierce ten-month struggle known as the Miike Strike.[27] Nikkeiren mobilized business nationwide, while Sōhyō mobilized labor support. Financially exhausted and politically defeated, in the end the union accepted the original layoff plan. The coal miners' unions lost their biggest postwar struggle against management. Many scholars regard this defeat as epoch-making in Japanese postwar labor history, arguing that labor began losing its militancy after this defeat and was domesticated.[28] The defeated coal miners, however, enjoyed extensive relief measures from the government. Why and how was it possible for defeated labor to have those relief measures? The answer to this question leads us to a new understanding of labor politics in Japan.

Policy Transformation Struggle

In the wake of this loss, and faced with oil import liberalization in 1963, Tanrō drastically changed its strategy and began to lobby the LDP government to introduce an industrial policy for coal mining. This tactic was called the Policy Transformation Movement. At this point the unions realized it was necessary to restore their cooperative association with management in order to lobby the government effectively. Union leaders did not mind naming this new strategy "*avec* struggle," in other words, a joint struggle with management against government. They demanded policies to protect the domestic coal industry against foreign competitors, such as a heavy tariff on oil imports, price supports, and public finance to rationalize industry. The unions actively lobbied the government and the LDP, in cooperation with management, by sending many miners to Tokyo to put pressure on the government. While some policy demands were met

[27] Okochi and Matsuo, *Nihon rōdō kumiai monogatari*, vol. 2, pp. 397–98. There are many studies on the Miike Strike. For a description in English, see B. Martin, "Japanese Mining Labor: The Miike Strike," *Far Eastern Survey* 30-2 (1961). A recollection from the union point of view is Miike Tankō Rōdōkumiai, *Miike 20 nen* (Twenty years of Miike) (Tokyo: Rōdō Junpōsha, 1967) and one from management is Miike Kōzan Kabushiki Kaisha, *Shiryō Miike sōgi*. Ministry of Labor, *Shiryō rōdō undōshi* (1959 and 1960) is also a useful source on the Miike strike. Kazuo Koike, "Miike," in Tsuneo Iida et al., eds., *Gendai Nihon keizaishi* (History of the modern Japanese economy) (Tokyo: Chikuma Shobō, 1976) is a well-balanced description of the Miike strike.

[28] E.g., Kawanishi, *Kigyōbetsu kumiai no riron*, p. 131.

by the government, the unions' main demand, to secure employment within the coal industry, was not achieved.

The coal industry seemed to be dying, and no one could stop it. However, several policies were introduced to alleviate unemployment in the coal industry. The most important was the active labor market policy, which helped redundant miners to find new jobs in the growing national economy. The government set up a new system to facilitate labor mobility and to decrease unemployment with retraining programs, an active job placement service, and subsidies for employers of some categories of unemployed workers (including miners). In sum, the coal industry almost died, but the union's final efforts cushioned the worst consequences for their members and left an active labor market "policy legacy."

On October 12, 1960, after the defeat in the Miike Strike, Tanrō adopted new tactics to protect its members' interests in its twenty-eighth extraordinary convention, arguing that it was impossible to protect its members' jobs and rights by totally rejecting any rationalization plan and subsequent layoffs. Tanrō decided it would try to prevent or alleviate negative impacts on miners as much as possible, while accepting the fact of rationalization in general. Instead of resisting every rationalization effort, Tanrō began making new demands: an extension of the term length of unemployment insurance, an increase in the allowance itself and other welfare benefits, the establishment of a Job Placement Public Corporation, the provision of temporary housing for those laid off, and a minimum wage for coal miners. Tanrō in sum became more eco-nomically rational in its demands, as it realized that it could not prevent rationalization.[29]

Based on this new strategy, in its meeting with the prime minister and ministers of MITI and MOL on November 11, 1960, Tanrō demanded the establishment of a new tripartite council on coal industry rationalization, arguing that the Coal Mining Rationalization Special Measures Law was an instrument helpful for monopoly capitalists at the expense of labor and that it did not have any mechanism to represent workers' interests. In sum, Tanrō demanded participation in the formulation and implementa-tion of industrial policy for the coal industry. The government in the beginning opposed this new demand. The reply from the minister of MITI to Tanrō stated three points: First, Rationalization based on the Coal Mining Rationalization Special Measures Law was necessary. second, the government would try to expand the demand for coal, but the protection of coal against other fuel was not desirable from the perspective of the

---

[29] Ministry of Labor, *Shiryō rōdō undōshi* (1960), pp. 576–77.

national economy. And third, cooperation between labor and management was necessary in order to implement a rationalization plan, and thus the government would develop an employment policy for redundant coal miners in cooperation with MOL. MITI put priority on rationalization rather than the employment security of miners.[30]

Tanrō sought an ally in management to demand that the government help coal industry rationalization by alleviating its restructuring cost, especially unemployment. In its meeting with the Coal Association on December 22, 1960, Tanrō declared that it would consult with management on issues of labor-management relations, making a fresh start. The next day, management and labor together met with the government and demanded special measures for redundant miners separate from the existing URPW program.[31] The government decision to liberalize oil imports in October 1962, as a part of a 90 percent trade liberalization plan negotiated with the IMF, further drove labor and management to demand government measures to help the coal industry. In a meeting of Tanrō and management on September 3, 1961, management announced that it was necessary to accelerate their rationalization process, with which labor concurred, and labor demanded extensive measures for possible unemployment. They both agreed that as measures to take care of unemployed workers were beyond the ability of individual firms, they would start a coordinated effort to demand government aid.[32] The Coal Association formulated its basic proposal for an energy policy, and demanded that the government financially support the rationalizing efforts, subsidize the transportation cost of coal, and build several coal-fired electric power plants, all of which would increase demand for coal. Because the coal industry crisis was the result of a national energy policy change, the Coal Association also demanded that government be responsible for implementation of a special policy package for unemployed miners, consisting of a job placement service, retraining, housing aid, and an income guarantee.[33] Tanrō, on the other hand, set up the Supreme Council on the Coal Policy Transformation with Sōhyō and the Socialist Party on September 25, but it also sought to consolidate labor across ideological lines. It asked for support from three other national union federations and set up a unified coal miners' movement with Zentankō and Tanshokukyo (a white-collar union in the coal industry). At the same time, Tanrō in September started mobilizing its members and led rallies in Tokyo to put

[30] Ibid., pp. 578–79.
[31] Ibid., p. 580.
[32] Asahi, September 4, 1961.
[33] Asahi, October 10, 1961.

pressure on the government; Tanrō continued to organize massive rallies when it had consultations with the government.[34]

In the beginning, these labor and management demands were rejected by members of the governing LDP because coal management was too eager to ask the government for aid when its business was in difficulty and also because Tanrō as well as Sōhyō and the JSP were allied in radical opposition to the LDP. However, faced with the strong demands of the coal industry, the government gradually responded. Some LDP politicians began arguing that Japan should maintain its coal industry as a valuable domestic energy source from the perspective of national security. In the cabinet meeting on September 29, the minister of MITI stated that as the Diet formed the Special Committee on Coal Industry in response to labor and management demands, the government should now formulate an integrated policy for the coal industry. On October 12, the Cabinet Meeting of the Related Ministers on the Coal Industry decided that the government would soon formulate a policy to secure the employment of the redundant miners, subsidies for coal companies, and some protective measures for the small and medium-sized companies. In the meantime, MITI and MOL were working to find an effective policy to smoothly transfer redundant miners to modern industries. Studying the experience in West Germany's coal industry, in which laid-off coal miners received differential earnings in new jobs from the government, MITI and MOL formulated the Employment Promotion Subsidies. The idea was that using revenues from the tariff on oil, the government would subsidize companies that employed the ex-miners, providing some portion of wages and a housing allowance for them. Furthermore, MOL started negotiations with MOF for increases in unemployment and training allowances, an extension of their terms of benefits, and some financial aid for ex-miners on new jobs leaving their families in mining areas. These new policies were strongly supported by the top leaders within the government and the LDP. Prime minister Hayato Ikeda said that he personally felt a deep responsibility for this difficulty in the coal industry, of which he as a minister of MITI had been in charge. Kakuei Tanaka, chairman of the LDP's Policy Affairs Research Council, also supported these new policies, saying that he would treat the coal industry problem as an important issue in the new policy set of the governing party.[35]

The government proposal consisted of three policies at this point. First

[34] Ministry of Labor, *Shiryō rōdō undōshi* (1961), p. 495.
[35] *Asahi*, September 30, October 7, 15, and 20, 1961; *Mainichi Shimbun*, October 12, 1961; and Ministry of Labor, *Shiryō rōdō undōshi* (1961), pp. 544–45.

was the rationalization policy, which would help coal companies to reduce the unit cost of coal. Second was the protective policy for the coal industry, including a tariff on oil and a government effort to increase the demand for coal. Third was an employment security policy, such as the Employment Promotion Subsidy. The government began seeking the employment security policy not to secure employment of redundant miners in the coal industry, but to find new jobs for them in growing industries.[36] In sum, the government tried to formulate a market-oriented employment policy rather than any form of direct job creation by the government. On October 26, 1961, the government submitted a bill to revise the Coal Mining Rationalization Special Measures Law as well as some related bills.

Tanrō originally wanted the redundant miners to be employed in the coal industry, most preferably by nationalizing the industry. It wanted priority to be put on employment security rather than rationalization, and it felt uneasy about the market-oriented employment policy, because it was dependent on the functioning of the labor market and might not guarantee jobs for laid-off miners. Therefore, after the government submitted the bill to revise the Coal Mining Rationalization Special Measures Law to the Diet, Tanrō made every effort to assure greater government commitment to provide the laid-off miners with stable employment. One of Tanrō's tactical goals was to pass a resolution attached to those bills that would declare that the employment goal should be prioritized. It set meetings with officials in the Ministries of Finance, International Trade and Industry, Labor, and Welfare, and with the cabinet secretary general to keep pressure on them. Furthermore, it mobilized its union members in its meeting with MITI officials, and it also threatened the government that if the resolution did not pass, it would organize a massive demonstration in Hakone, where the U.S.-Japan Conference on the Economic Affairs was to be held.[37] On October 31, those bills, together with the union-demanded resolution, passed the Diet.

Tanrō, on January 29, 1962, decided to continue pressuring the government to assure more job security for working miners and more generous policies for laid-off miners. In February, Tanrō and Sōhyō agreed that Tanrō would appeal for a strike for an indefinite term and would mobilize 100,000 miners for a demonstration in Tokyo in March. The Socialist Party in coordination with Tanrō and Sōhyō proposed the bill to regulate lay-offs in the coal industry on March 11.[38]

[36] *Asahi,* October 24, 1961.
[37] Ministry of Labor, *Shiryō rōdō undōshi* (1961), pp. 510–11, 552–56.
[38] Ministry of Labor, *Shiryō rōdō undōshi* (1962), pp. 414–18, 557–59.

These unions' tactics worked fairly well because MITI was afraid that a strike in the coal industry at this time would give coal consuming industries legitimate reasons to ignore the government rationalization plan and to shift their source of energy quickly to oil. MITI wanted to implement the Coal Mining Rationalization Special Measures Law as soon as possible, while Tanrō wanted to delay its implementation until a more intensive employment policy was introduced. This helped Tanrō to demand more employment measures from the government. Just before Tanrō went on strike for an indefinite period, the government and the JSP reached an agreement that Tanrō would cancel the strike in exchange for two promises from Prime Minister Ikeda. First, the government would form a neutral task force to investigate coal industry rationalization and let it recommend a new policy. Second, until the recommendation was made, labor would not appeal for a strike and management would not lay off any miners.[39]

On May 11, following the agreement, the Task Force on the Coal Mining Industry was established by the cabinet and started its investigation. Its final report was issued in October. It first proposed that coal consumption should be increased to 55 million tons by 1967 by encouraging the construction of coal power plants and increasing subsidies for coal companies in order to maintain the competitiveness of coal in the domestic market. Second, it proposed that laid-off miners be guaranteed three years' living expenses by the government as a preparation period for new jobs, and that government would introduce allowances for retraining, housing, job search, and subsidies for new employers hiring the laid-off miners. Finally, it advised that some part of the cost of these measures be covered by the consumption tax on heavy oil.[40]

Even after this report, Tanrō further kept up pressure to realize the government commitments and sought more generous measures, by organizing demonstrations and strikes. Tanrō was afraid that management in the coal industry might be satisfied with the reported government protection of the coal industry and might dissolve the joint struggle with labor against the government.[41] In November, the government decided on the First Coal Program following the Task Force report, and submitted bills to revise the Coal Mining Rationalization Special Measures Law, the Temporary Measures for Laid-Off Coal Miners, and other related laws.[42] These

---

[39] *Asahi*, March 23, 1962; and Ministry of Labor, *Shiryō rōdō undōshi* (1962), p. 426.
[40] Ministry of Labor, *Shiryō rōdō undōshi* (1962), pp. 454–66.
[41] Ibid., pp. 468–80.
[42] Samuels, *Business of the Japanese State*, p. 116.

bills eventually passed the Diet on January 16, 1963, and Tanrō's Policy Transformation Struggle ended.

Tanrō evaluated the struggle at its January convention and admitted that it failed to organize effective resistance against the rationalization plan per se, as it focused on the lay-off issue.[43] However, the employment measures for laid-off coal miners were very generous in comparison with those of the 1950s. As Tanrō in cooperation with coal management kept pressuring the government, it succeeded in extracting more and more generous measures to alleviate the cost of the coal industry crisis. In the course of this political exchange between government and labor, measures for the coal industry became so generous that some LDP politicians had to point out that the coal industry was not alone in suffering from economic problems.[44] The policy aim of finding new jobs for redundant miners functioned very well, and most laid-off miners found new jobs outside the coal industry in a very short transition period. From 1962 to 1964, 109,080 laid-off miners sought new jobs, and 95,770 (88 percent) found ones by the end of 1964.[45] This active labor market policy established a new unemployment practice in Japan.

INDUSTRIAL ADJUSTMENT IN THE MANUFACTURING SECTOR AFTER THE FIRST OIL CRISIS

Unions in the manufacturing industries were more concerned about wage increases than political issues in the 1960s. (It should be remembered that the Shuntō strategy was advocated by Kaoru Ota who criticized Takano's politically oriented movement.) On the other hand, these unions did not follow the path of typical business unionism as the United States had done, in which labor has an oppositional relation with company management. Rather, as described in chapter 3, unions and/or employees have sought to participate in company decision making, as the company is regarded as the property of the employees as well as the shareholders. At any rate, unions in the private manufacturing sector in the 1960s were apolitical. They were active in the macro-distributive sphere (Shuntō), the micro-distributive sphere (wage negotiation in the company), and the micro-productive sphere (production/management decisions), but less active in the macro-productive sphere (industrial/

---

[43] Ministry of Labor, *Shiryō rōdō undōshi* (1963), p. 386.
[44] *Asahi*, April 5, 1961.
[45] *Nihon rōdō nenkan* (1965), p. 476.

employment policies). Rapid economic growth enabled this labor accommodation because the unions did not have to worry about employment security or the competitiveness of their industries. This condition changed after the first oil crisis and brought about a transformation of labor politics in the 1970s. This transformation had begun quietly in the late 1960s, however, as the Japanese economy became internationalized.

As an industry matures and is faced with international competition which requires industrial restructuring, labor in that industry will become active in demanding industrial policies. The coal industry was the first such case in Japan, and was followed by the textile industry.[46] Many unions in the private manufacturing industries, however, began discussing their responses to industrial restructuring in the mid-1960s, even before they were actually faced with industrial restructuring and layoffs.[47] One important stimulus for these early discussions was the prediction of the possible impact of continuing trade and capital liberalization. The Japanese government started liberalizing trade in 1961 and achieved 90 percent liberalization in 1964 under Article 8 of the International Monetary Fund Charter. The government finally started liberalization of direct investment by foreign companies in 1967, though the process was slow. These changes created a strong sense of the vulnerability of Japanese industries among business, labor, and the government, and forced Japanese manufacturing industries to prepare for international competition by rationalizing their business.[48]

Unions began to formulate policies for this industrial restructuring, with Dōmei leading this new movement. From its establishment in 1964, Dōmei was eager to participate in industrial policy formation. In February 1967, Dōmei decided on a policy aiming toward capital liberalization and industrial restructuring.[49] It advocated the restructuring of Japanese industries in a way that would increase international competitiveness, but not in a way that exploited cheap labor. It proposed the introduction of well-balanced industrial planning and modernization, which would contribute to international competitiveness as well as a higher living standard.

---

[46] Hisamura, *Sangyōseisaku to rōdōkumiai*, chap. 2.

[47] The best and most comprehensive study of this process is Shinoda, *Seikimatsu no rōdōundō.*

[48] Motoshige Ito and Kazuharu Kiyono, "Bōeki to chokusetsu tōshi" (Trade and direct investment), in Komiya et al., *Nihon no sangyōseisaku*; Shinoda, *Seikimatsu no Rōdōundō*, pp. 83–94; Komiya et al., *Nihon no sangyōseisaku*, chap. 2.

[49] Ministry of Labor, *Shiryō rōdō undōshi* (1967), p. 451.

Dōmei did not just demand a government industrial policy, but also participation in policymaking. It called for establishing a prior-consultation (*jizenkyōgi*) mechanism between labor and management within each industry, as well as the participation of labor in various government deliberation councils (*shingikai*) on economic and industrial issues. The chairman of Dōmei, on March 16, 1967, met with ministers of MITI and MOL and the cabinet secretary general and received positive responses from them on Dōmei's demands. Especially on the request for union participation in the deliberation councils, the government replied on May 17, giving labor immediate representation on the Economic Deliberation Council of the Economic Planning Agency and promising positive consideration of union membership on the Industrial Structure Council of MITI and other groups.[50]

Dōmei pursued this new policy, forming an Industrial Policy Committee in April 1967. This committee had sixteen meetings in that year to formulate its first report.[51] In due course, it invited to its study meetings union leaders from outside Dōmei, such as, Yoshiji Miyata of the Steel Workers' Union (Sōhyō) and Shinsuke Kiyota of the Electric Equipment Industry Union (Chūritsurōren), as well as economists and government officials. Dōmei tried to use this new policy to establish its hegemony in the private-sector union movement.[52]

Within Sōhyō, there appeared a similar move toward industrial policy. In 1966, Tekkōrōren (Steel Workers' Union) and Tanrō (Coal Miners' Union) proclaimed that Sōhyō should have its own industrial policy. Their proposal was based on Tanrō's experience in the Policy Transformation Movement and Tekkōrōren member unions' experiences of participating in company production decision making. Sōhyō decided to let the Long-Term Strategy Committee consider this issue, but this caused a conflict within Sōhyō.

The chairman of the newly formed Private Sector Unions Conference within Sōhyō, Haraguchi, argued that unions should have their own industrial policy to quickly respond to management rationalization plans and should also pursue the establishment of tripartite deliberation councils on industrial restructuring as a mechanism to voice union demands. The president of Sōhyō, Toshikatsu Horii, concurred on this point, but the secretary general of Sōhyō, Akira Iwai, and ex-President Ota were against this industrial policy. Iwai and Ota argued that union participation in

[50] Ibid., pp. 452–53.
[51] Ibid., p. 453.
[52] *Sankei Shimbun*, evening edition, March 16, 1967.

government industrial policymaking would not change the nature of the rationalization, but rather unions should organize their own struggle against rationalization from the workshop level and support the Socialist Party in order to transform the Japanese economic system as a whole.[53] This controversy reflected the conflict between the pro-Structural Reform (*kōzōkaikaku*) group and its opponents, which imported the Italian Communist Party's strategy.[54] After serious internal conflict, Sōhyō could not adopt these new industrial policy tactics. It emphasized that workshop-level resistance to rationalization rather than participation in government deliberation councils or any tripartite consultation mechanisms would be the best way to protect workers' interests in industrial restructuring, and that it would oppose Dōmei's industrial democracy proposals and labor-management cooperation.[55] This was partly because Sōhyō was dominated by public-sector unions which were less vulnerable to international competition. However, within the private sector, Gōkarōren (Synthetic-Chemical Industry Workers' Union) was against the industrial policy tactics. As analyzed in chapter 4, this was a result of Gōkarōren's strategy. It focused mainly on wage demands and preferred oppositional relations with management in order to avoid being co-opted.

Although Sōhyō did not support this industrial policy tactic, Dōmei and Chūritsurōren as well as many private manufacturing sector unions in Sōhyō did. These unions were also members of the IMF-JC established in 1964. This was the start of the private-sector lead in the Japanese labor movement, although it was only after the first oil crisis that the private unions clearly took the lead.

An important institutional development for this private union movement was the establishment of a labor-management consultation mechanism at the industry level. As chapter 4 shows, the Japan Productivity Center (JPC) had been eager to promote labor-management consultation within the company, and it began advocating a similar consultation mechanism at the industry level, the Industrial Labor Management Council (ILMC, *sanbetsu rōshi kaigi*) in 1965. It argued that it is the company that introduces technological innovation, and thus labor-management consultation should be conducted there first. But the impact of technological innovation and subsequent increases in productivity are beyond a given company and affect the industry and the society as a whole. There-

---

[53] Ministry of Labor, *Shiryō rōdō undōshi* (1967), pp. 443–48.

[54] Gerald L. Curtis, *The Japanese Way of Politics* (New York: Columbia University Press, 1988), chap. 4.

[55] Sōhyō, "Undō Hōshin" (Movement tactics), annual conference, 1967, quoted in Ministry of Labor, *Shiryō rōdō undōshi* (1967), pp. 448–49.

fore, labor-management consultation should be elevated to the industry level, and labor should also be allowed to participate in the public policy formation.[56]

Dōmei and other private manufacturing sector unions were eager for this institutional development, while management was reluctant because it feared that unions would become irresponsible once outside the company system. The unions, in cooperation with the JPC, kept pressure on management to form this mechanism. When the JPC issued its Proposal for the Industrial Labor Management Council in 1969, the Unions' National Productivity Council (consisting mainly of private manufacturing sector unions) simultaneously advocated this institutional development.[57]

Management attitudes gradually became more positive, due to several factors. First, capital and trade liberalization convinced management of the necessity to cooperate with labor in demanding some industrial policies from government and in implementing them. Second, management could expect that these ILMCs might be used to control wage increases which began exceeding productivity increases in the late 1960s. The JPC actually used this reasoning to sell the ILMC idea to management. Third, this movement was led by Dōmei and the IMF-JC-affiliated unions against the radical unions in Sōhyō, a situation that motivated management to respond positively.[58]

Consequently, the number of ILMCs began increasing in the late 1960s (fig. 24). Before 1968 ILMCs were formed only in the industries of coal mining, textiles, and shipping. After 1968, ILMCs became established in the core industries such as automobiles, electric power, ship building, steel, and electric equipment. By 1977, ILMCs were established in most industries.

This change illustrates the development of a new labor-management accommodation, on which new labor politics flourished in the late 1970s. Furthermore, the establishment of Sanrōkon, the tripartite national-level meeting, continued the process of institutionalizing labor's participation in national policymaking.[59] Labor unions in the late 1960s and early

[56] *Seisansei undō 30 nen-shi*, pp. 614–22.

[57] Ibid., pp. 667–68.

[58] Katsumi Yakabe, "Sangyōbetsu rōshi kaigi no dōkō" (The trend toward industrial labor management councils), *Gekkan rōdōmondai* (April 1969). *Seisansei undō 30 nen-shi*, p. 644; *Nikkei*, October 27, 1969. Mori, ed., *Nihon no rōshikankei shisutemu*, p. 281.

[59] Hiroshi Nakanishi, "Sangyōbetsu rōshikaigi to rōdōundō no genkyokumen" (The industrial labor-management council and current aspects of the labor movement), *Gekkan rōdōmondai* (May and June 1971).

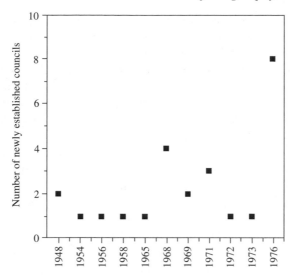

Figure 24. Number of industrial labor-management councils established. From Mori, ed., *Nihon no rōshikankei shisutemu*, p. 277.

1970s steadily expanded their policy network into the governing coalition.

The Employment Security Struggle

An economic downturn after the first oil crisis required the management of rationalization efforts, and thus labor was threatened by possible layoffs. Labor pursued the goal of protecting employment, not just by demanding employment security from management, but also by demanding an employment security policy from the government. The Employment Insurance Law was one example. The policymaking process resulting in the Special Measures for Laid-Off Workers in Targeted Depressed Industries shows how the new inter- and intra-class politics worked in practice.

The oil crisis hit several industries especially hard, such as textiles and open-hearth and electric-furnace steel. These were structurally depressed industries, in which production capacity far exceeded demand. In these industries, MITI usually tried to help reduce the production capacity to balance supply and demand in response to industry requests. This industrial restructuring resulted in work force reductions, and labor unions

began demanding government measures to solve the employment problems. The Special Measures for Laid-Off Workers in Targeted Depressed
Industries was one of labor's most important achievements.

First of all, how did labor and management in the open-hearth and
electric-furnace steel industry adjust to the crisis? Within the depressed
iron and steel industry, open-hearth and electric-furnace steel, consisting
of the small and medium-sized companies, was the hardest hit. The demand for this steel began declining because its main consumers were the
building and construction industries, which suffered from the recession.
The industry association, on August 8, 1975, asked the Fair Trade
Commission for permission to implement a recession cartel in order to
reduce production output, and their request was granted. The labor
unions supported this industrial adjustment from the beginning.
Tekkōrōren formulated its industrial policy for the small and medium-
sized steel makers in December 1975, arguing that while working conditions in this sector should be maintained, a fundamental restructuring of
the industry to reduce excess production capacity was inevitable. While
communicating with industry management through the labor-management discussion meeting, Tekkōrōren demanded that MITI introduce
this sort of industrial policy for the industry. In September 1976, MITI set
up the Research Group on Fundamental Problems of Open-Hearth and
Electric-Furnace Steel Makers as an advisory board for the bureau chief of
the Basic Industry of MITI, and a report was issued in 1977. It proposed
that 3.3 million tons of excessive capacity of steel output should be
scrapped (a 16 percent reduction) with steel makers themselves coordinating their share of reduction. Most companies in this industry, following MITI's advice, applied for an extension of the cartel and implemented
it. Furthermore, fifty-two companies in this industry were permitted by
MITI to establish an industry organization (*sangyo kumiai*) as prescribed in
the Small and Medium-Sized Companies Organizing Law, which enabled
them to implement a cartel among all the companies in this industry,
including twelve companies outside the organization. Management in this
industry restructured production.[60]

Tekkōrōren also appreciated this report, but expressed dissatisfaction at
its lack of discussion of employment concerns. Tekkōrōren had frequent
meetings with MITI and MOL in order to make the government incorporate an employment security program in their industrial policy, while it

---

[60] *Asahi nenkan* (1976), p. 353. Tekkōrōren, *Tekkōrōren undōshi* (A history of the steel
workers' union) (Tokyo: Nihon Tekkōsangyō Rōdōkumiai Rengōkai, 1981), p. 461. Ministry
of Labor, *Shiryō rōdō undōshi* (1977), p. 512. *Asahi nenkan* (1978), p. 341.

organized the unions within those companies implementing the rationalization plan in order to minimize work-force reduction and to maximize severance pay for the laid-off workers.[61] Tekkōrōren and the National Association of the Unions handed an official request to the minister of MITI on April 28, 1977, demanding special legislation to guarantee job transfers for redundant workers.[62] They reasoned that government was responsible for employment security because this restructuring was supported by the government. Unions appreciated government help in restructuring the industry, not just because it would help the industry's survival and maintain employment, but also because it would give them a legitimate reason to demand government guarantees of employment security for redundant workers. Politicization of industrial restructuring enabled labor to participate in the process and to demand benefits from it. Here labor and management cooperated with each other in demanding government help.

This kind of labor-management alliance existed in many structurally depressed industries, such as textiles, aluminum, and ship building. Both union and management in these industries began demanding special government measures for them. Dōmei integrated these individual demands and proposed the original idea for the Special Measures for Laid-Off Workers in Targeted Structurally Depressed Industries. On July 1, 1977, Chairman Amaike of Dōmei argued that the government should target the structurally depressed industries and provide living stipends for employees laid off in those industries until they could find new jobs.[63] On August 8, Dōmei presented its proposal on measures for the depressed industries. After this, four national union federations and the CPPU (Council of Policy Promotion Unions) had meetings with the minister of labor and the cabinet secretaries in order to realize their demands in the summer budget-making process. They all demanded a government employment security policy and the minister of labor replied positively and asked for labor's support of MOL's budget demands for the employment policy.[64]

However, MOL's response to Dōmei's proposal for the special measures was not as positive. MOL replied that although the proposal was understandable, it was difficult to introduce a comprehensive measure for the

---

[61] Ministry of Labor, *Shiryō rōdō undōshi* (1977), pp. 558–59. The fact that Tekkōrōren supported the rationalization plan does not mean it was less willing to organize the labor movement to protect employment at the company level.

[62] Ibid., pp. 463–64.

[63] Ministry of Labor, *Shiryō rōdō undōshi* (1977), p. 444.

[64] Ibid., p. 445.

depressed industries because these problems were beyond the jurisdiction of MOL. MOL planned to implement various existing measures prescribed in the Employment Insurance Law rather than formulating a new law. Sōhyō was also not eager for new legislation for the depressed industries, preferring general unemployment relief measures. On the other hand, Chūritsurōren, Shinsanbetsu, and the CPPU strongly backed Dōmei's proposal, as a result of which Sōhyō finally concurred with Dōmei in October. The government, under pressure from unions, also changed its stance. It declared that it would support this bill, although the cabinet would not sponsor it because it did not have enough time to establish consensus among the ministries (MITI, MOL, and the Ministry of Transportation).

On October 18, the five opposition parties submitted the bill to the Diet. The unions in the affected industries—Zensen (textiles) and Gōkarōren (synthetic chemical)—met with the minister of labor and lobbied strongly for the legislation. Negotiation between the opposition parties and the LDP followed, and on November 1, the LDP accepted this bill, which unanimously passed the Lower House. In the Upper House, however, its passage was tactically linked by the Socialists to revision of the Health Insurance Law, which the Socialist and Communist parties criticized and tried to prevent. In the middle of delicate negotiations on these two unrelated bills, Sōhyō organized a strike to prevent the passage of the Health Insurance bill. Dōmei criticized this political strike as illegal, afraid that Sōhyō's tactics would kill the Special Measures bill.[65] As Dōmei feared, the bill did not pass. Dōmei and the Chūritsurōren as well as the unions in the depressed industries harshly criticized Sōhyō, arguing that the public-sector-dominated Sōhyō was insensitive to difficulties in the private manufacturing sector. Even within Sōhyō, Tekkōrōren and Gōkarōren criticized Sōhyō's tactics. Most Sōhyō leaders countered that defeat of the Health Insurance Revision bill was a victory for labor.[66] Here the schism between the private-sector and public-sector unions became clear. Dōmei, Chūritsurōren, and Shinsanbetsu dissolved the joint struggle with Sōhyō, negotiated with the government, and succeeded in securing passage of the bill.[67]

This law prescribed that company management in consultation with the union set up a plan to retrain laid-off workers for new jobs. The government would also provide the laid-off workers with various allowances for job hunting as well as an extended unemployment allowance. Further-

[65] Ibid., p. 450.
[66] *Asahi*, December 3, 1977.
[67] Ministry of Labor, *Shiryō rōdō undōshi* (1977), p. 445.

more, the government would subsidize employers who hired the targeted laid-off workers. This was the policy repertoire that had been prescribed in the Employment Insurance Law. But this new law introduced more generous measures for laid-off workers, and also made it clear that if the government took part in industrial restructuring, it would be also specially responsible for the employment security of the laid-off workers.[68] This new law, together with the Special Measure to Stabilize the Targeted Depressed Industries, constituted a comprehensive industrial adjustment policy. The latter law was legislated in May 1978, at the request of management and labor in the depressed industries, in order for those industries to easily rationalize their production. The main measures were the formulation of a plan to bring about a new equilibrium in the industry by reducing production capacity, financial support for their rationalization efforts, and advising the cartel on rationalization. Most economists are critical of this law because it distorted the functioning of the market and may have made the restructuring process slower.[69] However, from the standpoint of the unions, this politicization of industrial adjustment provided a good opportunity to demand government help to secure employment. This comprehensive industrial adjustment policy might not have realized theoretically optimum restructuring, but it seemed to realize industrial adjustment at a lower social cost with labor's consent.

ANALYSIS: INTER- AND INTRA-CLASS POLITICS

The two cases discussed in this chapter show that unions, faced with industrial restructuring, succeeded in gaining government aid to establish secure employment and to alleviate the cost of dismissals. But the coal-mining union had to appeal to more militant tactics than did private manufacturing unions in the post–oil crisis period. This situation prompts two questions: Why were unions successful in their policy demands? And why did the private manufacturing sector unions achieve their policy gains with greater ease than did the unions in the coal industry?

First I will test what is called the resource-centered hypothesis. To what extent can these policy achievements be explained by the size of mobilized resources? The organization rate in postwar Japan reached a high of 55.8 percent in 1949, then declined to 31.6 percent in 1960. But from

---

[68] Takanashi, *Aratana Koyōseisaku no tenkai*, p. 128. See also Peck, Levin, and Goto, "Picking Losers."

[69] Komiya, et al., *Nihon no sangyōseisaku*, chaps. 3 and 13.

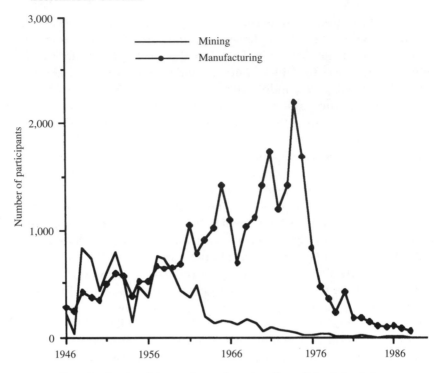

Figure 25. Size of strikes in mining and manufacturing. From *Shōwa kokusei sōran.*

1961 to 1976, it rose and stayed around 33 percent, although it began declining again afterward. In other words, in the periods of the cases examined here, the organization rate did not decline. In mining, the rate had been very high, around 90 percent, until 1961, while in the manufacturing industries, the rate exceeded 40 percent in 1975 for the first time since 1951. In both industries, organization rates were high when the policy struggles were fought.

Strike data show similar patterns. As described in chapter 1, strike activity had been intense until the early 1960s, and it again became intense in the early 1970s (figs. 1, 2, and 3). The size of strikes in the mining industry had been large until the early 1960s when it declined, while in the manufacturing industry it reached a maximum in 1974 (fig. 25). These data might be used to show that an increase in mobilized resources was an important factor enabling the unions to achieve their policy gains. Thus, a careful analysis of union movements, focusing on actual resource mobilization, contradicts the view that Japanese unions are just cooperative and docile.

A closer reading of these data, however, leads to a more interesting finding. Strike activity dropped just before the periods of our cases. In coal mining, the union mobilized its resources intensively in the Miike Strike in 1960, but it backed down after its defeat. In the case of the employment security struggle of the 1970s, union mobilization peaked in 1974, but it was after this peak that the unions began successfully seeking their policy gains. During the 1975 Shuntō wage bargaining, labor restrained its wage demands while reducing its strike activity. Many scholars have stopped their analysis there and concluded that the unions were defeated because union demobilization is regarded as evidence of their defeat. However, one important question remains. Why did labor achieve these policy gains described above? The resource-centered hypothesis is not enough to answer this question. So instead, I focus on the political opportunity structure of the labor movement, especially inter- and intra-class alliances and their institutionalization in the policy network.

In the two cases here, labor formed an alliance with management. In the case of coal, labor called the movement a joint struggle with management to demand government policies to help both the industry as well as the workers. In the case of the employment security struggle, too, management in the depressed steel industry supported union demands for government employment measures, while the union cooperated with management in demanding industrial policy. As described in chapter 4, when it is faced with economic difficulty and the need to reorganize its business, Japanese management usually seeks labor's cooperation by granting labor participation in managerial and production decision making. This is also true for national policymaking. Management supported union employment policy demands, because it could receive benefits from those policies in the form of employment adjustment subsidies to help it restructure its business. But it also needed union cooperation in its reorganization efforts, and cooperation on national policymaking was an important way to buy internal cooperation. This alliance between labor and management, thus, helped unions to realize their policy demands.

The origin of this labor-management alliance in the coal-mining industry can be found in its accommodation to labor in the late 1940s and 1950s, in which management made concessions to labor's wage demands as long as the labor cost could be transferred to coal consumers or the government. The alliance in the manufacturing industry in the 1970s was more solidly institutionalized than in the former case. Tanrō's Policy Transformation Struggle taught the unions that they could not totally oppose rationalization; instead, they had to have their own industrial policy and actively participate in the process of industrial restructuring. After its policy transformation struggle, Tanro became one of the most active advocates for the union industrial policy movement within Sōhyō. Also, the unions' experiences participating in production and management decision making through the management council made it easier for them to formulate their own industrial policy. Tekkōrōren as well as Dōmei-affiliated unions became anxious to develop their industrial policy movement. They concluded that union participation within the company should be developed into an industrial policy movement as industrial restructuring became necessary.

Furthermore, the unions succeeded in establishing the industry-level labor-management consultation mechanism (ILMC) in the late 1960s and the early 1970s. This institutionalization of labor-management consultation made it easier for those two groups to cooperate in demanding industrial policy for depressed industries and employment security measures from the government. The progress of institutionalization of this labor-management alliance explains the increasing ease with which unions realized their employment demands.

Intra-Labor Relations

On the issue of labor-management consultation on industrial policy, there existed a controversy within labor. Sōhyō (especially public-sector unions and Gōkarōren) was against this consultation, although Tekkōrōen and Tanrō were willing to develop the unions' industrial policy movement. Dōmei, however, was eager to set up the institutional mechanism of labor-management consultation. This conflict thus existed between the private manufacturing sector unions and the public sector unions (although Gōkarōren was an exception).[70] The former unions were more sensitive to the competitiveness of their industries, which was the foundation of their employment and their high wages, while the latter unions were not so sensitive because their industries were not directly influenced by market forces.

In the case of coal mining, this conflict was not so clear, but Sōhyō fully supported Tanrō's policy transformation movement. In the employment security struggle cases in the 1970s, this conflict emerged within labor. Sōhyō was not eager to demand concrete employment policy gains be-

[70] This was because Gōkarōren tried to follow a different union strategy, that is, pursuing high wage increases with less involvement in the production process of the company. See discussion in chap. 4.

176

cause it, instead, wanted to transform the political economy as a whole, while the private-sector unions and Gōkarōren wanted those policy gains. What is important is that this schism within the labor movement did not prevent private-sector unions from realizing their employment policy demands. Moreover, they seemed to succeed with more ease than the coal miners' union which enjoyed unified support from labor. Why did divided labor succeed?

This schism within labor seemed to strengthen the alliance with management. Management and the government had every reason to cooperate with the moderate private unions which were against radical leftist unionism. Therefore this schism promoted the development of the institutionalization of a labor-management alliance and the government incorporation of labor unions within the policymaking process. This situation ran parallel to the labor-management alliance formation at the company level in the 1950s described in chapter 3.

The LDP and the Government

As analyzed in chapter 5, the LDP, faced with electoral decline, opened up the policymaking process to unions in the early 1970s to appeal to workers. The same was also true in the early 1960s when coal miners organized their policy transformation struggle. The Ikeda cabinet was formed after the political turmoil caused by the demonstration against revision of the U.S.-Japan Security Treaty, and it adopted a more conciliatory approach to opposition groups. Also, some LDP politicians, anticipating a demographic change, began advocating a new effort to incorporate labor. It was, however, not until the 1970s that the LDP wholeheartedly began opening up the policymaking process to labor, and this fact explains why the coal miners needed more militant tactics to achieve their policy gains in the early 1960s than the manufacturing unions did in the 1970s.

In addition, the communication channels between the LDP and the unions have been institutionalized over time. It is true that Sōhyō and Dōmei had meetings with the prime minister and other high-ranking government officials in the 1960s, but the communication was rather sporadic. Establishment of the Sanrōkon meeting among the top leaders of labor, business, and the government in 1970 was epoch-making, and since then, this meeting has been held almost every month. Furthermore, the Private Sector Unions' Joint Action Council (the origin of the CPPU and Rengō) started meeting with government officials in order to present their policy demands at the beginning of the budget-making process in

1976.[71] This was perfect timing for demanding new policies, because in Japan the budget-making process before parliamentary deliberation is the real battlefield of competing new policy initiatives.[72] Since then, the private sector unions group, which ended up establishing Rengō in the 1980s, made it a rule to actively participate in budget making. This means that the private sector unions group became an "insider" of the policymaking process. In sum, the communication channel between labor, especially in the private sector, and the government became institutionalized in the 1970s. The cases of the employment security struggle in the 1970s show that this institutionalized network played an important role in helping labor to realize its demands, while the case of coal mining shows that without this network, labor had to use more militant and nonroutinized tactics to make its demands known to the government and to realize them.

The Bureaucracies

The fact that the LDP government opened the policymaking process to unions does not automatically guarantee development of an effective employment policy. As Weir and Skocpol show, the way past policy was institutionalized (the policy legacy) determines the kind of policy that can be developed.[73] It is important that MOL was willing to introduce new policies in the early 1960s and in the 1970s. In the late 1950s MOL's URPW was faced with many problems, and MOL began searching for a new employment policy. The coal crisis was a nice opportunity for MOL to transform its employment policy menu. In the early 1970s, MOL was again faced with a problem in developing an employment policy. Because the Japanese economy was booming and the labor market was so tight that the unemployment insurance account was running a huge surplus, some business leaders doubted the need for MOL. Faced with this criticism, MOL set up a research group to study a new employment policy in the era of full employment in 1973. The Employment Insurance Law was a product of this research.[74] MOL reasoned that although full employment had been achieved, it was in charge of preempting future unemployment and also promoting workers' welfare.

---

[71] Katsumi Yakabe, ed., *Zenmin rōkyō no kenkyu* (A study of the Association of the Private Sector Unions) (Tokyo: Nihon Seisansei Honbu, 1985), pp. 33–34.

[72] John C. Campbell, *Contemporary Japanese Budget Politics* (Berkeley: University of California Press, 1977).

[73] Weir and Skocpol, "State Structures and the Possibility for 'Keynesian' Responses."

[74] Koike, *Shigoto no keizaigaku*, p. 99.

In sum, just before the unions demanded employment measures, MOL began searching for a new employment policy. The policy windows were open for the unions. In the case of coal, MOL was ready for a new employment policy idea beyond the policy legacy of the URPW because it had already caused a lot of implementation problems. This situation made it easier for unions to entertain new market-oriented effective employment measures. In the case of the Employment Insurance Law, MOL was again ready for a new employment policy idea, and Dōmei's demand for the Employment Adjustment Grant Program was easily incorporated in MOL's new employment policy package. But at the same time, MOL's employment policy changed from a public job creation policy to a market-oriented employment policy. The Employment Insurance Law was a further development of the market-oriented employment policy. In this sense, it was an easier innovation given the legacy of the market-oriented employment policy. It was even easier for the employment policies formulated after the Employment Insurance Law, including the Special Measures for Laid-Off Workers in Targeted Depressed Industries, because the Employment Insurance Law set the basic policy repertoire for later policy development and also established a relatively autonomous fund for employment policy development in the form of the Employment Insurance Special Account.

It is also important that MITI was eager to intervene in the industry. As many political economists agree, the Japanese economy is more politicized than other advanced capitalist economies. Although there are controversies on the effectiveness of government intervention for Japanese economic success, it should be noted that the politicized nature of the Japanese economy makes it easier for unions to demand an intensive employment policy from the government. There is no strong reason against an intensive employment policy, if the government regards its intervention in industry as legitimate. The development of industrial policy in postwar Japan helped unions to legitimize their demands for government intervention to secure employment.

Labor's Policy Network

In short, these developments resulted in an extensive policy network connecting labor, business, and the government. Their channels of communication have been well institutionalized and contributed to union policy achievements. The final question is whether this policy network is just a token reward for domesticated labor. In other words, did these policy gains matter to the unions? Our case studies show that these achievements mitigated difficulties for laid-off workers and also helped to prevent lay offs in the first place.

This employment policy development strengthened efforts to avoid dismissals by constraining the actions of management. The case of the Hachinohe Kōgyō struggle is telling.[75] Hachinohe Kōgyō is a medium-sized steel maker using open-hearth and electric-furnace technology. In 1974 it was faced with a serious business downturn and announced a three month layoff of all workers, promising full reemployment after the layoff. It applied for an Employment Adjustment Grant immediately after the legislation of the Employment Insurance Law. But after receiving the grant, management announced the parmanent dismissal of all workers and closure of the factory. The union organized a strong movement against this dismissal, with support from Tekkōrōren. The union sued the company, arguing that the company had enough capital to continue its business and that the dismissal was an abuse of management privilege and thus was invalid. Furthermore, the union argued that because management had used the employment adjustment grant which was supposed to prevent dismissals, it should make every effort to continue to employ the workers. The court ruling supported the union's argument in 1977, although management appealed to the higher court. Finally, in 1979, the court declared the company bankrupt, and the union succeeded in forcing management to sell the company to the Taiheiyokinzoku Company, which would employ all the workers. The implementation of the employment policy bound management behavior. The implementation of the employment policy itself created the expectation of protecting employment.

The labor's policy network in the employment policy arena has been institutionalized and supports the protection of the employment of workers. Within this institutional development, private-sector labor succeeded in setting up a new alliance with management and the government.

These two cases show that unions achieved policy successes that exploited political opportunity structures, especially as a result of an institutionalized inter-class alliance, rather than by unilaterally mobilizing their resources. This interpretation answers the paradox of these two cases, that is, why unions gained policy successes after their apparent defeat or demobilization. Inter-class political dynamics provided the unions with policy gains.

[75] *Tekkōrōren undōshi*, pp. 455–60 and 560–62.

What is also interesting is that Sōhyō did not play an important role in the latter case. The driving force of the politics of employment security was the private-sector unions. However, this was not just because Sōhyō consisted mainly of public-sector unions. It played an important role in the case of the coal-mining restructuring, supporting the Tanrō union. But Tanrō's Policy Transformation Movement did not have significant impact on Sōhyō's strategy. We should remember that although Tanrō (coal mining) and Tekkōrōren (steel) proposed a new role for labor in industrial policy formation, mainstream Sōhyō members, not just public-sector unions but also Gōkarōren (synthetic chemistry), opposed this proposal. It was Dōmei and the IMF-JC that took Tanrō's experience seriously and developed their movement in the macro-productive arena, that is, by working toward an industrial policy to protect members' employment security. The private-sector unions which had developed the micro-level productivity coalition extanded the coalition to the industrial level labor-management collaboration. They led this new policy activity. Therefore, on this issue of employment security, the private-sector unions took leadership over mainstream Sōhyō members. This labor politics development, however, did not stop here, but further eroded Sōhyō's leadership in other political fronts.

CHAPTER SEVEN

The Conservative Resurgence:
Labor in the 1980s

On November 5, 1993, the president of the unified Rengō (the Japanese Trade Union Confederation),[1] Akira Yamagishi, and the chairman of Nikkeiren, Shigeo Nagano, visited Prime Minister Hosokawa of the non-LDP coalition government to demand a five trillion yen income tax cut to boost the Japanese economy, which was suffering from its worst recession in the postwar period. This event symbolized the development of Japanese labor politics. It was the first time the top leaders of labor and management had visited the prime minister together to make a common policy demand. The event suggests how far labor unions have come in their policy activities since beginning collaboration with management in national public policy formation in the 1970s.

Moreover, the coalition government which labor unions formally supported emerged after forty-five years of conservative party rule, although the new government was by no means leftist. The direct cause of the formation of the non-LDP coalition government was the split of the LDP. The LDP splinter groups, the Renaissance Party and the Sakigake, deprived the LDP of a majority in the powerful Lower House. In 1993 Prime Minister Miyazawa of the LDP government dissolved the Lower House but could not regain a majority in the subsequent general election. After intensive political negotiations, Masahiro Hosokawa of the small Japan New Party organized a non-LDP eight-party coalition government, and

---

[1] The private-sector Rengō absorbed Sōhyō on November 21, 1989, and contained 65% of organized workers in Japan, thereby unifying the private- and public-sector workers in one large national organization. Its membership comprised 9% of the nation's voters. Tsujinaka, "Rengō and its Osmotic Network." In this chapter, however, I will mainly analyze the private-sector Rengō. If I refer to the new Rengō, I will call it the unified Rengō.

the Socialist party and the LDP formed a coalition government in July 1994. The unified Rengō actively supported the splinter groups in the election and played a key role in the process of this political realignment. The union vote in national politics has increased in importance because of these events.

This is a significant phenomenon. In the late 1970s and 1980s, unions in the advanced industrial democracies suffered from loss of power. Lowell Turner posed a question on the future of the union: "Are contemporary unions, once critical bastions in the historical development of political and industrial democracy, now a spent force, increasingly irrelevant in highly differentiated modern societies (playing important roles only in countries in earlier stages of development such as Poland and South Korea)?"[2] As Frances Fox Piven writes, the decline of labor politics varies in particular nations. Under the neo-conservative administrations of Thatcher and Reagan, unions in Britain and the United States were among the hardest hit. In this context, if Japanese unions are as weak as the orthodox view maintains, Japan should be in an even worse position. In the early 1980s Prime Minister Nakasone advocated neoconservatism following Reagan and Thatcher and introduced administrative reform to resolve the fiscal crisis without a tax increase. The privatization of the Japan National Railway, the Nippon Telegraph and Telephone, and the Japan Tobacco and Salt Public Monopoly Corporation was an important pillar of administrative reform. As Mike Mochizuki argues, an implicit objective of this privatization was to transform the leftist public-sector labor movement to resemble the accommodationist big business unions.[3] However, as I will show in this chapter, the private-sector unions deepened their participation in national policymaking and achieved hegemony within the labor movement.

It is true that the organization rate decreased in Japan from 35 percent in 1970 to 24.4 percent in 1992. However, the absolute size of labor unions did not decrease as much. In 1989 the total number of union members was 12,230,000 and constituted almost 10 percent of the Japanese population. The unified Rengō alone boasts 8 million in membership. Furthermore, the organization rate in companies employing more

---

[2] Turner, *Democracy at Work*, p. 1.
[3] Frances Fox Piven, ed., *Labor Parties in Postindustrial Societies* (Oxford: Oxford University Press, 1992), chap. 1; Hideo Otake, "Nakasone seiji no ideorogii to sono kokunai seijiteki haikei" (The ideology of Nakasone's politics and their domestic political background), *Leviathan*, no. 1 (Autumn 1987); Mike Mochizuki, "Public Sector Labor and the Privatization Challenge: The Railway and Telecommunication Unions," in Allinson and Sone, eds., *Political Dynamics in Contemporary Japan.*

than 1,000 workers is 62 percent. Big business unions, which have been a leading force in the labor movement since the first oil crisis, maintain their strong position.

In this chapter, I show that Japanese labor deepened its participation in the policymaking process, according to a survey of union leaders. I analyze how the private-sector unions were able to maintain their position in the policy process in the era of neoconservatism and argue that their success is attributable to the formation and institutionalization of the big business–labor coalition. In order to decide whether the union has been co-opted by the business or not, I analyze the conflict between Nikkeiren and labor over the formation of the work-hour reduction policy. The introduction of this policy demonstrates that labor was not co-opted by the government, but rather held a critical and autonomous position in the policy process. Finally, I focus on the general direction of changes in the labor policy network, analyzing survey data on bureaucrats. In the 1980s, the labor policy network became supportive of union participation in policymaking. In conclusion, the Japanese unions survived the neoconservative era and increased their influence as a result of international pressure, domestic political realignment, and the development of the labor policy network.[4]

Unions in Politics in the 1980s: Private-Sector Hegemony

In the summer of 1989, I conducted a survey of top union leaders, using the same questionnaire format and targeting the same unions as the 1980 Interest Group Survey conducted by Michio Muramatsu, in order to find how labor leaders' perceptions had changed in the 1980s.[5] I targeted four national-level unions and forty-seven industry-level union organizations.[6] In this period, the LDP government implemented neoconservative

[4] The data and cases in this chapter are based on Ikuo Kume, "Cooptation or New Possibility? Japanese Labor Politics in the Era of Neo-Conservatism," in Frieder Naschold and Michio Muramatsu, eds., *State and Administration in Japan and Germany* (Berlin: Walter de Gruyter, 1996).

[5] The Interest Group Survey by Michio Muramatsu targeted not just unions but various other social groups. The analysis of the survey data is published in Michio Muramatsu, Mitsutoshi Ito, and Yutaka Tsujinaka, *Sengo nihon no atsuryokudantai* (Pressure groups in postwar Japan) (Tokyo: Tōyō Keizai Shinpōsha, 1986).

[6] In the ten years between surveys, some unions changed their organizations, so I tried to use the offspring of the surveyed unions of 1980. For instance, Rengō (Japanese Confederation of the Private Sector Unions; not the current Rengō covering both public and private unions) was the Council for Policy Promotion Unions in 1980. Furthermore, Shinsanbetsu existed as the national union federation in 1980, but was dissolved in 1989. Therefore, the

Table 7. Union success in policy promotion

Type of union	1980 (%)	1989 (%)	Number of unions
National federation	100.00	50.00	4
Manufacturing	81.30	75.00	16
Service	58.10	54.80	31
All combined	68.60	60.80	51

SOURCE: Labor union survey by the author.

Table 8. Union success in policy revision

Type of union	1980 (%)	1989 (%)
National federation	75.00	75.00
Manufacturing	75.00	37.50
Service	71.00	51.60
All combined	72.50	49.00

SOURCE: Labor union survey by the author.

administrative reform and unions were also reorganizing themselves into a large unified labor confederation, the unified Rengō. Using these two sets of data, I analyze how labor participated in national politics and what change occurred in the 1980s.

The first question is to what extent do the unions have influence in the policymaking process. The survey asked whether the union had any success in getting the government to adopt favorable policies or in stopping the government from adopting unfavorable ones. In 1980, 68.6 percent of the unions were successful in promoting new policies, and 77.1 percent were successful in resisting unfavorable government policies (tables 7 and 8). These data seem to show that unions in Japan have more influence than what the orthodox weak labor thesis has asserted. Furthermore, in comparison with other interest groups, labor's influence is not small (fig. 26). Tables 7 and 8 show that the number of unions that succeeded in the policy process had decreased by 1989, however, the decline is not conspicuously low when compared with the 1980 data for all groups. (Unfor-

1989 survey data does not include Shinsanbetsu. The four national-level unions surveyed are Rengō, Sōhyō, Yuaikaigi (previously Dōmei), and Churitsu Rōso Renrakukai (previously Churitsurōren). For more information on this survey, see Ikuo Kume, "1980 nendai ni okeru riekidantaiseiji no henyō" (Transformation in interest group politics in the 1980s in Japan), *Kōbe hōgaku zasshi* 41-2 (September 1991).

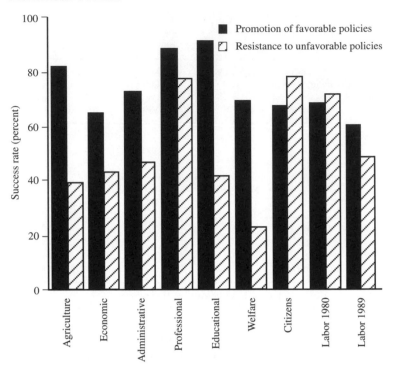

Figure 26. Success rate in influencing the policy process (by sector). From Muramatsu, Ito, and Tsujinaka, *Sengo Nihon no kanryōsei*, p. 250. Data for labor 1989 comes from the results of the author's survey. All other data is for 1980.

tunately we do not have data for non-labor groups in 1989.) Table 9 also shows that the perceived influence of the union did not decrease much in the 1980s.

This comparison also shows another important change in the influence of labor on policy. In 1980 labor and citizens' groups were more successful in resisting government policy, while other groups were better at promoting policy. Muramatsu, Ito, and Tsujinaka explain that because labor and citizens' groups are "outsiders" to the political system, they tend to oppose government policy.[7] In 1989, the pattern of labor's influence on policy had changed, and it became more successful in promoting new policies than in resisting them. This indicates that labor became more of an "insider." This was especially true for private manufacturing unions which have been the driving force for labor's participation in

[7] Muramatsu, Ito, and Tsujinaka, *Sengo Nihon no atsuryokudantai*, p. 263.

Table 9. Perceived policy influence

Type of union	1980	1989
National federation	2.50	2.25
Manufacturing	2.75	3.06
Service	2.65	2.68
All combined	2.67	2.76

SOURCE: Labor union survey by the author.
NOTE: This table shows the self-perception of union leaders with regard to union influence in policymaking. Numbers represent average score out of a range from 1 = very high influence to 5 = no influence.

policymaking (tables 8 and 9). This findimg requires us to disaggregate our data in order to understand changes in labor's influence in the 1980s.

First, let us focus on the national-level union organizations. The data seem to be contradictory at first glance, in that perceived influence among the national unions increased, while the percentage of the unions reporting success in promoting new policies decreased. If we disaggregate the data, we see that while Chūritsurōren perceived a decline in influence, Dōmei (now Yūaikaigi) perceived an increase. On the promotion of new policies, Sōhyō and Chūritsurōren recognized a decline in their influence, while Rengō and Dōmei recognized no change. In all, the data suggest that the losers in the 1980s were Sōhyō and Chūritsurōren, while the winners were Rengō and Dōmei. In its resistance to government policies, Dōmei achieved no success in 1989, while others did. But this data can be interpreted as evidence of Dōmei's further penetration into insider politics, as previously described.

Second, the manufacturing unions also show contradictory data. They seem to have entered insider politics in that they reported more successes in promoting new policies and less in resisting. However, their self-perception of their influence declined. Why was this? First, the nature of the policy they pursued changed from specific to general. According to the qualitative answers from union leaders, in 1980 they referred to more specific industrial and employment policies as their successful cases, while in 1989 they referred more to general policies, such as the revision of the Labor Standards Law for the purpose of workhour reduction. Consequently, the place of negotiations seems to have moved to the national level, and the industry-level unions became less concerned with their role

Table 10. Degree of government consultation of labor

Type of union	1980	1989
National federation	3.00	2.25
Manufacturing	2.88	3.06
Service	3.62	3.42
All combined	3.33	3.22

Source: Labor union survey by the author.
Note: Two unions' leaders did not answer this question in 1989. Numbers represent average scores ranging from 1 = often consulted to 5 = never consulted.

in national policymaking. The second factor in their low estimation of their success rate was reorganization of the national federation, that is, the formation of the private-sector Rengō. Although the private big business unions led this process by rallying the unions to make policy demands, after Rengō's formation in 1987, it began centralizing the private-sector unions' policy activities. The top IMF-JC leader, for example, said that the IMF-JC was organizing policy-related activities as a member of Rengō.[8] The unions themselves delegated policy activities to Rengō. These two factors contributed to a decline of the perceived influence among the manufacturing unions.

As a result of these changes, Rengō became the main force for labor participation in the policymaking process. Given these qualifications, it was very important that Rengō maintained its perceived influence and boasted of its successful policy activities in 1989 as well as in 1980, even though the LDP government introduced a neoconservative administrative reform and enjoyed a conservative resurgence. In this period, the national union organizations, especially private-sector Rengō, deepened their participation in the policymaking process.

In addition, the national labor organizations were consulted more by the government on policy issues (table 10). Even more interesting were the changing patterns of contact between the government and the unions (table 11). The national unions increased their contact with top-level government officials (that is, the prime minister and ministers), while maintaining frequent contact with the bureaucracies (vice ministers, bureau chiefs, and section chiefs). The manufacturing sector unions had relatively frequent contact at the top level in 1980, but much less in 1989.

[8] Yoshiji Miyata, interview with author, Tokyo, August 25, 1989.

Table 11. Frequency of contact with government officials

Type of union	Prime minister	Minister	Vice minister	Bureau chief	Section chief	Other
National federation						
1980	3.75	2.75	3.25	1.75	1.75	1.75
1989	3.00	2.50	2.25	1.50	1.25	1.25
Manufacturing						
1980	3.63	2.50	2.75	2.13	1.88	2.00
1989	4.88	3.38	2.94	2.38	1.88	2.19
Service						
1980	4.68	3.48	3.39	2.13	1.90	2.03
1989	4.71	3.55	3.23	2.63	1.73	2.10
All combined						
1980	4.27	3.12	3.18	2.10	1.88	2.00
1989	4.63	3.41	3.06	2.46	1.74	2.06

SOURCE: Labor union survey by the author.
NOTE: Numbers represent average scores ranging from 1 = often to 5 = never.

Table 12. Union contact with LDP

Type of union	1980	1989
National federation	3.75	3.00
Manufacturing	3.69	4.13
Service	3.94	4.03
All combined	3.84	3.98

SOURCE: Labor union survey by the author.
NOTE: Numbers represent average scores ranging from 1 = often to 5 = never.

Their frequent contact with the bureaucracies remained unchanged. The service-sector unions had less contact with government at all levels, and this did not change. Contact with the LDP followed the same pattern (see table 12), in that the national unions intensified their contact, while the manufacturing unions experienced a loss of contacts. These data are consistent with my interpretation of changes in the unions' policy influence. The private manufacturing unions started their policy-oriented movement in the 1970s upon which Rengō was established. They then delegated policy activities to Rengō. In the 1980s, the private-sector unions kept contacts with the bureaucracies for their particularistic policy goals. Consequently, the national unions, especially Rengō, became the main actors in the policy process.

In this process, the unions came to put more confidence in the actions

Table 13. Union confidence in administrative agencies

Type of union	1980	1989
National federation	2.75	2.50
Manufacturing	2.50	2.25
Service	2.87	2.42
All combined	2.75	2.37

SOURCE: Labor union survey by the author.
NOTE: Two union leaders in the service sector did not answer the question in 1989. Numbers represent average scores ranging from 1 = very high to 5 = no confidence.

of the government. The unions had more trust in the administrative agencies with which they had contact in 1989 than in 1980 (table 13), and their evaluation of government policies improved during the 1980s (table 14). It is noteworthy that the unions especially the manufacturing unions and national federations evaluated the government economic policy highly. This finding is interesting considering the conservative resurgence and the neoconservative admimstrative reform.

In sum, the private-sector Rengō (and its predecessors) maintained its influence and succeeded in centralizing labor's policy activities in the 1980s. Rengō deepened its participation in the policy process. And the unions, especially the manufacturing unions, put more trust in the conservative LDP government.

Neoconservative Administrative Reform and the Union

Let us now examine how private manufacturing unions and Rengō (and its predecessors) participated in the policy process during the conservative resurgence and the neoconservative reform.[9] Faced with an increasing budget deficit, the Suzuki cabinet initiated administrative reform in 1981, establishing the powerful Second Provisional Council for Administrative Reform (SPCAR), and the successor Nakasone cabinet pursued it further.[10] The term "administrative reform" is rather misleading, because it was a multifaceted package of policies, the common ideology of

[9] Kume, "Cooptation or New Possibility."
[10] The first commission was established in 1961, although its impact was not large. A brief review of the administrative development in postwar Japan is in Michio Muramatsu and Ikuo Kume, "Country Report: Recent Administrative Development in Japan," Governance 1-4 (October 1988).

Table 14. Union evaluation of government performance

Type of union	Welfare	Crime control/order	Public service	Economic policy	Foreign/defense
National federation					
1980	3.25	2.50	3.25	3.00	3.50
1989	3.50	2.50	3.50	2.75	2.75
Manufacturing					
1980	3.69	2.38	3.50	3.33	3.73
1989	3.31	2.25	3.31	2.50	3.00
Service					
1980	3.81	2.87	3.74	3.35	3.57
1989	3.68	2.68	3.58	3.06	3.32
All combined					
1980	3.73	2.69	3.63	3.32	3.61
1989	3.55	2.53	3.49	2.86	3.17

SOURCE: Labor union survey by the author.
NOTE: Scores given by union leaders regarding the performance of government policy; numbers represent average scores ranging from 1 = doing very well to 5 = doing poorly.

which was laissez-faire liberalism. Small government, deregulation, and privatization were the political banners of this reform. Therefore, this was, in principle, a neoconservative policy package similar to those in the Reagan and Thatcher administrations.

A substantial number of the SPCAR's proposals, though not all, were implemented. Government regulation was loosened: telecommunications, for example, was deregulated. Three public corporations—Nippon Telegraph and Telephone, Japan National Railway, and Japan Tobacco and Salt—were privatized. And the government restrained budget increases following SPCAR's proposals. Consequently, the ratio of the budget to GNP decreased in 1984 for the first time since 1973. A policy of no-budget-increases continued for five years. These efforts were enacted to reduce government functions and public expenditures but were related to the new tide of neoliberalism in which market and individual initiative were regarded as central. According to Michio Muramatsu, "the most significant effect of administrative reform is not so much its visible results, such as the JNR reform, as the growing resolve to reduce expenditures. . . . its pressures for a reexamination of governmental activities along the principles of small government and autonomous, independent action have been extremely successful."[11]

[11] Michio Muramatsu, "In Search of National Identity: The Politics and Policies of the Nakasone Administration," *Journal of Japanese Studies* 13 (Summer 1987).

The administrative reform mobilized wide support, ranging from business groups to private-sector unions as well as the general public, under the banner of "Financial Reconstruction without a Tax Increase." Administrative reform boosted the popularity of the Nakasone cabinet. Business groups supported this reform in the hope of avoiding possible tax increases that had been planned by MOF in the late 1970s. This contrasts with business demands for more spending in the 1970s.[12] However, this change was not just opportunistic, but also structural. Mitsutoshi Ito argues that big business groups survived the two oil crises and became confident enough in their economic power to pursue a more autonomous position from the government.[13]

Union response to administrative reform differed. When the government passed the legislation to establish SPCAR in December 1980, the unions began formulating their own policies to deal with this issue. Sōhyō although critical of SPCAR, decided to send its vice president to the council. Sōhyō advocated joining with the Socialist Party in order to demand a new administrative and fiscal structure. It argued that the fiscal crisis was a product of the LDP's irresponsible rule. In its formal statement, Sōhyō argued that most of the rationalization and administrative reform in the name of fiscal reconstruction could not but victimize people's livelihoods and the jobs of public-sector workers, and Sōhyō would not accept any reforms at the expense of workers and the people. It also contended that the public-sector should assume more responsibility to control the economy for building the welfare state.[14]

On the other hand, private-sector unions supported administrative reform from the beginning. The private-sector-dominated Dōmei argued that the public sector should introduce the principle of efficiency and productivity increase in its management practice and also argued for privatization as a way to pursue the goal of small government.[15] The other private-sector unions, the CPPU (later Rengō), the IMF-JC, and the Council of Chemical and Energy Workers' Unions basically shared this attitude

[12] Shinkawa, *Nihongata fukushi no seiji keizaigaku*, p. 157.

[13] Ito, "Daikigyō rōshirengō no keisei."

[14] Sōhyō, "Gyōzaisei no minshuteki kaikaku, kōtekikigyō minshuka no tatakai oyobi daini rinjigyosei chōsakai ni taisuru torikumi ni tsuite" (On the democratic administrative and fiscal reform: the struggle for democratization of public corporations, and tactics to deal with the Second Provisional Council for Administrative Reform), February 23, 1981, quoted in Ministry of Labor, *Shiryō rōdō undoshi* (1981), pp. 506–7.

[15] Dōmei, "Gyōseikaikaku ni kansuru kokumin undō no tenkai to dainiji rinji gyōsei chosakai e no taiōhōshin" (Tactics to organize a national movement for administrative reform and to deal with the Second Provisional Council for the Administrative Reform), March 12, 1981, quoted in Ministry of Labor, *Shiryō rōdō undōshi* (1981), p. 510.

with Dōmei, and they established the National Council for Promoting Administrative Reform. Here we can find the same dividing line within the labor movement, between the private and public sectors, that appeared in the 1970s. The private-sector unions' support for administrative reform and the small government goal was a logical response in line with their tactics to raise real wages while restraining nominal wage increases in the 1970s. It is interesting that Dōmei wanted to emphasize tax payers' interests in arguing for administrative reform.[16] These unions did not want tax increases for any reasons and preferred small government. Furthermore, they wanted to reduce the internationally high consumer prices in Japan and, for that purpose, criticized such policies as agricultural protectionism, which supported higher prices on food, and the health care system, which guaranteed higher incomes for medical doctors. The CPPU had been a strong advocate for the policies of small government well before the administrative reform movement and boasted of its early initiative for administrative reform.[17]

The private-sector unions naturally formed a coalition with management to promote the reform and were eager to use this opportunity to establish their hegemony over the public-sector leftist unions within the labor movement. This was not a co-optation of the private-sector unions by government or business, however. The private-sector unions had their own interest in pursuing reform. In addition, the business groups needed union support in order to formulate and implement this reform. In their meeting in March 1981 Dōmei and Nikkeiren agreed on the basic position on administrative reform, and Nikkeiren argued that, in order to break through the bureaucrats' resistance to reform, they should rally for public support. Toshio Doko, chairman of the SPCAR and former president of Keidanren, acknowledged that the establishment of the union-led National Council for Promoting Administrative Reform was an important move for popular support. He also asserted, in his meeting with the CPPU in April, that he would be responsive to various social groups in order to show that SPCAR was not led arbitrarily by business interests.[18]

Furthermore, the possibility that Sōhyō and the bureaucracies would form an implicit coalition against administrative reform required business to get support from the private-sector unions. In March 1981, Sōhyō leaders, the vice ministers (who were career bureaucrats) or secretary generals of all ministries, and the vice presidents of three public corpora-

[16] Ministry of Labor, *Shiryō rōdō undōshi* (1981), p. 514. Ibid., p. 510.
[17] Ito, "Daikigyō rōshirengō no keisei," pp. 56–57. Ibid., p. 56.
[18] Ministry of Labor, *Shiryō rōdō undōshi* (1981), p. 515.

tions met to discuss administrative reform. Their agreement showed the possibility of an anti-reform coalition. Together they argued that although the idea of a small and efficient government was good, it would be very difficult to realize that goal because it was also important to maintain a democracy. They decided that the level of administrative service should not be reduced and that they would continue to coordinate their opinions on reform.[19] Actually, in the processes of the privatization of public corporations, opposition emerged based on an implicit labor-management coalition within those corporations.[20] For business, it was necessary to cooperate with the private-sector unions to pursue administrative reform.

This was also true for government leaders, especially for Nakasone, who was in charge of administrative reform as a director of the Administrative Management Agency and who then became prime minister. Nakasone committed himself to administrative reform to promote his political advance to the prime ministership and to maintain his power after his inauguration.[21] After a landslide victory in the 1986 election, Nakasone attributed the LDP's victory to his strategy to accommodate the moderate left groups. In the process of administrative reform, Nakasone resorted to this strategy. This meant that the private-sector unions had an opportunity to bargain with the government to realize their own interests.

The case of welfare reform demonstrates this clearly.[22] The 1983 Law on Health Care for the Aged put an end to the unconditional free medical service for the elderly over seventy, although the government, after intensive negotiation with various actors including the unions, introduced an extremely small copayment. The Pension Reform Law of 1985 also lowered the benefit level. At first glance, these seem to be typical anti-welfare policies. However, the private-sector unions generally supported them. Dōmei agreed that a copayment should be introduced for elderly health care to control costs, although Sōhyō opposed it.[23] Dōmei also endorsed pension reform, because it wanted to reduce future contributions in the aging society.[24] The private-sector unions did not endorse all welfare reforms. All unions opposed the Health Insurance Reform bill of 1984, which demanded that insured workers pay a 10 percent copayment until

---

[19] Ibid., p. 513.

[20] Mochizuki, "Public Sector Labor."

[21] Muramatsu, "In Search of National Identity."

[22] For a detailed analysis of these processes, see Campbell, *How Policies Change*.

[23] Shinkawa, *Nihongata fukushi no seijikeizaigaku*, p. 165.

[24] Ministry of Labor, *Shiryō rōdō undōshi* (1984), pp. 531–33. The purpose of this pension reform was to establish the welfare state with a middle-level benefit and a lower burden. See Yamazaki, "Kōsei nenkin seido no 'bapponkaisei' katei."

April 1986, and a 20 percent copayment thereafter. Although, after intensive negotiations within the Diet, the government proposed that implementation of the 20 percent copayment should require Diet approval again, the unions continued to oppose it.[25] Although they did not succeed, the private-sector unions and Nikkeiren worked very closely to control increasing medical costs.[26]

These cases show that the private-sector unions prefered a middle-level welfare state with less burden to a big welfare state with a heavy burden. The National Council for Promoting Administrative Reform, which consisted of the private unions, in 1981 advocated the principle of fair burden-sharing among the policy benefit recipients. It claimed that the handicapped should be entitled to free benefits, while able recipients should pay the fair cost of public services. It also proclaimed that the unfair tax system in Japan which gave benefits to small and medium-sized merchants, industrialists, doctors, farmers, and others, should be reformed. Big business concurred on this principle, and from time to time, the private-sector unions and management cooperated in demanding a fair policy for workers in the private sector. Mitsutoshi Ito calls this the big business and labor coalition.[27] We can find a similar pattern of labor politics development at the micro-level in the 1950s and the 1960s, when management and labor in the private sector formed a productivity coalition. In the 1980s, at the national level, the private-sector unions and management worked to introduce the "vigorous welfare society" that SPCAR advocated. The logic of the productivity coalition within the firm is consistent with the logic of the "vigorous welfare society": both principles emphasize the well being of workers based on private initiative and economic rationality and are opposed to groups that depend on the state for their "unfair" benefits, whether they are public-sector unions or protected industries.

Employment Policy–Small Government for Labor?

As shown above, private-sector unions committed themselves to the principle of small government in general. However, this principle was not applied to their main interest, that is, employment security. As I show below, employment policy was not influenced by this principle.[28]

Especially after the first oil crisis, labor succeeded in making the govern-

[25] Ministry of Labor, *Shiryō rōdō undōhi* (1984), p. 526.
[26] Shinkawa, *Nihongata fukushi no seijikeizaigaku*, pp. 168–69.
[27] Ito, "Daikigyō rōshirengō no keisei."
[28] Kume, "Cooptation or New Possibility."

ment intervene in the necessary industrial adjustment process to protect members' employment. Most economists, however, criticized this government intervention, alleging that it would distort the functioning of the market and might make the restructuring process slower.[29] If the 1980s principle of neoliberalism had been taken seriously, the employment policy could have been the target of the administrative reform.

This type of employment policy not only survived administrative reform, however, but was extended. The two laws establishing special measures for targeted industries and regions were to expire in 1983, and MOL wrote a new law by integrating the two previous laws, creating a single law, Special Measures for Stable Employment in Targeted Industries and Regions. This law anticipated a continuing employment problem in some industries and strengthened the employment measures on two points. First, it did not require implementation of the industrial policy as a precondition. In other words, MOL had more autonomous discretion in implementing the new law which enabled the ministry to take employment into direct consideration. And second, the new law introduced subsidies to companies that educated laid-off workers.[30]

What is more important is the fact that MOL succeeded in enacting this new law just when the Nakasone administration adopted the no-budget-increase principle for the 1983 fiscal year. While the general account budget increase was kept at 0 percent (except for redemption of national bonds and tax money allocated to local government), MOL's budget, including its special account budget, increased by 5.2 percent. This increase was largely attributable to the new law.[31]

This pattern can be found in the 1987 fiscal year, when the revaluation of yen after the Plaza Accord of 1985 caused a serious economic recession in Japan. In that year, the government was still committed to the surplus budget principle, but MOL's budget (including its special account) increased by 7.4 percent. The Program to Create 300,000 Jobs was possible because of this budget increase. Furthermore, the Special Measures for Stable Employment in Targeted Industries and Regions, which was to expire in 1988, was extended, first as the Law to Facilitate Regional Employment Development (1987) and then as the Law to Stabilize Employment in Targeted Industries (1988).

This employment policy development shows that state-labor relations in the employment policy arena did not experience significant change in the

---

[29] Komiya et al., *Nihon no sangyōseisaku.*
[30] Takanashi, *Aratana Koyōseisaku no tenkai,* pp. 147–48.
[31] *Nihon rōdō nenkan* (1984), p. 462.

days of small government. MOL eagerly develped these employment policies, and management and unions supported this policy development in the 1980s as it had in the 1970s.

LABOR AS A FULL ACTOR? THE WORKHOUR REDUCTION POLICY

I argued that labor and management in the private sector formed a coalition in several important policy arenas, such as employment security and administrative reform. Did labor have influence beyond this coalition base? If the answer is no, then it is somewhat difficult to tell the difference between such a coalition and management's co-optation of labor. Labor politics in the 1980s in Japan, however, shows cases in which labor went beyond this coalition. The unions achieved several important policy victories over business resistance. In these cases, the government, especially the Ministry of Labor, took labor's side against business. The Equal Opportunity for Male and Female Workers' Law of 1985 and the Law to Facilitate Employment of Elderly Workers of 1986 are two examples.[32] Labor unions had been demanding active government intervention to guarantee equal opportunity for female workers and to extend the retirement age to sixty, yet, management had been strongly opposed to government intervention on these issues. These new laws prescribed an active role for government, so Nikkeiren, in 1986, criticized MOL's intervention as "the Labor Ministry offensive." It claimed that MOL was intervening in spheres that should be the sole purview of labor and management, that these two groups in each company should voluntarily negotiate, and that the new laws were against the general government policy of deregulation.[33] The workhour reduction policy illustrates how labor succeeded in achieving its policy victory in this field in the era of neoconservatism.

The postwar workhour regulation started as part of the occupational reform. The Labor Standards Law of 1947 introduced the eight-hour day and forty-eight-hour week principle in Japan for the first time. The Ministry of Labor, which was established in 1947 under the Katayama Socialist-Democrat coalition government, was in charge of regulating workhours. In the latter half of the 1960s, MOL started its efforts to further reduce working hours by advocating two days off per week. However, at this stage, MOL did not try to revise the Labor Standards Law to promote further workhour reduction. Instead, it used administrative guidance and other

---

[32] Kume, "Cooptation or New Possibility."
[33] *Nikkeiren taimuzu*, January 23, 1986.

public relations methods. For instance, MOL conducted large-scale surveys to investigate the prevalence of the five-day work week among companies in 1971 and 1973. The purpose of this survey was not just for research but also to promote this practice while interviewing the management of individual companies. MOL did not choose to directly regulate management practices but to facilitate labor-management efforts for workhour reduction. Average annual working hours decreased from 2,315 in 1965 to 2,064 in 1975.[34]

The workhour reduction, however, stopped in the middle of the 1970s. This was because many companies restructured their business and assigned more work to employees to survive the economic downturn after the oil crisis. Faced with this new situation, the unions advocated further workhour reductions by shortening the legal workhour standards in the Labor Standards Law. However, the unions' demand was not met. In 1976, the Central Labor Standards Council (CLSC), which is the formal tripartite advisory council for the minister of labor, started its deliberations on the workhour issue. In its concluding report, the CLSC endorsed the idea of work sharing, that is, pursuing workhour reduction as a way of increasing employment. However, it did not recommend revising the Labor Standards Law. Its report said that because of the stark diversity in the capacity to reduce working hours among industries as well as companies, it was better for MOL to continue to use administrative guidance rather than direct legal regulation of management practices. MOL's 1980 plan to introduce a five-day work week followed the same logic, though it more strongly advocated the workhour reduction. MOL stated that the workhour reduction should be negotiated between labor and management, and thus its own role was to facilitate and support their negotiations.[35]

The ministry's approach in the 1980s became more aggressive and active. In May 1982, the Research Group on the Labor Standards Law, an informal advisory group for the Minister of Labor, started research on workhour regulations as well as wage and labor contract issues. The second committee of the Research Group, in charge of the workhour regulation issue, drafted an interim report in August 1984. It proposed introducing the principle of a forty-five-hour week and a nine-hour day instead of the forty-eight-hour week and eight-hour day principle in the

[34] Ikuo Kume, "Gyōseikikan no jiritsusei to nōryoku: rōdōjikan kisei gyōsei o tegakari to shite" (Autonomy and capacity of the state agency: The case of the workhour regulation policy), *Kōbe hōgaku nenpō*, no. 6 (1990).

[35] Masayuki Nomiyama, *Rōdōjikan: Sono dōkō to kadai* (Workhours: Trends and problems) (Tokyo: Rōdō Kijun Chōsakai, 1987), pp. 120–24.

new Labor Standards Law. It also advocated that if the union and management agree on a workhour reduction to forty hours a week, MOL would deregulate its workhour policy to admit a flexible workhour allocation. This was progress toward workhour reduction, in that for the first time since the Labor Standards Law of 1948, shortening the legal workhour standard became a serious policy option.

The Second Committee held a series of hearings with eleven unions including five national unions, and twelve business associations, including Nikkeiren. Labor criticized the report for its hesitation in introducing a bolder policy and advocated the forty-hour week and eight-hour day principle. On the other hand, business also criticized the report but from the opposite direction, arguing that working hours should be negotiated between labor and management and that the government should not interfere.[36] Although both parties criticized the report, it was business that was on the defensive.

Despite management opposition, MOL continued to make efforts to mobilize support for the workhour reduction policy. It was necessary not just because business groups were opposed to MOL's policy, but also because some LDP members were against it. In November 1984, newly appointed Labor Minister Toshio Yamaguchi, who was a member of the small conservative party, the New Liberal Club, that formed the coalition government with the LDP, proclaimed that MOL would put its policy priority on workhour reduction. He subsequently established a liaison conference with MITI for reducing working hours. In February 1985, MITI and MOL had their first formal meeting on this issue and jointly argued for further working hour reductions.[37] This strategy was useful for MOL to upgrade the workhour policy from a peripheral concern to a central issue of the government.

MOL also used international pressure to sell its workhour policy. In June 1985, after getting the CLSC's endorsement, MOL publicly announced its policy proposal, the Prospects and Guidelines for Reducing Work Hours, and it tried to link the workhour issue to the trade surplus issue. The logic was that Japanese workers worked so long that Japanese companies enjoyed strong cost advantages and earned too many benefits, which contributed at the national level to the huge trade surplus. Thus, it was allegedly necessary to shorten working hours.[38] Immediately after the newspapers reported management criticism against MOL's policy, Minis-

[36] Toshiyuki Hiraga, *Kaisei rōdōkijunhō* (The Labor Standards Law revision) (Tokyo: Nihon Rōdō Kyōkai, 1987), pp. 114–15.
[37] *Nikkei*, November 22, 1984, January 9, 1985, and February 28, 1985.
[38] Nomiyama, *Rōdōjikan*, p. 124.

ter Yamaguchi responded to this criticism by emphasizing the workhour reduction as an effective way to solve the trade friction.[39]

MOL, furthermore, combined these two tactics by incorporating its workhour reduction policy in a series of cabinet-level decisions to deal with trade problems. In October 1985, the cabinet meeting of economic ministers adopted the Measures to Increase Domestic Consumption as a policy package to reduce the trade surplus. MOL's workhour reduction policy was one of the major policies in that package. Since then, fourteen cabinet-level decisions, including the Maekawa Report of 1986, have advocated the workhour reduction policy. These cabinet-level decisions supported MOL in its efforts to sell its new workhour policy.

In December 1985, the second committee of the Research Group presented its final report to the labor minister. The report clearly advocated new legal restrictions on working hours, justifying the need for legal changes because of Japanese enterprise unionism, the low organization rate in small and medium-sized companies, and harsh inter-company competition, which made it difficult for the unions alone to realize workhour reductions within their companies. The report also proposed a forty-five-hour week and an eight-hour day. Originally, it had advocated a nine-hour day, but it shortened the day to eight hours in response to union pressure. Finally, while it continued to advocate flexible workhours as a means to facilitate total workhour reduction, it also proposed more restrictions than the interim report did in response to union demands.

MOL submitted this report to the tripartite CLSC in March 1986, and the CLSC held a series of deliberation meetings. Management continued to oppose this report, arguing that workhour reduction was a matter concerning the distribution of productivity gains and that, therefore, management and labor in an individual company should decide on the matter, and that the government should stay out of it. Furthermore, the government was to legally set a shorter workhour standard, individual companies would have to pay the extra cost of overtime work, and this would curtail the competitiveness of those companies. Labor, by contrast, basically supported the research group report, although it advocated greater workhour reductions. Consequently, the CLSC was almost deadlocked. It was the public representatives, scholars, and ex-bureaucrats of the CLSC who took the initiative to break through this deadlock. They formulated their own proposal and actively persuaded both management

[39] *Nikkei*, August 7 and 8, 1985.

and labor to endorse it. The main point was that the legal work week should be reduced to forty hours in the end, but for the time being it would be forty-six hours, later to be reduced to forty-four hours. This was a compromise to management, by setting the immediate workhour reduction to forty-six hours not forty-five. But it also formally announced its plan to introduce a fouty-hour week as demanded by labor. After intensive negotiation, management and labor representatives endorsed the proposal.[40] In this process, the winner was labor. The post-proposal comments by labor and management representatives are telling evidence. Labor appreciated this proposal while management regretted it.

MOL formulated the bill to revise the Labor Standards Law based on this proposal and submitted it to the Diet in March 1987. The unions set the agenda in the Diet deliberations. Five national labor organizations presented their demands to MOL in June while lobbying politicians, including those of the LDP. Their demands were that the forty-hour week should be implemented in three years and that the maximum legal daily work hours based on the flexible work allocation agreement between union and management should be ten hours. In the process of the Diet deliberations, the government compromised on these two points. First, Prime Minister Takeshita promised that the government would do its best to implement the forty-hour week principle in the early part of the 1990s. Second, the labor minister promised to introduce the ten-hour day limit for the flexible workhour allocation. Furthermore, the chairman of the LDP workhour subcommittee also promised to implement the forty-four-hour week principle in three years and the forty-hour principle in ten years. This bill finally passed the Diet in September 1987.[41] Since then, the average working hours for Japanese workers has decreased.

This case seems to show that MOL was on the union side and pursued the introduction of a more active workhour policy. My survey data, which included several specific questions regarding the process of this new workhour legislation, supports this observation by showing that this policy was a success for the unions, and that the unions gained this victory without forming a labor-management coalition, but by forming an MOL-labor coalition. First, although some labor scholars and leftist union leaders criticized this new law as a change for the worse, 68.6 percent of union leaders evaluated the new Labor Standards Law positively (table

---

[40] One member of the CLSC and a prominent labor scholar published a detailed description of this process. See Taishiro Shirai, "Rōdōjikan hōkaisei o megutte" (On revising the workhours law), *Nihon rōdō kyōkai zasshi*, no. 339 (October 1987).

[41] For a more detailed description, see Kume, "Gyōseikikan no jiritsusei to nōryoku."

Table 15. Evaluation of the new Labor Standards Law by union leaders (1989)

	Excellent (%)	Very good (%)	Good (%)	Poor (%)	Very poor (%)
National federations	—	50.00	50.00	—	—
Manufacturing	—	12.50	62.50	25.00	—
Service	—	16.10	45.20	25.80	12.90
All combined	—	17.60	51.00	23.50	7.80

SOURCE: Labor union survey by the author.

Table 16. Perceptions of other agencies' eagerness for workhour reduction (1989)

	MOL (%)	LDP (%)	Management (%)
National federations	2.00	3.50	4.00
Manufacturing	1.56	3.63	3.56
Service	2.45	3.87	3.42
All combined	2.14	3.76	3.51

SOURCE: Labor union survey by the author.
NOTE: Numbers represent average scores ranging from 1 = very eager to 5 = not at all eager.

Table 17. Frequency of contact between union leaders and others in workhour legislation (1989)

	LDP (%)	JSP (%)	DSP (%)	Management (%)	MOL (%)
National federations	3.50	2.75	3.50	3.00	1.75
Manufacturing	3.69	3.25	3.00	3.13	2.69
Service	3.61	2.52	3.26	3.32	2.48
All combined	3.63	2.76	3.20	3.24	2.49

SOURCE: Labor union survey by the author.
NOTE: Numbers are average scores: 1 = often, 2 = several times a year, 3 = one to three times in the whole process, 4 = never.

15).[42] One national union leader said that he personally believed that the new law was a big victory.[43]

Second, the union leaders believed that MOL was eager to introduce a more active policy for workhour reduction and that management and the

[42] Takeo Morooka, "Jitan to rōkihō no yukue" (The future of workhour reduction and the Labor Standards Law Revision), *Rōdōjihō* (August 1987).
[43] Author interview with a director of the Policy and Law Department of Rengō, Tokyo, September 11, 1989.

LDP were much less eager (table 16). In addition, union leaders had more frequent contact with MOL than with management on this issue (table 17). These data seem to support the interpretation that the unions and MOL formed a coalition to introduce the new workhour policy. In all, Japanese labor did not just survive the conservative resurgence but, in fact, strengthened its position in the policymaking process.

ANALYSIS OF THE LABOR-MANAGEMENT COALITION

After the first oil crisis, the private-sector unions started changing their goals from demanding a high nominal wage increase to pursuing a real wage increase and secure employment. They demanded a tax cut and an anti-inflation policy as well as an employment policy. In this process, they formed a coalition with management. The policy package of administrative reform was partially a development of these policies. The unions as well as management preferred fiscal reconstruction without tax increases. They both were against big government providing social groups with policy benefits at the expense of the competitive private sector.

The big business unions and management were against the "unfair" tax system that provided various tax favors to protected sectors in Japan, such as farmers, small and medium-sized merchants and industrialists, and doctors. They also criticized the three major sources of the government deficit, that is, the national railway, the food control system, and the national health insurance system. They argued that these systems were protecting various vested interests—such as railway workers, farmers, and doctors, as well as politicians and bureaucrats involved in related activities—all at the expense of private competitive sectors.[44] The private-sector unions and management had relatively few stakes in these systems and thus supported small government.

International pressures to open up the Japanese economy facilitated this labor-management coalition. In the 1980s, international pressure hit the traditional supporters of the LDP, such as the farmers and the small and medium-sized merchants, pressure in the form of liberalization of agricultural products and deregulation of the large retail stores.[45] In

---

[44] Very often, private-sector union leaders criticized the public sector as inefficient due to lack of market competition. The saying, *oyakata hinomaru*, which literally means "the boss is the Japanese government," is commonly used to criticize the public sector.

[45] Frank Upham, "Privatizing Regulation: The Implementation of the Large-Scale Retail Stores Law," in Allinson and Sone, eds., *Political Dynamics in Contemporary Japan*.

responding to these international pressures, the LDP government appealed to the private-sector unions and workers for support. This appeal fit well with the LDP's long-term strategy of trying to attract workers. The LDP electoral victories in the 1980s convinced the LDP politicians of the effectiveness of this strategy.[46]

The development of the labor policy network helped private unions actively support the administrative reform. They were the formal members of the SPCAR. More importantly, the CPPU (later the Private Sector Unions Conference [Zenminrōkyō]) was consulted intensively by the government in that process. As a result of the development of communication channels with the government and bureaucracies, the private-sector unions could play a formal and essential role in the process of administrative reform.[47]

Employment policy has not been the target of administrative reform, however. This is because management and labor in the private sector which supported administrative reform did not want to back off of employment policy development. At the same time, the coalition for small government supported this development. In addition, institutional development in this policy arena is important. As shown in chapter 6, a stable fund for employment policy was established in the form of employment insurance. Because this insurance account is outside the general account, it is relatively free from the pressure of fiscal reconstruction. Finally, Japanese private-sector unions are not dependent on public job creation programs. They secured their members' employment within the firm based on the productivity coalition. The employment policies facilitated this practice by providing companies in difficulty with subsidies to restructure their business and employ redundant workers. These policies were, in this sense, embedded in the economic institution not the political institution and thus were free form neoconservative criticism. Labor accommodation at the micro-level supported the private unions' macro-level small government orientation. The private-sector unions did not become the victim of the neoconservative tide in Japan; instead, they were riding on this tide, as a result of the development of postwar Japanese labor politics.

Atsushi Kusano, *Nichibei orenji kōshō* (The US-Japan orange negotiations) (Tokyo: Chūōkōronsha, 1984).

[46] Prime Minister Nakasone's comments on the 1986 landslide victory confirms this interpretation. He said that the LDP's victory was due to its successful incorporation of moderate leftist groups within its camp.

[47] Tsujinaka, "Rengō and its osmotic network."

BEYOND THE LABOR-MANAGEMENT COALITION

The case of the workhour reduction policy demonstrates that labor could achieve substantial policy victories over business resistance. Labor was not co-opted by management; rather it increased its power in national policymaking in the 1980s. In this case, too, international pressure played an important part. Criticism against the longer workhours in Japan as one cause of the trade surplus helped labor and MOL to formulate the workhour reduction policy. The Rengō official in charge of the workhour issue recollected that the Maekawa Report of 1986 was very useful in overcoming business resistance at the final stage of deliberation in the tripartite CLSC meeting.[48] The Nakasone cabinet, faced with an intensified trade conflict, established the Maekawa Committee to formulate a policy proposal to solve the trade problem. The Maekawa Report was submitted to the prime minister in April 1986 and advocated the expansion of domestic demands to balance the trade surplus. It explicitly argued for workhour reduction as a means to attain such a goal and consequently made the workhour reduction an international commitment. International pressure to transform the Japanese economy favored labor on this issue.

However, it is insufficient to give complete credit to international pressure because it has not been effective in changing a number of domestic policies in Japan, as is evident by the difficulty in opening the Japanese rice market and other regulated sectors to foreign competition. The success of the workhour reduction policy was not just a result of international pressure. The domestic political process played as essential role.

MOL is the key institution within the labor policy network, a situation we can better understand through the results of a 1985 survey of bureaucrats, in which 251 high-ranking bureaucrats in eight bureaucracies were interviewed.[49] As described previously, MOL introduced various pro-labor policies since the mid-1950s, although they differed from those advocated by Sōhyō. Although MOL tried to be a fair arbitrator between management and labor, conservatives sometimes criticized it as being too pro-

[48] Author interview with a director of the Policy and Law Department of Rengō, Tokyo, September 11, 1989.
[49] This survey was conducted by Professor Michio Muramatsu. I would like to thank Professor Muramatsu for permission to use this data. The interviewed ministries are the Economic Planning Agency, Ministry of Finance, Ministry of Welfare, Ministry of Agriculture, Forestry, and Fishery, Ministry of International Trade and Industry, Ministry of Labor, Ministry of Construction, and Ministry of Home Affairs.

labor.[50] Table 18 summarizes the outcome of a multifactor analysis of answers to six selected questions in the survey about the bureaucrats' policy views. They were asked about the relative importance of four factors in their policymaking decisions—"balance of interests" vs. "national interest," "coordination" vs. "efficiency," cooperation with social groups (necessary or not so necessary), and income redistribution as a policy goal (important or not so important)—as well as about their party support (LDP vs. non-LDP) and their perception of policy difference between LDP and opposition parties (large or small). First, we conducted a multifactor analysis and extracted two dimensions. We labeled the first "societal concerns." The positive end of this dimension represents national interest, efficiency, less cooperation with social groups, and negative attitudes toward income redistribution; the negative end represents balance of interests, coordination, cooperation with social groups, and positive attitudes toward income redistribution." The second dimension is "conservative orientation. "The positive end is LDP support and a perception of little policy difference; the negative end is non-LDP support and a perception of large policy difference. The average scores of each ministry on these two dimensions show that MOL as well as the Ministry of Welfare has a distinctive policy orientation, that is, more "societal concern" and less "conservative orientation."[51] This finding is consistent with the observation that MOL has a pro-labor orientation.

MOL has been depicted as one of the weakest bureaucracies in Japan. Its share in the national general budget decreased from 2.35 percent in 1960 to 0.94 percent in 1985.[52] However, the 1985 survey data of bureau-

[50] Mamoru Naka, *Rōdōshō kenkyū* (A study of the MOL) (Tokyo: Gyōsei, 1988); Nakasone, "Hoshutō wa shisei wo tadase."

[51] Ikuo Kume, "Tōchikatei to gyōsei kanryōsei: Tōchirengo no kakudai to sono seidoka" (Governing process and the bureaucracies: Expansion of the governing coalition and its institutionalization), *Kōbe hōgaku nenpō* 9 (1993). I used a factor analytic type of quantitative analysis developed by Chikio Hayashi and known as Type III Quantification Scaling. The statistical techniques assume that all variables, whether independent or dependent, are measured at the nominal level, and hence these techniques are most useful for categorical variables and for ordinal variables that do not conform to linear relationships. This method is useful in finding the underlying structure of the relationships between the different scales. See Ichiro Miyake, "Types of Partisanship, Partisan Attitudes, and Voting Choices," in Scott C. Flanagan, Shinsaku Kohei, Ichiro Miyake, Bradley M. Richardson, and Joji Watanuki, *The Japanese Voter* (New Haven: Yale University Press, 1991), pp. 233–34. This technique is similar to homogeneity analysis in which one alters least squares by quantifying nominal data, which is done by assigning numerical values to the cases and categories.

[52] Tsujinaka, "Rōdōkai no saihen," p. 67. A low budget does not automatically mean a weak ministry, however. The allegedly powerful MITI does not enjoy such a large budget. And furthermore MOL's budget is dependent on the unemployment rate, which has been low in Japan. Finally, the policies that called attention to the MOL were regulatory policies that did not need much money. The fact that MOL is not a big spender seems to be partly

Table 18. Multifactor analysis of policy orientation of government bureaucrats

Variables	Number of respondents	Extracted dimensions	
		Societal concerns scores	Conservative orientation scores
Standards in using discretion[a]			
Balance of interests	131	0.85	−0.45
National interest	88	−1.45	0.78
Coordination or efficiency[b]			
Coordination	166	0.80	0.42
Efficiency	85	−1.54	−0.82
Cooperation with social groups[c]			
Necessary	45	1.98	−1.21
Not so necessary	205	−0.42	0.26
Income redistribution[d]			
Positive	136	0.94	−0.30
Negative	113	−1.13	−0.35
Party support			
LDP	159	0.17	0.89
Non-LDP	92	−0.27	−1.55
Policy difference between LDP and opposition[e]			
Large	148	−0.39	−1.05
Small	102	0.60	1.52

Ministry	Number of respondents	Average scores[f]	Average scores
Economic Planning	21	−1.46	−0.94
Finance	41	−1.70	0.12
Welfare	41	1.02	−2.07
Agriculture	34	1.84	2.88
MITI	40	−1.97	0.55
Labor	27	1.69	−2.13
Construction	31	0.96	0.11
Home Affairs	16	0.06	2.05
Correlation		0.51	0.49

SOURCE: Bureaucrats survey, 1985.

[a] Standard the bureaucrats use in policymaking, "balance of interests" or "national interest."

[b] Standard the bureaucrats use in policymaking, "coordination" or "efficiency."

[c] Whether cooperation with social groups is necessary in policymaking or not.

[d] Whether income redistribution should be pursued in policymaking.

[e] Perception of policy difference between LDP and opposition parties.

[f] Average scores of each ministry on the extracted dimension.

Table 19. Frequency of bureaucrats' contact with the prime minister

Ministry	(%)
International Trade and Industry	27.5
Economic Planning Agency	19.1
Labor	18.5
Finance	14.7
Construction	3.2
Agriculture, Forestry, and Fishing	2.9
Welfare	2.4
Home Affairs	0

SOURCE: Bureaucrats survey, 1985.

NOTE: Numbers represent the percentage of bureaucrats in the ministry meeting the prime minister more than once a week.

crats' opinions show that 44 percent of the interviewed MOL bureaucrats recognized an increase in its rank within the government, and this percentage was second only to the Ministry of Construction among the eight interviewed ministries. In addition, 44.4 percent of MOL bureaucrats replied that it became easier to get the budget it asked for. Again only the Ministry of Construction showed higher results. Based on the same bureaucrat survey data analyzed here, Yntaka Tsujinaka argued that MOL increased its importance as a policy maker within the information network of the government, although it could not increase its budget share.[53] The percentage of bureaucrats who met the prime minister more than once a week was high for MOL (table 19). This result seems to support the observation that MOL became a central player in national policymaking.

Furthermore, MOL had intensive negotiations with related political actors. Tsujinaka's analysis of the bureaucrats' survey data demonstrates that MOL bureaucrats perceived a strong influence on themselves from the political actors closely representing social groups, that is, policy tribes and the LDP's Policy Affairs Research Council. MOL also worked closely with these political actors (table 20). Putting these data together with the recent appearance of a group of LDP politicians representing salaried

---

a result of the private-sector union movement, since the employment policy needs less money, as long as the private unions force management to maintain high employment.

[53] Ibid.

Table 20. MOL's perception of other political actors

Influential actors[a]	(%)	Cooperative actors[b]	(%)	Uncooperative actors[c]	(%)
Policy tribes[d]	44.4	Policy tribes	62.9	Opposition party	44.4
MOF	25.9	Deliberation council	33.3	Other ministries	44.4
PARC[e]	25.9	PARC	29.6	MOF	33.3
Lobby groups	22.2	Mass media	7.4	Lobby groups	18.5
Top LDP	14.8	Top LDP	7.4	Deliberation council	14.8

Source: Tsujinaka, "Rodokai no saihen," p. 68.

[a] Percentage of MOL bureaucrats who regard the following actors as the most and the second-most influential.

[b] Percentage of MOL bureaucrats who regard the following actors as the most and the second-most cooperative.

[c] Percentage of MOL bureaucrats who regard the following actors as posing the most and the second-most difficulty in MOL's policy formulation.

[d] Policy tribes are groups of LDP politicians who have specific interests and knowledge in the given policy area.

[e] The Policy Affairs Research Council, the powerful policy formulation body within the LDP.

employees, Tsujinaka concludes that MOL has become more open to private-sector union policy demands.[54] A further analysis of the data supports his interpretation. MOL also has a greater tendency than other ministries to regard the deliberation councils (which in the case of MOL are mostly the tripartite body) and groups (including unions, in MOL's case) as influential (table 21). At the same time, MOL bureaucrats most often saw the deliberation councils as the most difficult actors to deal with.[55] This means that the tripartite council of MOL is not a token body but a real forum of policy negotiation. All these data seem to substantiate Tsujinaka's interpretation.

Now let me summarize these various findings in a more simplified form by using multifactor analysis of the variables that affect the interaction between bureaucracies and the political actors. Table 22 shows the outcome. We used nine variables in the analysis. Four are related to power perception: whether Diet is influential or not; whether "top" political actors (prime minister, top LDP politicians, and MOF) are more influential than "bottom" actors (policy tribes, deliberation councils, PARCs, and lobby groups); whether party or bureaucracy is more influential; whether the respondent's ministry gained more influence in ten years or not. Five

[54] Takashi Inoguchi and Tomoaki Iwai, *Zokugiin no kenkyū* (A study on policy tribes) (Tokyo: Nihon Keizai Shimbunsha, 1987).

[55] The results are 14.8% for MOL, 9.8% for MOW, and 7.3% for MOF.

Table 21. Ministries' perceptions of the influence of lobby groups and the deliberation councils

Ministry	Lobby groups (%)	Deliberation councils (%)
Labor	22.20	11.10
Finance	4.80	9.80
Economic Planning Agency	0.00	9.50
International Trade and Industry	25.00	7.50
Welfare	14.60	7.30
Home Affairs	6.30	6.30
Construction	6.50	3.20
Agriculture, Forestry, and Fishing	26.40	0.00

SOURCE: Labor union survey by the author.

NOTE: Numbers are the percentage of bureaucrats in the ministry who perceive either lobby groups or the deliberation councils to be the most or second-most influential body among all political actors.

variables are related to their activities; whether top or bottom political actors are more cooperative with the respondent's ministry, and frequency of ministry's contact with the prime minister, with LDP members, with opposition party members, and with lobby groups. We extracted two dimensions, "political contact" and "political leadership." The positive end of the first dimension represents more contact with societal interests; the negative end, less contact with such actors than with high-ranking political actors. The second dimension represents whether power is perceived as centralized (negative) or decentralized (positive). Then we calculated the average scores of each ministry on these two dimensions. The perceived increase in the rank within the government parallels the first dimension. This means that the more the ministry had contact with social groups, the more it perceived an increase in its status. This might be a common phenomenon in which the administrative agency mobilized its supporters to increase its power. This seems to have been the case with MOL as well as the Construction Ministry. However, the second dimension, political leadership, separates MOL from the Construction Ministry and tells another story. With regard to this second dimension, MOL and MITI have similar characteristics: both had intensive interaction with social actors (in the case of MOL, unions and management) and saw core political actors (not lower-ranking actors, such as policy tribes) as having more influence on their policymaking. This finding supports the interpretation that MOL became an arbitrator between top government officials

Table 22. Multifactor analysis of the interaction between bureaucrats and political actors

Variables	Number of respondents	Extracted dimension Political contact	Extracted dimension Political leadership
Diet[a]			
Influential	168	0.08	0.71
Not influential	82	−0.19	−1.42
Influence[b]			
Top political actors[c]	109	−0.83	−1.08
Bottom political actors[d]	118	0.98	1.05
Power balance between party and bureaucracy			
Party	123	−0.04	1.05
Bureaucracy	104	−0.02	−1.26
Respondent's ministry's position[e]			
Up	93	1.39	0.01
Equal and down	157	−0.86	0.02
Cooperation[f]			
Top political actors	37	−1.78	−1.22
Bottom political actors	176	0.61	0.19
Frequency of contact with prime minister			
Often	95	−0.07	−1.92
Rare	156	0.00	1.17
Frequency of contact with LDP members			
Often	141	1.09	−0.72
Rare	109	−1.47	0.94
Frequency of contact with opposition party mencbers			
Often	128	1.11	−0.40
Rare	123	−1.21	0.42
Frequency of contact with lobby groups			
Often	152	0.98	−0.43
Rare	99	−1.57	0.66

Ministry	Number of respondents	Average scores[g]	Average scores
Economic Planning	21	−3.14	−0.29
Finance	41	−2.41	−1.17
Welfare	41	1.10	2.05
Agriculture	34	0.38	1.90
MITI	40	0.74	−2.74
Labor	27	0.85	−0.40
Construction	31	1.10	0.26
Home Affairs	16	0.87	1.23
Correlation		0.48	0.43

SOURCE: Bureaucrats survey, 1985.
[a] Whether Diet is influential or not.
[b] Whether "top" or "bottom" political actors are more influential.
[c] "Top" political actors are the prime minister, top LDP politicians, and MOF.
[d] "Bottom" political actors are policy tribes, deliberation councils, RARCs, and lobby groups.
[e] Whether the respondent's ministry gained more influence in ten years or not.
[f] Whether "top" or "bottom" political actors are more cooperative.
[g] Average scores of each ministry on the extracted dimension.

and unions, a situation that consequently increased its status within the government.

This interpretation fits my argument that the LDP has tried to incorporate labor in its camp and has introduced pro-labor policies. In addition, the data show that the policy network of MOL has been well-embedded in the government system. This in turn provides the policy-oriented, private-sector unions with a stable and important channel of influence. Furthermore, MOL became a closer ally with private-sector unions, because the unions themselves became more moderate and "realistic" in their policy demands—as their support for small government shows—and closer to MOL's original pro-labor policy stance. This helped MOL to increase its status within the government, and at the same time helped the unions to pursue their policy goals. The unions consequently began enjoying a more central role in the national policymaking. The success of the workhour reduction policy seems to support this interpretation. The policy network for labor became so well institutionalized that unions were able to achieve several policy victories over business resistance.

Japanese labor, especially the private-sector unions, survived the neoconservative tide and succeeded in deepening their participation in national policymaking. As described in this chapter, that success is attributable to the formation of the labor-management coalition for small government in the 1980s. This coalition was the product of the union movement started in the 1950s. The private-sector union within the company, after a series of harsh struggles with management, began cooperating with management to increase the productivity of the company and demanding its fair share of the profit, ans so the productivity coalition was formed. The unions pursued their own interests within this privatized framework. They were active in the micro-distributive and micro-productive arenas.

In the 1960s, the unions developed their activities in the macro-distributive arena, in the form of the Shuntō wage struggle. However, the private unions still worked within the privatized framework and did not actively engage in politics. This changed in the 1970s, especially after the first oil crisis, when the unions realized it was impossible to protect their members' interests within the privatized framework alone. They thus organized political activities, demanding secure employment and increases in real wages, both of which were beyond the capacity of the internal management-labor relationship. Subsequently, unions became active in the macro-productive arena. This development, however, did not cancel out the micro-level productivity coalition. Rather, the private unions developed their political activities based on the micro-level productivity coalition and expanded this coalition at the macro-level. In this process, the private-sector unions finally established their hegemony over the public-sector unions. The labor-management coalition for small government in the 1980s completed of this transformation. The private-sector unions developed their political agenda from within the company and extended it to the national level. But labor politics in the 1980s had its own characteristics—a preference for privatized political economy, which drove them toward the goal of small government.

This developmental path enabled labor to participate deeply in national policymaking and to institutionalize its position within the policy network. This institutional base was an important factor in labor's success against management in the case of the workhour reduction policy. This, however, does not mean that labor became antagonistic to management. Rather, labor achieved a stature in which it could negotiate with management on a more equal footing. Establishment of the labor-management coalition provided a foundation for the ongoing negotiation between management and labor, which was by no means without conflicts.

The birth of a non-LDP government in 1993 seems to have been supported by this development in labor politics. The end of the cold war contributed to the formation of this new government by blurring the dividing line between socialist and conservative, but the development in labor politics played a central role as well. It eroded the leftist hegemony within the movement and narrowed the policy difference between labor and the conservative groups. The LDP's splinter groups could count on the unions as an ally to help transform the Socialist party into a more realistic political actor.[56] It is telling that the Hosokawa and Hata administrations advocated deregulation as a way to transform the Japanese political economy for the sake of consumers. This was the goal the private-sector unions pursued with management in the 1980s.

---

[56] Hitoshi Igarashi, "Seiji-seitō to rōdōkumiai" (Politics/party and the labor union) in Hoseidaigaku Ohara Shakaimondai Kenkyūsho, ed., *Rengōjidai no rōdōundō*.

CHAPTER EIGHT

The Distinctiveness of
the Japanese Solution

Japanese labor politics has developed since the Pacific War, from the enterprise level to the national level. This experience casts strong doubt on the conventional understanding of labor politics, which proclaims that only a unified and centralized union movement can promote workers' interests against capitalists and the state. Japanese enterprise unionism, which is often characterized by decentralization and fragmentation, however, has achieved some notable successes in the postwar period–substantial improvement of working conditions, employment security, and an intensive employment policy. Japanese labor played an important role in bringing about these achievements. It gained substantial power in the enterprise as a result of workers' skills, internal political dynamics, and postwar labor offensives supported by the occupation forces. Individual management tended to be accommodationist, as it depended on the cooperation of unions in order to operate in a highly competitive market. Labor's internal divisions within the company (accommodationists versus confrontationists) often helped the accommodationist union gain more participation in management's production decision making. The establishment of a norm in which workers were viewed as legitimate members of the enterprise, rather than mere production factors, has allowed unions to become more active on both productive issues and distributive issues. This development facilitated a cross-class micro-level accommodationist alliance. Based on this micro-level accommodation, enterprise unions successfully developed national level activities, such as Shuntō wage bargaining and participation in public policymaking. Here again, cross-class political dynamics helped unions to achieve favorable outcomes. All of these situations demonstrate that a divided and decentralized union movement like enterprise unionism is not necessarily weak.

Against this conclusion, the students of the weak labor thesis have two main counterarguments. First, although unionized workers may enjoy favorable achievements, unorganized workers—who are the majority of Japanese labor—are still suffering from poor working conditions and are excluded from policy benefits. Second, weak-labor proponents argue that the unions were merely co-opted and integrated in the company system on management's terms. I will respond to these two points in turn.

The first counterargument can be characterized as dualist. It is clear that some segments of labor may gain more benefits than others, but such an outcome is not always the case. As described in chapter 2, an inter- and intra-class politics approach does not judge labor politics in a dichotomous way (that is, in terms of victory or defeat), using the "real interests of the working class as a whole" as the sole criterion. It is very natural for some segment of labor to pursue its own self-interest, and there may or may not be relative losers in the labor camp as a result. Did organized workers in big companies enjoy their benefits at the expense of other workers or, on the contrary, was there a positive spillover effect for other segments of workers in Japan?

Dualists argue that such spillover effects did not exist in Japan. The question then is does dualism correctly characterize Japanese labor politics? Kazuo Koike shows that dualism is not a characteristic of Japanese labor. He argues that the wage structure in Japan is not very dualistic. Differences in wage levels between large and small companies decreased drastically in the postwar period. Furthermore, such wage differentials did not exist at all before World War I in Japan.[1] Thus, Koike argues, wage differentials emerged as the result of differences in skill formation in large and small companies. The composition of workers of various skill levels differed between large and small companies and is probably the main reason for wage differences, not a deliberate management effort to control workers. According to dualist logic, however, if there were no difference in workers' skill levels, an omnipotent management in a large company would recruit cheap labor from the small and medium-sized enterprises (SMEs) instead of retaining expensive organized workers. Since this does not happen, the dualists must be wrong. Furthermore, Koike finds that wage differences across different sized companies in Japan are no larger than those in European countries.[2] In other words,

---

[1] Koike, *Shigoto no keizaigaku*, pp. 113–17; Konosuke Odaka, *Rōdōshijō bunseki* (Analysis of the labor market) (Tokyo: Iwanami Shoten, 1984).

[2] Koike, *Shigoto no keizaigaku*, pp. 118–19. His analysis is based on European Community,

the assertion that comparatively weak Japanese labor suffered from a dualistic wage structure cannot be supported.

Second, it is well known that a "life-time" employment practice exists in large Japanese companies and not in SMEs. Workers in large companies tend to work more years in the same company than do those in SMEs. The degree of long-term employment for SMEs in Japan, however, is the same as in European countries.[3] It is not true that SMEs' managements arbitrarily dismiss workers in order to adjust to a changing business environment. In the period of economic difficulty after the first oil crisis (1975–78), 20.3 percent of companies with more than 1,000 employees laid off workers, while the same rate for companies with 5 to 29 employees was only 16.9 percent, although larger companies much more often than smaller ones appealed to voluntary retirement instead of designated dismissals.[4] According to another survey, among those who actually quit jobs from 1983 to 1991, 9.16 percent did so because of management initiatives in companies larger than 1,000 employees, while the counterpart ratio for companies with 30 to 99 employees is 5.70 percent. The majority of workers who quit their jobs did so voluntarily in both groups of companies (73.7 and 76.6 percent, respectively).[5] The assertion that workers in SMEs are dispensed with easily and used as shock absorbers for the well-organized workers in the core economy cannot be supported.

What spillover effects did union achievements based on micro-level accommodation have on other segments of labor? This study shows that the Shuntō wage practice introduced by the unions contributed to wage standardization and evidently had some positive spillover effect for workers in SMEs. Koike attributes wage standardization to the enhanced skills of workers in SMEs. Such skills could provide an effective platform for workers in SMEs as well as in large companies during wage negotiations in the Shuntō framework. An intensive information flow across companies and industries in the Shuntō bargaining system helped workers in the unorganized sectors to achieve substantial wage increases. In this way, Shuntō has had a positive spillover effect on the unorganized sectors.

The unions in Japan have been very eager to protect employment

---

Structure of Earnings in Industry for the Year 1972 (vol. 13, 1975–76) and United Kingdom Department of Employment, *New Earnings Survey*, 1975, and Ministry of Labor, "Showa 51 nen chingin kōzō kihon tōkeichōsa" (Statistical survey of basic wage structure), 1976.

[3] Koike, *Shigoto no keizaigaku*, pp. 37–43.

[4] Ibid., p. 100. The data source is Ministry of Labor, "Koyō hendō sōgō chōsa" (Analysis of employment changes), 1979.

[5] Ministry of Labor, *Rōdō hakusho* (1993), p. 350.

security. They did so first within the enterprise and then gradually developed their activities in the policymaking process toward that goal. In response, a series of intensive employment policies were successfully introduced, especially after the first oil crisis. These organized unions demanded an employment policy in order to protect their self-interest rather than to protect employment in the unorganized sector. However, once such an employment policy was formulated, recipients of the benefits were not confined to the organized sector. For instance, many SMEs received employment adjustment subsidies, the per-worker amount of which was higher than that for large companies, in order to keep their employees. In addition, as chapter 6 shows, implementation of such an employment policy seems to have strengthened employment protection in all companies.

The workhour reduction policy had a similar spillover effect for peripheral workers. Workers in the large companies enjoy relatively shorter workhours than those in the SMEs, as management in large companies is not as antagonistic to workhour reduction. For instance, when Matsushita Company eagerly introduced a workhour reduction, it was management in SMEs that opposed the policy. Unions as well as MOL preferred government regulation to self-regulation by the union and management, although management (especially Nikkeiren) preferred the latter. Workhour reduction in the form of public policy had more of a spillover effect than did labor-management self-regulation that was conducted within the enterprise.

In sum, Japanese unions based on decentralized and fragmented enterprise unionism won not only favorable achievements but also brought about some positive spillover effects for workers in SMEs.

The second criticism of this book's thesis, the co-optation argument, can be made not just by students of the orthodox "class politics" approach but also by scholars who emphasize the importance of labor's role at the micro-level. The former group believe that labor's incorporation within the company inevitably results in its co-optation, but the latter group argues that such participation, if correctly combined with labor's national-level strength, enhances labor's interests in the process of work reorganization. These scholars successfully refute the class politics argument through their analysis of the process of work reorganization (see chapter 2). What is important to this study, however, is whether national-level strength is a precondition for labor's successful participation within the company, as the latter scholars emphasize. This question leads us to a comparative view of labor politics in the advanced industrial democracies.

Lowell Turner emphasizes unions' integration in company decision making as an important way to protect workers' interests in work reorganization in today's changing world economy. He first argues that labor's strategy is critical in achieving this integration. "Where labor-management relations were adversarial and arm's-length at the outset of major efforts at industrial restructuring and work reorganization, unions had little leverage from which to influence processes of change." However, unions' willingness is not enough. The institutionalization of labor's power at the national level, Turner says, is a necessary precondition for labor's successful participation at the micro-level.[6] Closely studying the U.S. and German automobile industries in broader institutional frameworks in the two countries, he concludes that German unions fare significantly better in representing workers' interests in work reorganization than do the U.S. unions. He attributes this difference to national institutional conditions for the union. The existence of a legal and political framework in Germany that regulates union integration in managerial decision making from outside the firm (the Works Constitution Act, codetermination, bipartite and tripartite bargaining, and so forth) enables the unions to participate in and influence management's decision making in a stable and autonomous way. Without this institutional characteristic, the U.S. unions could not achieve stable and effective representation of workers' interests in the process of work reorganization.

Based on this understanding, he summarizes cross-national variations. In Britain and Italy, as in the United States, where unions have adversarial and arm's-length relations with management within the company and lack centralized corporatist institutions, they are vulnerable to management's unilateral attack in the process of work reorganization. Lacking both conditions for successful union participation at the micro level, these countries' unions allegedly fare more poorly than German unions.

What happens in cases where one of the two prerequisites for successful participation is lacking? Turner's treatment of Sweden and Japan shows that he regards the national-level institutional setting, not the unions' orientation for micro-level participation, as crucial. In countries such as Sweden, where unions have not been integrated into managerial decision making but have enjoyed a strong national-level power to bargain, they can protect workers' interests in the process of work reorganization through the national-level institutions. On the other hand, in Japan, where unions participate in company decision making but do not have an

---

[6] Turner, *Democracy at Work*, pp. 163–66, 222. Cf. Thelen, *Union of Parts*, pp. 214–24.

institutionalized channel of influence at the national level, unions cannot protect workers' interests and are gradually losing their influence.

In Turner's understanding, union participation in company decision making without institutionalized power at the national level results in work reorganization at the expense of workers. In terms of workers' interests, labor's participation at the company level without national-level power either makes no difference or leads to a worse outcome.

The problem with Turner's understanding is twofold. First, he is still obsessed with the "resource centered class approach" and seems to assume that a national-level labor victory is possible only if a centralized and united union movement mobilizes sufficient resources to overwhelm the capitalists or the state. Labor's strength, based on the centralized and unified organization, is regarded as the reason why Swedish unions, although slow in developing micro-level participation tactics, gained better representation of workers' interests in work reorganization. However, recent studies show it is problematic to believe that Swedish labor has achieved its various victories by unilaterally mobilizing its resources based on a centralized and unified labor organization. Peter Swenson, James Fulcher, and Jonas Pontusson all show that cross-class politics played an important role in bringing about what used to be regarded as labor's victory in Sweden.[7] Pontusson, for instance, demonstrates that the limited but real success of codetermination in Sweden was attributable to an alliance between labor and business in the competitive sector, while the practice of industrial policy was supported by labor and business in declining industries.[8] As the present study shows, Japanese private-sector unions succeeded in achieving substantial employment policy benefits in alliance with management in manufacturing industries, despite a divided labor movement. A dynamic political process at the national level which from time to time enables labor to enjoy policy benefits should not be discounted. A divided labor movement may not be an obstacle for successful labor politics.

Second, Turner tends to discount labor's micro-level potential. Without prior institutionalization of labor's power at the national level, he presumes that labor will end up being co-opted. I have shown here, however, that unions can reap favorable benefits, such as employment security and fair work reorganization, as a result of their micro-level participation, and furthermore they can successfully develop their national-level movement

---

[7] Swenson, *Fair Shares*; Fulcher, *Labour Movements, Employers, and the State*; Pontusson, *Limits of Social Democracy*. See also Swenson, "Bringing Capital Back In, or Social Democracy Reconsidered."

[8] Pontusson, *Limits of Social Democracy*, chaps. 5 and 6.

starting from this micro-level participation. The potential of micro-level labor politics should not be discounted. What Turner is missing is an understanding of the micro-level political dynamism in which management and labor negotiate. If we take micro-level dynamics seriously, we see another aspect of the development of labor politics.

The cases of the United States and Italy, which are characterized as a failure to represent workers' interests in work reorganization, seem to teach us a different lesson about the development of labor politics. U.S. unionism is often called "business unionism," in which workers' interests are secured not through politics but through collective bargaining and industrial action on the shop floor, or "job-control unionism," in which seniority rules prevail, job classifications are narrow, and relations with management are adversarial. These practices prevented the U.S. workers from influencing management decisions and put them on the defensive in work reorganization. However, these characteristics of the U.S. unionism are not endemic nor are they a natural outcome of economic development. Recent literature shows that an alternative form of unionism once existed in the United States and that the current U.S. unionism became institutionalized through historical and political processes. Victoria Hattam shows how the decentralized state structure of the United States enabled the courts to sustain judicial obstruction of labor policy reform and led the unions to choose business unionism after the Civil War.[9] However, this transformation did not bring about job-control unionism. As Stephen Amberg argues, producerist schemes of workplace participation and planning and their macro-political counterparts persisted within the labor movement until the postwar settlement in the 1940s.[10] The American Plan of the 1920s, for instance, was a system of company welfarism. Management realized that it would be profitable to secure workers' loyalty and dedication to the firm by offering various intra-company benefits, such as company-sponsored pensions and the opportunity to purchase the firm's stock at favorable prices.[11] Under this plan,

[9] Hattam, *Labor Visions and State Power.*

[10] Stephen Amberg, "Democratic Producerism: Enlisting American Politics for Workplace Flexibility," *Economy and Society* 20-1 (February 1991). Hattam herself argues that a shift from the producers' concept of class, based on skilled workers, to the wage-earners' concept of class, based on semi-skilled workers, played an important role in this transformation. This was not an automatic result of industrialization. Ideology played an autonomous role. Hattam, *Labor Visions and State Power,* p. 206.

[11] David Brody, "The Rise and Decline of Welfare Capitalism," in David Brody, ed., *Workers in Industrial America: Essays on the Twentieth Century Struggle* (New York: Oxford University Press, 1980).

labor-management consultation, in the names of works councils or shop committees, was developed.[12] Michael Piore and Charles Sabel regard this trend not as a management effort to forestall union organization and to extend employer control over the labor process, but as a lost opportunity for an alternative labor-management settlement. They attribute the failure of the American Plan and the rise of job-control unionism, not to management's resistance to the plan, but to an accident of economic history, that is, the prolonged depression. Nelson Lichtenstein also shows that Keynesian emphasis on sustained growth and productivity gain-sharing replaced labor's earlier commitment to economic planning and social democracy after World War II. Economic success in the late 1940s—again, not management resistance—discredited the union proposal to democratize the political economy and increase participation within the firm (through, for example, the Industry Council Plan advocated by the CIO) as a way to boost the U.S. economy.[13] These students assume that micro-level labor politics had the potential to promote workers' interests.

In Italy, the labor movement has been divided into three rival federations: CGIL (Confederazione Generale Italiana del Lavoro) linked to the ex-Communists, CISL (Confederazione Italiana dei Sindicati Lavoratori) linked to the ex–Christian Democrats, and UIL (Unione Italiana dei Lavoratori) linked to the Socialists.[14] Despite a relatively high organization rate around 55 to 60 percent in 1980, the Italian labor movement has not been regarded as strong, because of this organizational fragmentation. However, after the Hot Autumn of 1969, unions strengthened their power within factories by forming factory councils and exploiting shop floor mass uprisings which were not led by the unions.[15] The elected shop stewards (*delegati*) for factory councils are important power bases for unions at the micro level. Furthermore, in 1972, three federations started a semi-unification. Given these developments both at the micro level as well as the macro level, labor unions forced employers to accept automatic wage indexation, called *scala mobile*.

---

[12] Piore and Sabel, *Second Industrial Divide*, p. 126.

[13] Nelson Lichtenstein, "From Corporatism to Collective Bargaining: Organized Labor and the Eclipse of Social Democracy in the Postwar Era," in Steven Fraser and Gary Gerstle, eds., *The Rise and Fall of the New Deal Order* (Princeton: Princeton University Press, 1989).

[14] The following description is mainly based on my reading of Turner's compact discussion of Italian experience and the articles and books cited therein. Turner, *Democracy at Work*, pp. 205–11.

[15] Charles F. Sabel, "The Italian Politics of Trade Unions," in Berger, ed., *Organizing Interests in Western Europe*.

However, increasing labor power at both the national and micro levels did not result in labor's effective integration into managerial decision making within the firms. Italian labor, like that in Britain, used its power on distributive issues but failed to use it effectively on productive issues. This strategic choice by the union led to labor's defeat in Fiat in 1980, as described by Richard Locke, Thomas Kochan, and Chris Heye.[16] In 1980, when Fiat was at the brink of bankruptcy, it proposed to place 24,000 workers in a state-financed redundancy fund, to save the firm from bankruptcy. The union rejected this proposal and in return management planned to fire 15,000 workers. The union then escalated its tactics. Supervisors and foremen, however, succeeded in organizing workers in a demonstration against the union, calling for a return to work. After this rally, the union had to sign the agreement, which represented a major defeat for the union. As union influence in the plants was based on the balance of power between labor and management. Turner attributes the union defeat to a lack of institutionalized labor power in Italy.[17]

However, it seems that this defeat was actually attributable to the union's inability to propose a feasible alternative to the company's plan. The union instead appealed to a showdown strategy, in vain. This event calls to mind a typical labor conflict on the issue of "production rationalization" in the 1950s in Japan (see the description of the Amagasaki Steel Strike in chapter 3). In other words, the union might have been able to reduce the cost of restructuring in Fiat, if it had developed intensive collaboration within the firm. Even if there was no legal protection of workers' right to participate in management decisions backed by national-level labor power, the union might have been able to protect workers' interests based on its micro-level labor power.

Richard Locke's recent study of the Italian politics of industrial change show this alternative. He finds that faced with new world market situations, two automobile companies in Italy, Fiat and Alfa Romeo, implemented successful industrial adjustment in very different ways. "Whereas Fiat reorganized by asserting managerial control and repressing the unions, Alfa experienced a more negotiated process. . . . Alfa's unions managed to preserve, perhaps to even enhance their strength while Fiat's unions lost membership and practically all influence on the shop floor."[18]

[16] Richard M. Locke, Thomas A. Kochan, and Chris R. Heye, "Industrial Restructuring and Industrial Relations in the U.S. and Italian Automobile Industries," paper presented at the Conference on Managing the Globalization of Business, Capri, Italy, October 28–29, 1988. This description is quoted in Turner, *Democracy at Work*, p. 207.

[17] Turner, *Democracy at Work*, p. 208.

[18] Richard M. Locke, *Remaking the Italian Economy* (Ithaca: Cornell University Press, 1995), p. 33.

Locke attributes the divergence to "the very different local socio-political networks in which the two companies are embedded and which shaped the alternative managerial and union strategies."[19] This analysis shows that how labor politics is developed at the local level or at the micro level is important in determining the nature of labor politics, and that labor's national-level institutionalized power may not be a precondition for successful union participation in the process of work reorganization.

I would not argue, however, that national-level labor power is irrelevant, but that it is not a precondition for labor's success at the micro level. The two possibilities, that labor could have substantial power at the micro level and that divided labor could form a cross-class alliance at the national level, if combined, lead us to the conclusion that labor can successfully develop its activity from the micro level to the national level. This does not mean labor can get favorable benefits everywhere. The quality of labor politics is determined through a dynamic political process at both the micro and macro levels. We should not disparage the bottom-up development of labor politics without taking seriously political dynamics which may enable labor to win victories.

Does this bottom-up development have any characteristic features? The cases of the United States and Italy do not provide an answer, because bottom-up development has not been completed in these two countries. Some networks appeared at the micro level, but they have not developed to the national level. It is the Japanese case that tells us what characteristics such development from below gives to labor politics. The increasing national-level participation of Japanese unions did not make labor politics in Japan finally resemble that of Germany or Sweden. Different developmental paths themselves influence the nature of labor politics. Labor politics is path dependent. From this perspective, a contrast between Japanese and Swedish cases is interesting. As opposed to a common-sensical understanding of these two political economies as polar opposites, they share several important characteristics. Phenomena such as relatively better economic performance from the first oil crisis to the late 1980s, highly egalitarian income structure, and the existence of a dominant party in the postwar period are common in these two countries.[20] A similarity between the Swedish solidaristic wage policy and the Japanese Shuntō wage practice analyzed in chapter 4 shows how similar labor

---

[19] Ibid. See also chap. 4.

[20] T. J. Pempel, "Japan and Sweden: Polarities of 'Responsible' Capitalism," in Dankwart A. Rustow and Kenneth Erickson, eds., *Comparative Political Dynamics: Global Research Perspective* (New York: Harper and Row, 1990).

politics can become, even when the two countries start from very different points.

As in Japan, Swedish labor is now eager to participate in and influence managerial decision making on issues such as work reorganization. These two countries interestingly rank the highest in terms of robotization of the production process. Rigid job control unionism does not exist in either country. But in Japan flexible production has been introduced mainly through labor-management negotiations within the company, while in Sweden it has been an issue mainly at the national level. The Metal Workers' Union's Solidaristic Policy for Good Work and the LO's Developmental Work programs can be seen as just two recent examples in which national-level union organizations tried to strengthen workers' influence in the production process. Since the late 1960s and early 1970s, when increasing turnover, absenteeism, and wildcat strikes posed threats for both management and unions, such issues as work reorganization and quality of work have been negotiated mainly on the initiative of national-level actors.[21] Different paths of development for labor politics have influenced how a similar issue of work reorganization and flexible production is politically negotiated.

Similarly, different developmental paths seem to have determined the nature of labor politics in these two countries. Until the early 1970s, Swedish unions mainly concentrated on distributional issues, such as wages and other related working conditions. The Saltsjöbaden Agreement of 1938 was an epochmaking event for this development. This distribution orientation is the result of the strength of the unions in the labor market as defined by high union density. Although the Swedish unions' achievements, such as a solidaristic wage practice, cannot be interpreted as the product of the unions' unilateral resource mobilization, recent studies show that the centralized and encompassing nature of the Swedish union movement induced unions to concentrate on distributional issues, while leaving productive issues in the hands of management. The centralized labor movement naturally wanted to bargain with management at the national level in order to maximize its advantage as a monopolistic supplier of labor. The electoral strength of the Social Democratic Party in Sweden also induced unions to pursue their interests at the level of national politics. As Mancur Olson argues, an encompassing and broadly based "interest group" (such as LO) is the basis for "explicit redistribu-

---

[21] Åke Sandberg, et al., *Technological Change and Co-Determination in Sweden* (Philadelphia: Temple University Press, 1992); Robert E. Cole, *Strategies for Learning: Small-Group Activities in American, Japanese, and Swedish Industry* (Berkeley: University of California Press, 1989).

tion" (social welfare) not for "implicit redistribution" (like protectionist policies).[22] General characteristics of Swedish labor politics, that is, wage-centered industrial relations and social welfare policy, may be largely attributable to the nature of the labor organization, although its specific outcomes are brought about through inter- and intra-class politics.

On the other hand, in Japan, labor politics developed from the micro level to the macro level. Private-sector labor from the beginning tried to participate in managerial decision making. Micro-productive issues have been important for the unions. After achieving legitimate status within the company system, labor gradually developed its national-level activities based on micro-level achievements. As analyzed in chapter 6, experience in the micro-productive arena made it easier for unions to participate in the macro-productive arena, such as industrial and employment policy formulation. Faced with economic difficulties, Japanese unions first tried to force management to keep as many people working as possible before demanding public policies. Once unions began demanding public policies, they often preferred industrial policies to help their company or industry to keep their workers. Employment policy often has a similar aim. Japanese employment policy after the 1960s has had a strong orientation toward preventing workers from being laid off and urging rapid reemployment, as is evident by the subsidies for employers who continue to employ or who newly hire targeted redundant workers and/or who implement retraining programs within their companies. In other words, the cost of economic change first tends to be compensated for within the privatized framework rather than the public welfare framework. Once this cost has became too great for private firms, unions as well as management then pursue productive public policies rather than distributive or redistributive ones. This productive orientation can be attributed to the developmental path of Japanese labor politics from the micro-productive area to the national level.

The small-government orientation of the private-sector unions in the 1980s was based on this productive orientation, which may have had some negative spillover effect on the peripheral workers. Big business unions did not want to have a heavy tax burden to support a big welfare state. A lower tax burden and a medium-sized welfare state might be more beneficial for core workers than peripheral workers. But we should remember two things. First, the basic welfare policies were introduced in the 1970s

---

[22] Mancur Olson, *How Bright Are the Northern Lights? Some Questions about Sweden* (Lund: Lund University Press, 1990). See also *The Rise and Decline of Nations* (New Haven: Yale University Press, 1982).

in Japan, and welfare reform in the 1980s did not eliminate the welfare program, as shown in chapter 5. Second, as low unemployment in Japan shows, a privatized framework functioned well not just for core workers but also for peripheral workers. Furthermore, protected sectors, such as agriculture, construction, and most service sectors, all provided implicit though inefficient redistributive functions.[23]

This contrast between Sweden and Japan shows how different developmental paths of labor politics can result in different types of labor politics. But this study also shows that the unified and centralized union movement is not the only way for workers to promote their interests in a capitalist political economy. Furthermore, the recent demise of the Swedish model may show that the centralized labor movement cannot be an effective way to protect workers' interests in the new world market where flexible production instead of standardized Fordist mass production comes to have a competitive edge.[24] Labor politics is more complicated and dynamic than what students of the orthodox class-analysis model assumed.

This study has implications for the debate on the Japanese political economy. The market-centered approach emphasizes the apolitical nature of the success of the Japanese economy, at least in the competitive manufacturing sectors. The state-centered approach views Japanese success as a result of state intervention, typically industrial policy. Against these two widely accepted explanations of the Japanese political economy, an institutionalist or network approach reviewed in chapter 2 has recently been gaining influence. The students of this approach find that dense networks among the participants in the political economy played an important role in achieving economic success in Japan. Long-term relations among corporations enabled various firms to improve the quality of manufactured products. It is well known that iron and steel makers produced high-quality, specialty steel in close cooperation with automobile companies. Banks as well have had long-term relationships with their customer companies, as both stockholders and lenders. Consequently, banks monitor their customer companies, and when the companies are in financial difficulty, the banks tend to organize rescue operations for them. The institutionalized, long-term relations between large manufacturing firms and SMEs are also important in enabling Japanese manufacturers to establish flexible mass production. The co-existence and strategic coop-

[23] E.g., Calder, *Crisis and Compensation.*
[24] See, e.g., *Western European Politics: Special Issue on Understanding the Swedish Model.*

eration among them made possible the constant variation of high-quality, high value-added products. The support from local governments as well as the national government for SMEs helped them to have autonomous but cooperative relations with larger companies. Furthermore, although the government industrial policy from time to time might not have realized its original goal, such government intervention created intensive and extensive networks among market actors and provided some companies with favorable opportunities for success.[25]

These networks also provided workers with benefits not just in the form of a larger paycheck resulting from economic growth. The corporate group functioned as a safety net for redundant workers, as member companies would usually employ them. The main bank's propensity to help their customer companies in financial difficulty has been also beneficial for employees. The government industrial and employment policy has helped these networks to function in this way. In other words, these dense networks within the Japanese political economy have provided labor with various benefits by buffering workers from market forces.

I have shown that labor is not a free rider in these institutional networks but rather that it contributed to establishing them. The incorporation of labor within the enterprise resulted in an extensive network which supported labor-management collaboration and flexible production. Labor's participation in the national political economy was also important in establishing the basic condition for the "virtuous" cycle of wage restraint, lower inflation, and secure employment after the first oil crisis. Labor's incorporation, not its subordination or exclusion, is the basis for flexible adjustments to changing economic conditions both within the enterprise and in the national political economy. This does not mean the adjustment process is conflict-free, but conflict is solved in institutionalized negotiations. An intensive and extensive network among labor, management, and the government made these adjustments easier by reducing transaction costs.

As many argue, a capitalist political economy should satisfy two basic functions: it should legitimate its existence and maintain its economic growth. Neo-Marxists such as James O'Connor and neoconservatives such

---

[25] Aoki, *Information, Incentives, and Bargaining in the Japanese Economy*, p. 148. Toshiya Kitayama, "Local Governments and Small and Medium-sized Enterprises," in Kim et al., eds., *The Japanese Civil Service*; Richard Florida and Martin Kenney, *The Breakthrough Illusion: Corporate America's Failure to Move from Innovation to Mass Production* (New York: Basic Books, 1990), chap. 8; Kume, "Party Politics and Industrial Policy." Imai, "Komento," in Komiya, et al., *Nihon no sangyōseisaku*; Seiichiro Yonekura, "Fukyō karuteru to autosaidā" (Recession cartel and outsiders), Kindai Nihon Kenkyūkai, ed., *Nenpō Kindai nihon kenkyū* 15 (1993).

as Daniel Bell both find these two functions, legitimation and accumulation, contradictory. But my case study shows that labor under private-sector union hegemony can form the basis of political legitimacy for the capitalist state without damaging capital accumulation. Private-sector-led labor tends to stimulate workers' interests in the privatized framework, as opposed to the political framework. The unions supported an employment policy to keep workers employed within the firm rather than in a public employment program. They preferred retraining of redundant workers within the company rather than through a public retraining program. Japanese private-sector unions have pursued the goal of "continuous commodification" of labor, not its "decommodification." Their small-government orientation is consistent with this preference. In the privatized framework, public social welfare is regarded as a supplementary mechanism for protecting labor's interests. Kuniaki Tanabe found that an income transfer mechanism in Japan was built into the tax system rather than into welfare social security. His finding is consistent with my argument. The Japanese labor accommodation may be an alternative way to tame the deteriorating effects of the market on the society, and this type of accommodation has made the postwar Japanese political economy distinctive.[26]

This privatized framework might have contributed to the LDP's dominance and the weakness of leftist opposition parties in Japan. The Socialist Party in particular has been obsessed with social democratic policy based on the class-politics view of labor and has failed to develop its own strategy based on the micro-level labor accommodation. It is telling that the Socialists were not interested in productive issues at the micro level (worker participation in production decision making) nor at the macro level (industrial policy). Rather, they tried to appeal to ideological and foreign policy issues. By doing so, they missed a precious opportunity to develop an alternative to the LDP government. Various polls show that even supporters of the Socialist Party were concerned about its governing ability.[27] Consequently, the LDP established its legitimacy as the guardian

---

[26] E.g., Lindblom, *Politics and Markets.* James O'Connor, *The Fiscal Crisis of the State* (New York: St. Martin's Press, 1973); Daniel Bell, *Cultural Contradictions of Capitalism* (New York: Basic Books, 1976). Maria Oppen characterizes German employment policy as an "externalisation" policy, which means that it helps redundant workers outside the labor market. "Labour Policy in Germany: Regulation of the Age Limits to Paid Employment," in Naschold and Muramatsu, eds., *State and Administration in Japan and Germany.* Kuniaki Tanabe, "Social Policy in Japan," in Naschold and Muramatsu, eds., *State and Administration in Japan and Germany.* Karl Polanyi, *Great Transformation: The Political and Economic Origins of Our Time* (Boston: Beacon Press, 1944).

[27] Tetsuro Morimoto, "Ittō yuui to seitōsei: Jimintō taisei to Gaulist taisei" (One party

of the Japanese political economy. However, the hegemony of the LDP paradoxically paved the way for its demise. After the end of Cold War, which marginalized ideological and foreign policy issues, there remained no clear-cut dividing line between the right and the left on domestic economic issues. This made it easier for socialists and the conservative splinter groups from the LDP to form a coalition government, which finally terminated the LDP's long-term, single party rule.

It is true that in the 1990s the worst economic recession in postwar-era Japan has provoked predictions that the Japanese management system verges on crisis because this recession is regarded as structural rather than cyclical. Many economists believe that the Japanese economy has become so mature that future economic growth will be slow. They argue that the seniority wage system and life-time employment have been efficient and possible because of the continuous expansion of the Japanese economy. Company size has expanded and most workers have been provided with sufficient opportunities for advancement with increasing wages within one company. As this economic condition changes, a new model more like what Dore calls the Company Law Model or the Anglo-Saxon liberal model is thought to develop, one that has more labor mobility across companies and a merit-based instead of seniority-based wage system.

It is telling, however, that some companies that have violated a basic principle of Japanese labor accommodation are faced with severe criticism from the public. Two episodes show how past developments have influenced the course of recent industrial adjustments. In January 1993, faced with a serious business downturn, the audio-visual equipment maker Pioneer designated thirty-five middle-rank managers over the age of fifty for dismissal, unless they would accept voluntary retirement with an additional retirement bonus by the end of January.[28] As they were not union members, the union was not involved in this management decision. However, this plan brought criticism both from within as well as from outside of the company. Employees and the union argued that the criteria for the dismissals were not clear and that management did not share the burden. Management explained that these designated managers had been poor at their jobs, but the union and the employees complained that such evaluation was not based on any objective criteria, only on the personal judgment of higher-ranking managers. The fact that while other companies in

---

dominance and legitimacy: The LDP regime and the Gaulist regime), *Leviathan*, special issue (Winter 1994).

[28] *Nikkei*, January 8, 1993.

this industry introduced salary cuts for top management, and Pioneer did not, made them feel management was being unfair. The mass media picked up this story, and the company's stock price tumbled.[29] Pioneer was not the only company implementing a plan to reduce its workforce, but other companies tried to do it in a more careful way with intensive union-management consultation, voluntary retirement rather than designated dismissal, and intensive after-care for retiring employees.

Pioneer's management, faced with these criticisms, established a Special Labor-Management Committee for Middle-aged Employees to deal with this problem. Management also intensified its efforts to find new employment for the designated managers, introduced salary cuts for top managers by 5 to 20 percent, and abandoned the deadline for voluntary retirement at the request of the union.[30] In May, management and the union agreed on three points: 1) together they would start a joint program to formulate a new management system; 2) management would admit being wrong in unilaterally designating employees for retirement; and 3) decisions regarding future employment and personnel plans would be open to the union.[31] Management learned that it is essential to make every effort to maintain employment before implementing a reorganization plan.

Successful management reform is contingent not just on cooperation from the union, but also on the social norms and the labor policy network. In January 1994, the management and union of the machine-tool maker Okuma, which suffered from a business downturn and did not anticipate business recovery in the near future, jointly decided to reduce the compulsory retirement age from sixty to fifty-six and to call for the voluntary retirement of 380 employees by paying two years' wages in addition to the regular retirement bonus.[32] In this case, the union participated in the planning process from the beginning. For both the management and the union, the business downturn after the first oil crisis had taught them a vital lesson. At that time, Okuma management could not reduce employment by voluntary retirement and designated seventy employees for dismissal. A serious labor conflict occurred because the criteria for dismissal were not clear and the company lacked enough money to add a special bonus. Management and the union agreed to use age as an objective

---

[29] *Nikkei Sangyō Shimbun*, February 9, 1993.

[30] *Nikkei Sangyō Shimbun*, February 18 and 20, 1993.

[31] *Nikkei*, May 22, 1993. As of May 20, all twenty-eight retired managers were given jobs in other companies in Pioneer's group, and Pioneer was looking for new jobs for the remaining seven managers it still employed.

[32] *Nikkei*, January 10, 1994.

criterion this time and to start restructuring before the company became unable to offer a sufficient bonus for the retiring employees.

This decision was severely criticized by MOL, however, because the ministry was eager to conduct various measures to extend the retirement age from sixty to sixty-five, by revising the Employment Security Law for Old Aged Employees. MOL announced its concern that such a practice might be followed by other companies in business downturns and directed an intensive investigation of this case. MOL started its investigation and efforts to persuade Okuma to cancel its decision to reduce the retirement age. The MOL also demanded that Okuma management make every effort to find new jobs for retiring employees. The top managers at Okuma replied that it was actively helping retiring employees to find new jobs if they wanted, and that its decision to reduce the retirement age was an emergency measure to survive the severe business downturn. It promised that it would reinstate a retirement age of sixty as soon as possible. Nikkeiren criticized MOL's intervention in a managerial decision agreed on between management and the union, while the unified Rengō criticized the union's decision to follow management's plan.[33] MOL continued to criticize Okuma's decision.

After the voluntary retirement plan was successfully implemented and the re-employment of retired employees in other companies made good progress, the president and two executive directors resigned admitting that they were to blame for cutting employment and drawing public criticism. President Maeda explained that the reason for his resignation was that he was forced to cut employment, which should be the last resort for an employer, and that he had also failed to treat a management problem properly and had made it a social problem.[34]

These episodes show that the norm of protecting employment is deeply embedded in the Japanese political economy. Recently, the presidents of Nikkeiren and the unified Rengo jointly announced that the Japanese management system should be protected. Moreover, the Nikkeiren president stated that employment should be protected at the expense of shareholders' interests because the company is not the private property of shareholders but a social institution.[35] Of course, Japanese employees are not entirely protected from dismissal. (It is impossible to protect employ-

---

[33] *Nikkei*, January 11, 1994. *Nikkei*, January 27, 1994. *Nikkei*, Nagoya edition, January 28, 1994.

[34] *Nikkei*, February 19, 1994.

[35] *Nikkei*, March 3, 1994. Nikkeiren did not want to protect the Japanese employment system unconditionally, but it did begin searching for a new system and established a study group to that end. *Nikkei*, December 20, 1994.

ment unconditionally in a market economy.) And Japanese companies do dismiss employees in various ways. However, Japanese labor accommodation at the micro level as well as at the macro level makes such reorganization less costly for workers.

Certainly Japanese labor accommodation may very well change in the future if faced with new economic conditions. But the adjustments will be made within the institutionalized framework of Japanese labor accommodation. For instance, recent efforts by Honda Motors to introduce a fixed term for managers in order to reduce labor costs and promote younger workers into managerial positions is an attempt to reform the seniority wage system for a new economic situation. The union has supported this plan,[36] and there has not been any serious criticism from the public or from MOL. Over all, Japanese management seems reluctant to totally transform the Japanese system, preferring to adjust it to changing economic situations within the framework of Japanese labor accommodation.

The generally accepted tenet, that workers are legitimate members of the company, is now deeply embedded in the Japanese political economy. Economic crises can, of course, change the nature of labor politics in Japan as it did in Sweden, but Japanese labor politics tends to be more resilient than Sweden's because it is more deeply rooted in micro-level labor accommodation than in centralized political bargaining. After all, labor politics is path-dependent, and economic change is mediated by the institutional settings Japanese labor politics has created.

[36] *Nikkei*, March 18 and 19, 1994.

Author Index

General Index

accommodationist cross-class alliance, 47–48
active labor market policy, 99, 148–49, 159, 164
Administrative Management Agency, 194
administrative reform, 99, 185, 190, 194, 196, 203
Alfa Romeo, 222
Allied occupation, 22, 46
Amagasaki Steel, 77, 222
American Plan of the 1920s, 220
anti-inflation policy, 42, 134–37, 203
anti-rationalization movement, 156
Anti-Subversive Activities Law, 79
Anti-Yoshida conservatives, 85
arm's-length relations with management, 105, 218
Association to Help Laid-Off Coal Miners, 156
AT&T, 29
Austria, 38
"avec struggle," 158

base-up practice, 86
big business and labor coalition, 184, 195
Bismarckian paternalists, 113
Britain, 1, 7, 13, 218, 222
British workers, 9
budget-making process, 136, 178
business unionism, 5, 164, 220

Central Labor Standards Council (CLSC), 198–99, 205
centralized union movement, 21, 22, 219
Chamber of Commerce, Japan, 135

chemical industry, 105
Chūritsurōren (Federation of Independent Unions of Japan), 88, 124, 172, 187
class politics, 19, 33–35, 85, 118, 142–43, 151, 214, 217, 219, 225
Coal Association, 156, 160
Coal Distribution Public Corporation, 151
Coal Mining Rationalization Special Measures Law, 155–57, 159, 162–63
coal mining industry, 19, 143, 151–64
codetermination, 218
Cold War, 229
collective bargaining, 22, 70
Communist Party, 56
"community model," 5
"company law model," 5, 229
company-specific skills, 25–26
competitiveness, 111, 139, 165
constitution, Japan, 144
co-optation of labor, 43, 46
corporatism, 3, 20–21, 33; in Austria and Switzerland, 37–38, 42
cost-push inflation, 129
Council for Policy Promotion Unions (CPPU), 135, 138, 171–72, 192, 204

decentralization, 2, 22, 44, 48
decommodification of labor, 51, 228
Deliberation Council on Industrial Structure, 110
deliberation councils (shingikai), 3, 166
Densan, 49, 75
Densan-Tanrō disputes, 80, 154
deregulation, 191, 203

Cornell Studies in Political Economy

EDITED BY PETER J. KATZENSTEIN